Lucy Letby

The Complete Story

Katherine Smith

© Copyright 2023 Katherine Smith
All Rights Reserved

Other Books by Katherine Smith

Kim Edwards - The Twilight Murders

Mary Bell

Shannon Matthews

Tia Sharp

Contents

5 - Author's Note
6 - Chapter One
20 - Chapter Two
32 - Chapter Three
47 - Chapter Four
58 - Chapter Five
69 - Chapter Six
79 - Chapter Seven
90 - Chapter Eight
107 - Chapter Nine
130 - Chapter Ten
148 - Chapter Eleven
158 - Chapter Twelve
175 - Chapter Thirteen
185 - Chapter Fourteen
202 - Chapter Fifteen
209 - References

AUTHOR'S NOTE

This book concerns an awful and distressing crime case that is still very fresh in the memory. I hope that this book approaches the case in a sensitive, informative and tactful way. The thoughts of everyone are of course with the victims in this case and the families involved. A list of salient references used in the research for this book can be found at the conclusion of the final chapter.

CHAPTER ONE

It has been estimated by some studies that around 15% of serial killers are women - though some might find this surprising or even dispute the veracity of such studies. Female serial killers are generally more likely to know their victims. Female serial killers are also more likely to work in the medical profession in some capacity than their male counterparts. A recent study in the United States found that 40% of female serial killers worked in the health care system - most commonly as nurses. Female serial killers are much less likely to have prior criminal convictions than male serial killers and this, one might argue, makes it harder to see them coming. Serial killers in the medical world tap into primal fears because we and our loved ones are at our most vulnerable in hospital and must put our faith in the kindness and professionalism of doctors and nurses.

    Lucy Letby was born in Hereford in 1990. She was an only child. Her father John was a furniture salesman and her mother Susan was an accounts clerk. When they retired, Letby's parents are said to have started a home business selling radiators. Lucy Letby grew up in a semi-detached house in Hereford's Arran Avenue, a small cul-de-sac off Hinton Road. Letby, in comparison to most convicted serial killers, had a perfectly normal and pleasant childhood. Hereford is located on the River Wye and is surrounded by beautiful countryside, making it a popular destination for outdoor activities such as hiking and canoeing. From a young age, Lucy Letby was taken to church each Sunday at the Hope City Church. There were no obvious signs which marked Letby out as a disturbed or potentially dangerous person. Lucy Letby was described as 'geeky' by many of her friends. She was seen as a kind person who liked to have fun. Letby was also a good student who took school seriously. She attended Aylestone School before going on to Hereford Sixth Form College.

    Aylestone School was established as a comprehensive following the merger of Hereford High School for Girls and Hereford High School for Boys in 1976. Former pupils of this school include the weather forecaster Susan Powell and the Bath rugby player Josh McNally. Lucy Letby's fame would eventually outstrip anyone who had previously attended this school. That was tough luck on Aylestone School because Letby obviously became famous in the worst way imaginable. Lucy Letby had always wanted to be a nurse ever since she was a child. To this end her academic studies were designed to move her in this direction. Letby was the first person in her family to go to university (her parents actually took out a celebration advert in the local newspaper when she graduated - something which most teenagers, one would imagine, would probably find a bit embarrassing) and studied paediatric nursing at the University of Chester.

Paediatric nursing is a specialised field of nursing that focuses on providing care to infants and children. Paediatric nurses are responsible for a wide range of duties, including conducting physical examinations, administering medications, monitoring vital signs, and assisting with procedures and treatments. They also educate patients and their families about health conditions and provide support during difficult times. A paediatric nurse is someone with a profound responsibility because there is nothing more precious and priceless than a person's child. During her studies, Letby had a number of work placements. These were mostly at Liverpool Women's Hospital and the Countess of Chester Hospital. It was the latter rather than the former where Letby spent the most time (this was obviously a consequence of its closer proximity to the university).

Letby qualified as a Band 5 nurse in September 2011. She now had a Bachelor of Science degree in Child Nursing from the University of Chester. A Band 5 nurse is someone who is newly qualified or works within one of the four core NHS specialisms: adult, child, mental health and learning disabilities. Letby's salary as a starting Band 5 nurse would have been about £28,000 a year. Although there appears to be no evidence yet that Letby was involved in any suspicious deaths during placements at Liverpool Women's Hospital a full investigation into her time there has yet to be completed. It was at the Countess of Chester Hospital where Letby worked after qualifying as a nurse.

In 2013, Letby was interviewed by the Chester Standard newspaper as part of a fundraiser for the hospital. "My role involves caring for a wide range of babies requiring various levels of support," said Letby. "Some are here for a few days, others for many months and I enjoy seeing them progress and supporting their families. I am currently undergoing extra training in order to develop and enhance my knowledge and skills within the Intensive Care area and have recently completed a placement at Liverpool Women's Hospital."

By 2015 Letby had become qualified to work with babies in the intensive care unit and so worked in the neonatal unit. A neonatal unit, also known as a neonatal intensive care unit (NICU), is a hospital unit that provides intensive care for newborn infants who require medical attention. These infants, often referred to as neonates, may be premature, have a low birth weight, or have medical conditions that require immediate intervention and monitoring. Neonatal units are equipped with advanced medical equipment and a highly skilled healthcare team, including neonatologists, nurses, respiratory therapists and other specialists. A neonatal unit is designed to provide a controlled environment with specialised incubators and equipment to maintain the temperature, humidity, and oxygen levels optimal for the newborns' well-being.

Lucy Letby had her first shift as a student nurse at the neonatal unit in the Countess of Chester Hospital on June 1, 2010. At the time the infant mortality rate at the hospital have the same average as any other hospital. In the months to follow this would - tragically - no longer be the case. The Countess of Chester Hospital was designated as a 'level two' unit. This meant it could provide care for fragile babies up to 48 hours. After this they would be transferred to a level 3 unit (a level three unit is designed to care for babies who have more serious medical conditions) in another hospital. The neonatal unit which Letby worked in had four rooms - each with different specialist care. Letby, as we shall see, was always especially eager to be in room one - which supplied the most intensive care. Babies would be moved around the rooms if they required a specific treatment. The unit was a very secure place with two locked doors. One was for staff and one was for the public (parents and grandparents of the babies). Both of the doors were controlled with electronic swipe cards so that it would be difficult for any unauthorised person to enter the unit.

To those that knew Lucy Letby, she seemed perfectly normal. Letby attended salsa classes and went to the gym. She liked to go out eating and drinking with friends and enjoyed holidays abroad (Letby would sometimes also go on holidays in Britain with her parents - which you could say was a trifle odd for a grown adult woman). Letby was considered to be a normal fun loving young woman. Some have suggested that there is something a little 'off' about the photographs of Letby with her friends. Her habit of pulling funny faces, some contend, is a sign of someone trying too hard in pretending to be a normal person. It's impossible now not to look for hidden clues in Letby's past in light of the knowledge of what would happen in her future. Whether these clues are really there is hard to say. If they do exist they are a long way from obvious.

Letby lived in hospital staff accommodation for a time before moving to a flat in Chester. Lucy Letby eventually lived on Westbourne Road when she became infamous. Her parents had helped her purchase a semi-detached house. The house was about a mile away from the hospital. Letby had two cats (Tigger and Smudge) and a fondness for cuddly toys - the latter betraying a childlike quality. Those that worked with Letby in the hospital had found her to be competent and caring. That was the facade which Lucy Letby apparently presented to the world. Letby has since been called a sociopath and psychopath - though there was no sign of these conditions in Letby prior to her employment as a nurse. Sociopaths lack a sense of responsibility or a social conscience. They are prone to antisocial behaviour. They can then tilt into becoming a psychopath. People with a sociopathic disorder typically exhibit a lack of empathy, remorse, and a disregard for the rights and feelings of others. They often engage in manipulative and deceitful behaviour, and may have difficulty forming meaningful relationships. Sociopaths may also display impulsive and aggressive tendencies, and may engage in criminal behaviour.

A psychopath has even less of a moral compass than a sociopath. 'Psychopathy,' wrote NCBI Resources, 'is a constellation of psychological symptoms that typically emerges early in childhood and affects all aspects of a sufferer's life including relationships with family, friends, work, and school. The symptoms of psychopathy include shallow affect, lack of empathy, guilt and remorse, irresponsibility, and impulsivity. While the typical non-psychopathic felon may ponder and struggle with life on the outside and with changing his criminal ways, the typical psychopath returns to his life of crime, and often violent and sexual crime, in the same way he does everything—impulsively, selfishly and without any regard to the rights of others, rights he does not even notice.'

Lucy Letby's friends and family never saw anything of the 'night' about their friend and relative. In fact, they all supported Lucy Letby throughout her trial and refused to believe she could be guilty. Even after the trial some friends and nursing colleagues still couldn't accept that Letby could have done these awful things. This is certainly not unusual in true crime cases. The most famous example of this phenomenon is Ted Bundy's mother Louise. Louise steadfastly refused to accept that her lovely kind son Ted was a serial killer. "Ted Bundy does not go around killing women and little children!" she told The News Tribune in 1980 after Bundy was convicted for the Florida killings. "And I know this, too, that our never-ending faith in Ted - our faith that he is innocent - has never wavered. And it never will." On his last night before execution, Ted Bundy called his mother twice. She told him he was still her son whatever had happened.

Harold Shipman's wife supported her infamous husband to the bitter end and simply refused to countenance that her dear Harold could deliberately have killed all those old ladies. Friends and relatives of killers only see a public side of their loved one - the side that person wants them to see. It is often difficult for relatives of serial killers to accept that the person they have known for many years and in many cases lived with was not the person they thought. This is perhaps a perfectly understandable instinct and reaction. The friends and relatives of serial killers often go into denial because they don't want to believe the terrible things being said about their loved one.

Letby's first charged victim, Baby A (the babies in this case obviously have their identity protected and can't be named in public), was a male twin who was born premature. This was the 8th of June, 2015. The baby was in the neonatal unit as a precaution but not considered to be in danger. Lucy Letby as a specialist was the baby's designated nurse when her shift began. Around 90 minutes after Letby began her shift the child was dead. Letby is believed to have injected the baby with air. An air embolism occurs when a bubble of air or gas enters a blood vessel and blocks the flow of blood. This can happen if air is accidentally injected into a vein during medical procedures such as surgery, catheter insertion, or intravenous therapy. It can also occur if a wound is open to the air, allowing air to enter the bloodstream.

The consequences of an air embolism are dependent on the size and location of the bubble. Small bubbles may be harmless and eventually dissolve on their own, while larger bubbles can cause significant problems. If the air embolism travels to the heart or lungs, it can impair blood flow and oxygen delivery, leading to symptoms such as shortness of breath, chest pain, rapid heart rate, or even cardiac arrest. If the embolism travels to the brain, it can cause stroke-like symptoms, including confusion, numbness, or weakness on one side of the body. Only two weeks before the death of Baby A, Letby had done a training course which qualified her to inject patients. This training course featured a module on the dangers of air embolus.

As far as Letby's MO went, she would resort to different methods of murder. The end result was - tragically - usually the same. It is impossible for any normal person to comprehend how anyone could harm an innocent and vulnerable baby. Normal people have a human failsafe system. We have compassion, empathy, guilt, and an instinct to look after and protect the most vulnerable. Serial killers do not have these qualities. This is what makes them capable of doing the most awful things. It was perhaps inevitable that Lucy Letby would come to be compared to Beverly Allitt. Until Allitt and Lucy Letby at least, Britain didn't seem to have suffered as many 'Angel of Death' medical killers as other places but one such tragic case was Allitt. Beverly Allitt was a nurse who killed four infants and children and tried to kill many more. She is a deeply disturbed and dangerous woman.

Alliitt was born in Lincolnshire in 1968. She was pretty odd from a young age and would fake illness to get attention. She famously had a healthy healthy appendix removed for no reason - such was her ability to pretend she was poorly or suffering from something. Allitt trained to be a nurse as a young woman and despite her poor attendance record, an incident where she was suspected of smearing excrement on a wall, and often failing her nursing exams, she somehow managed to secure a position at Grantham and Kesteven Hospital in Lincolnshire in 1991. Allitt's first victim was seven-week-old Liam Taylor. She was caring for Liam when he began suffering from breathing problems. He eventually ended up on life support with brain damage and his parents had to give their consent to turn the machine off. The alarm monitors had not sounded when Liam stopped breathing but although this was (in hindsight) suspicious at the time no foul play was suspected.

Two weeks later 11-year-old Timothy Hardwick died in Allitt's care when his heart stopped. Timothy suffered from cerebral palsy and his death was felt to have been a consequence of his epilepsy. The next victim was one-year-old Kayley Desmond. Kayley was making good progress after being admitted to the hospital with a chest infection but she went into cardiac arrest while Allitt was looking after her. The staff noticed a puncture mark near Kaley's armpit indicative of an injection but - once again - no foul play was suspected. Allitt continued to prey on children in the hospital. Five year-old Paul Crampton suffered from insulin shock while in the care of Allitt. He was sent to another hospital and thankfully managed to survive. Amazingly, Allitt was the nurse who looked after him during the journey. She still wasn't suspected of anything.

A day later five-year-old Bradley Gibson went into cardiac arrest at the hospital but was saved. On two occasions he was found to have dangerously high levels on insulin and his main nurse was (of course) Beverley Allitt. That same day two-year-old Yik Hung Chan nearly died in the hospital after his oxygen levels dropped alarmingly. On the 1st of April, two-month-old

Becky Phillips died in the hospital from convulsions. Becky had only been admitted for a stomach virus. Her sister was admitted for tests but stopped breathing while at the hospital. By now the authorities should have deduced that foul play was involved in all these strange and tragic incidents.

About three weeks later 15 month old Claire Peck was treated at the hospital for asthma and suffered a cardiac arrest while on a ventilator. Clare was brought into a stable condition but tragically died of another cardiac arrest shortly after. The nurse looking after her was Beverley Allitt. Traces of Lignocaine were found in Clare's system after tests. This is a drug for heart problems but it is never prescribed for children. This naturally raised all manner of alarm bells in the hospital. The investigation deduced that a common denominator in the incidents was that the children had dangerously high levels of insulin. It was no co-incidence that Allitt had reported the key to the insulin cabinet was missing. There were also missing nursing logs - which was obviously suspicious. The other common denominator in this case was Beverley Alitt. The hospital soon realised that she had been looking after all the children who died or nearly died. Allitt had attacked thirteen children over a 59 day period and killed four of them. She was sentenced to 13 concurrent terms of life imprisonment in 1993 and sent to Rampton Secure Hospital.

Allitt was deemed to be suffering from Munchausen's Syndrome by Proxy. There is certainly some plausible evidence for the theory that Lucy Letby suffered from this too. Munchausen syndrome by proxy is a rare disorder but one that has cropped up before in tragic cases where a killer operated in the medical world. Munchausen syndrome by proxy (MSBP), also known as factitious disorder imposed on another, is a psychological disorder in which a caregiver, typically a parent or guardian, intentionally causes or fabricates illness or injury in a dependent, often a child. The caregiver may exaggerate symptoms, tamper with medical tests, or even induce harm to the child in order to gain attention, sympathy, or admiration from healthcare professionals. The motivations behind Munchausen syndrome by proxy can vary, but they often include a need for attention, control, power, or a desire to assume the role of a loving and caring caregiver. The disorder is obviously considered to be a form of child abuse since the child's medical care and well-being are deliberately compromised. At its most extreme this condition can drive people to murder.

Lucy Letby alerted a doctor when Baby A began to change colour and worsen. Resuscitation failed the baby was pronounced dead at 8:58pm. The tragic death of the baby aroused no suspicion. In fact, Letby was praised by colleagues for her conduct (these colleagues obviously had no idea that it was Letby who might be responsible for the death). In response to one text from a nurse, Letby replied - "It was the hardest thing I've ever had to do. Just a big shock for us all. Hard coming in tonight and seeing the parents." Far from being distraught and in shock or wracked with guilt and regret, Letby actually seemed excited by all the attention she received. It was addictive to her. There are many cases where medical killers have become addicted to the power over life and death they wield in a hospital or care facility. They develop a 'God complex' and engineer medical emergencies so that they can play the hero.

Psychopaths tend to have an inflated sense of self-worth and may have an exaggerated view of their abilities and achievements. Lucy Letby displayed some of that during the time frame of the awful crimes. There certainly appears to have been some disturbing Munchausen's Syndrome by Proxy element with Letby too. Letby enjoyed the sympathy she got for being on duty when a child had died. Professionals in the health care services do heroic or difficult things all the time. They also witness sad and tragic things. They don't do this for attention or to feel like they are some great special person. They do it because that's their job and they are decent kind people who care about their patients. Lucy Letby, by contrast, did not care about her patients. They were simply a means to an end and the 'end' in this case was some extra attention and sympathy from colleagues.

Around twenty-eight hours after the death of the first baby, Lucy Letby, monstrously and unconscionably, apparently tried to murder the twin sister of the dead child. Baby B was, it is believed, injected with air by Letby and had her airwaves blocked. As with the first victim, the baby began to change colour and go into a critical condition. An on-call registrar rushed to the scene and, thankfully, the baby was resuscitated. Although it was Lucy Letby who was the designated nurse for both of these incidents at this very early stage she had yet to attract any undue suspicion. In fact, a few days later Letby actually requested to be assigned more shifts.

Letby continued to discuss the death of Baby A in text messages to colleagues. In hindsight it is plain to see that Letby was enjoying all the drama and attention from this tragedy. Letby said to a colleague that from a 'confidence' point of view she needed to 'take' another ITU baby soon. She obviously meant that she needed a baby to look after to mitigate what had happened but the use of the word 'take' has a rather sinister hue in retrospect. It is certainly evident that Lucy Letby was a disturbed young woman. Normal people don't murder babies. Normal people would be incapable of murdering an adult let alone a baby. There was something seriously wrong with Letby but she was able to hide this dark and troubled side of herself from friends, relatives, and colleagues.

The ability of serial killers to appear normal to those around them has been described as the 'mask of sanity'. The term "mask of sanity" was coined by psychiatrist Hervey Cleckley in his 1941 book, "The Mask of Sanity: An Attempt to Clarify Some Issues About the So-Called Psychopathic Personality." In the book, Cleckley explores the concept of psychopathy and describes how individuals with this disorder often present themselves to others as seemingly well-adjusted and normal, while internally lacking empathy, remorse, or a sense of moral responsibility. He refers to this outward display of normalcy as the "mask of sanity."

The mask of sanity allows psychopathic individuals to easily blend into society and manipulate others, appearing charming, charismatic, and often highly successful. They are skilled at mimicking normal emotional responses and social behaviours, making it difficult for others to detect their true nature. If you knew Lucy Letby in real life you would get no sense of any danger from her at all. In most of her photographs she is smiling or goofing around. She was described as 'carefree' and fun by her friends. Letby was also able to play the role of an empathetic and caring nurse at work - though the reality was of course tragically different.

On the 14th of June, 2015, Letby claimed a third victim. Baby C was a male baby born ten weeks premature. The baby was making good progress though and doctors judged the child to be getting better and growing stronger. Letby was not the designated nurse of this baby but was working on the shift. When the designated nurse of Baby C was doing something else, Letby, according to prosecution experts, injected air into the baby's stomach - which sadly caused his death. When the monitor alarm for Baby C sounded, Lucy Letby was found standing over the child. However, Letby has still yet to arouse any alarm or suspicion. It would take some time for an investigation to deduce that Letby was the common factor in the three incidents which had occurred with babies in such a short space of time (and tragically there would be more incidents to come).

Only hours after the death of Baby C it was later established that Lucy Letby had done online searches through Facebook to find out more about the child's family. Letby was also once again fishing for sympathy from colleagues through texts. 'It's all a bit much,' wrote Letby - which got the desired result with a return message of sympathy. 'It's heartbreaking but it's not about me,' replied Letby. 'We learn to deal with it.' Letby's assertion that 'it's not about me' was patently hollow and insincere. In reality, it was ALL about Letby. She displayed classic symptoms of narcissistic personality disorder.

Narcissistic personality disorder (NPD) is a psychological disorder characterised by a pattern of grandiosity, a need for admiration, and a lack of empathy. People with NPD have an exaggerated sense of self-importance and often believe they are special and unique. They constantly seek attention and praise from others and have a strong sense of entitlement. They may have a lack of empathy and have difficulty understanding the needs and feelings of others. They often exploit and manipulate others to fulfil their own desires and are prone to fits of anger or rage when their needs are not met. Although it obviously doesn't explain Letby's awful crimes and her parents (as with the parents of any serial killer you might care to mention) are not to blame, the fact that Lucy Letby was an only child who was spoiled by her parents and very close to them would perhaps provide for a partial explanation for why she had this psychological craving for constant attention. The reason why Letby was killing babies was an altogether more complex and unfathomable conundrum.

On the 21st of June, Lucy Letby took another life. Baby D was born with a suspected infection but not considered to be in any danger. The child was 36 hours old when Letby injected air into her bloodstream. The baby collapsed three times and required emergency medical attention by doctors. As with the previous incidents a discolouration on the baby's skin was apparent. The baby tragically died after the third collapse. Once again Lucy Letby went on Facebook shortly after to research the child's family. Letby also solicited sympathy from colleagues through text messages (in addition to the sympathy she solicited in an actual sense in the hospital). In the text messages after the death of Baby D, Letby ponders whether the death was 'fate' and wonders if these things happen for a reason. Letby claims that she has been constantly crying - though clearly she hadn't.

Guilt, remorse, sorrow, empathy. These would be alien emotions to someone capable of doing what Lucy Letby did.

Several days later there were text messages between Letby and another nurse in which the nurse noted there was something 'odd' about the fact that these babies had all died in such a short space of time. Lucy Letby was quick to deflect this observation, replying - 'Well Baby C was tiny, obviously compromised in utero. Baby D septic. It's Baby A I can't get my head around.' There had now been three deaths in a fortnight. This equalled the total number of deaths in the neonatal unit for the entirety of 2014. This was plainly a situation which merited an investigation and one was instigated. This was the first sign that the hospital authorities were becoming if not suspicious (as in thinking that foul play might be involved) but concerned that something was wrong and someone might not be doing their job correctly.

The same month as the latest tragedy, Dr Stephen Brearey, the head consultant on the neonatal unit, carried out a review. One inescapable fact quickly established by the review was that

Lucy Letby was the only nurse on shift for each of these deaths. The findings of the review were passed to the trust's committee. However, the committee decided that the deaths were most likely the result of medication mistakes or natural causes. As a consequence of this a full investigation was blocked and Lucy Letby remained on the neonatal unit. This was plainly a huge mistake in hindsight. Letby not only continued to work on the unit but was also still receiving sympathy and support. After the deaths Letby had been offered counselling but declined to take up this service.

On the 4th of August there was another tragic death at the hospital when Baby E, an identical twin boy who had been born premature, began screaming and showed sign of blood coming from his mouth. The baby's mother walked in on Letby standing over the child but presumed (as one would) that the nurse was lending assistance. Letby told the mother that the blood was nothing to worry about and due to a stomach tube. In her medical notes though Letby made no mention of this blood. A doctor later noticed the blood and the soon ailing child was given CPR. It is believed that the child's death was a result of an air embolism and trauma caused by the interference of the nasogastric tube. A nasogastric tube is a flexible tube that is inserted through the nose and down into the stomach. This medical device is used to remove fluids or air from the stomach, or to deliver medications and nutrients.

The following day, the twin brother of Baby E crashed and had to be given emergency treatment when synthetic insulin was used on him. Mercifully, this baby was saved by doctors.

It is believed that Letby took the insulin from the medical cabinet and injected it into the IV bag. No other child in the unit had been prescribed insulin (Baby G had been prescribed a tiny amount) so this was clearly not a mix up of medications. This was the first time that Letby had used insulin to try and kill a child. Letby later went a dancing class. As was her custom by now, she continued to research her victim's families on Facebook and solicit sympathy from colleagues.

'I said goodbye to Baby F's parents as Baby F might go tomorrow,' texted Letby. 'They both cried & hugged me saying they will never be able to thank me for the love & care I gave to Baby F & for the precious memories I've given them. It's heartbreaking.' Lucy Letby lived in a bizarre delusional world. She tried to portray herself as some great hero when the complete opposite was true. By now though one didn't need to be Dr Gregory House to see a pattern in these tragic and awful incidents at the hospital. There was one common factor in all of these incidents. That common factor was a nurse named Lucy Letby.

On the 7th of September, Letby attempted to murder Baby G. Baby G was a girl born prematurely. Letby attempted to murder the child by overfeeding her but was not successful.

On the 21st of September, Letby made another attempt to murder Baby G. This involved overfeeding and injecting air into the baby. At one point the baby stopped breathing but a doctor managed to stabilise the condition of the baby. However, the baby was left disabled as a result of all of this trauma. Letby would be found guilty on two charges of attempted murder of Baby G but not guilty on a third. As we shall see in the trial later, this was an incredibly complex case.

Once again, it was later established that Letby did Facebook searches on the baby's family after the incidents. Once again too, Letby was in text communication with other nurses and as usual painting herself as some dutiful, caring nurse who just seemed to be suffering from a lot of bad luck lately when it came to incidents on her shifts. What is detectable from the texts in relation to this timeframe is that Letby is now becoming somewhat defensive. It is clear that gossip in the hospital is portraying Letby as incompetent - or even worse.

On the 30th of September, Letby attempted to murder another baby at the unit. This was Baby I. Letby injected air into the baby's stomach through a nasogastric tube. Letby made two more attempts to kill the baby in similar fashion. Tragically, Letby killed the baby on the 23rd of October by injecting air into the child. Letby sent a sympathy card to the grieving parents of the child. By now Letby was again asking for extra shifts at the hospital. Letby was also though beginning to attract suspicion. You might reasonably suggest that it was about time. It was remarkable that Lucy Letby had got this far. The fact that she was the common link between all of these deaths and incidents would appear to have been apparent by now.

Letby was later accused of attempting to kill Baby H twice on September 26 and 27. This child recovered. Letby was found not guilty of attempted murder on three counts in the specific case of Baby H because there were other circumstances. The baby was intubated for ventilation after an 'unacceptable' delay and also had a needle incorrectly removed. It was decided that there were too many other factors to definitively say that the baby had been deliberately harmed (though the prosecution obviously begged to differ in court). Baby I died on October 23, 2015. Letby is believed to have made more than one attempt to kill this infant. The baby was fine until it arrived at the Countess of Chester. The cause of death was air embolism. Letby was there when the last attempt to resuscitate the child was made.

CHAPTER TWO

By now the unit's lead consultant Dr Stephen Brearey was beginning to have grave suspicions concerning Lucy Letby. At first he had refused to believe it could be possible because 'Lucy was so nice' and the last person you'd suspect of this. The baby deaths in the hospital though were now well above the national average. There was clearly something seriously wrong at the baby unit. The possibility that the hospital might have a Beverly Allitt on their hands was clearly something that they refused to even consider. Dr Stephen Brearey, despite his initial reluctance to accuse Letby of anything, now feared that it was Letby who was harming these babies - whether by incompetence or design. In October he passed these suspicions onto the unit manager and director of nursing but neither seemed interested in investigating these claims or even showed much interest in them at all. An independent expert, Dr Nimish Subhedar, was asked to carry out a review of the infant deaths. The review noted that the babies had seemed fine then rapidly deteriorated. This was highly unusual. The review also noted that the incidents happened on night shifts - where Lucy Letby happened to be present.

In November there was another death at the hospital. Baby J was a female baby who had bowel surgery. The baby's sudden death was later linked to Letby. At the trial it was suggested at one point that Letby may have smothered Baby J but the jury could not reach a verdict on this specific charge. Another consultant, Dr Ravi Jayaram, also alerted the management over his concerns over Letby at this time but he was basically told to keep quiet and not make a fuss. Jayaram had good reason to be suspicious of Letby because he was there when Baby K died in February. Baby K was a female baby born premature. Letby wasn't the designated nurse but Dr Jayaram found her standing over the baby's incubator. What struck Jayaram as odd is that the baby's oxygen levels had fallen but Letby had not called for assistance. The baby's breathing tube was dislodged and the alarm had been paused. The baby, tragically, died three days later. Letby was not convicted of this death at the trial (the jury could reach no verdict) - though her presence that day was highly suspicious to say the least.

By now there was ample evidence that something was seriously wrong at the hospital but no one wanted to hear the evidence because the evidence seemed to lead to the worst possible explanation. There were a range of possible explanations for why the baby mortality rate had substantially increased at the hospital. The possible explanations included medical incompetence, some sort of bug or infection in the hospital, or simply even bad luck. There was of course another explanation but it was apparently too awful for anyone to contemplate. That explanation was the 'nice' young nurse named Lucy Letby who always seemed to be on shift when these tragedies occurred.

In cases involving medical killers, or even alleged medical killers, there is obviously an awful lot of investigating to do. Because of the nature of hospitals and the medical world it is clearly more complex to prove a patient was deliberately murdered than it is, for example, to prove that a more conventional murder (which didn't occur in a hospital) was a result of foul play. If someone dies as a result of strangulation or knife wounds in an alley, well that's obviously murder. But someone dying in a hospital presents a much more complex mystery. It could be that they were simply ill, it could have been a medical mistake, and - in rare cases - it could be foul play. There are actually still complex cases involving famous convicted medical killers where not everyone is convinced they were even guilty. One such case is that of Colin Norris.

Colin Norris was born in Glasgow in 1976. Norris worked in a travel agency when he left school but he decided he wanted to do something different in the end so he trained to be a nurse. He studied for a Higher Nursing Diploma at Dundee University's School of Nursing and Midwifery and then worked at the Royal Victoria Hospital, Dundee on a placement scheme. Norris also spent some time working in a nursing home. The experiences of Colin Norris in the hospital and nursing home were not to his liking because he was working with geriatric patients. Norris, it seems, didn't like caring for old people very much. He especially disliked having to bathe elderly female patients. Norris was gay and it has been speculated that it made him uncomfortable having to wash female patients but it seems unlikely that his sexuality had anything to do with it. It was more the case that Norris wanted to work in a more general (and 'exciting' - as he put it himself) medical environment rather than simply look after old people. While Norris is alleged to have had a distaste for elderly patients there is no evidence that he harmed any of them in his student nurse years.

Much is made in this case of the fact that while he was training to be a nurse, Norris was taught about the story of Jessie McTavish. Jessie McTavish was a Glasgow nurse who was convicted in 1974 of murdering a patient with insulin. McTavish had learned that insulin was soluble and thus a potential homicide agent through which one might plausibly get away with the crime (she was obviously wrong about the second part of this deduction). The case of Jessie McTavish is said to have stuck with Colin Norris and inspired his own alleged medical crimes. Added to this was the fact that as part of his training he was taught how to care for patients with diabetes.

After his training was completed in Dundee, Norris got a job as a staff nurse at Leeds General Infirmary in Yorkshire. Norris would also work at St James's University Hospital in the city too. It was here in Leeds that his crimes took place. Norris is alleged to have been frustrated and unhappy at having to care for some elderly patients on his ward in Leeds. It is said that he tried to kill 90 year old Vera Wilby by way of insulin overdose in 2002 but she actually survived this murder attempt. In June of that same year, Norris was later found in court to have killed Bridget Bourke, 88, and then in October he murdered Irene Crookes, 79. These women were judged to have been killed by insulin overdose - despite the fact that they were not diabetic.

At the time of the deaths no foul play was suspected by the hospital - although Colin Norris was starting to get noticed by the staff. One colleague would later say that Norris seemed quite amused when a patient died - which was certainly what you could describe as odd and unprofessional behaviour for a nurse. Norris was also said to be bad tempered with the elderly patients on his ward and not exactly a barrel of laughs in his treatment of these ailing old folk. At his later trial there were many accounts by colleagues and patients about Norris being angry and verbally abusive with elderly patients on the wards. Norris was also later accused of murdering 86-year-old Ethel Hall on his ward. The trouble began for Colin Norris when Ethel Hall was found unconscious. Dr Emma Ward found that Hall, who was being treated for a broken hip, had been given 1,000 units of insulin. A diabetic is usually given 50 units (not that Mrs Hall was even a diabetic anyway). This was all highly suspicious and alarming and so an investigation was launched by the police.

The police found that 18 deaths at the hospital were - retrospectively - deemed to be suspicious and that a common denominator in these deaths is that they often seemed to occur during the shifts of Colin Norris. Another salient detail was that these incidents seemed to occur at weekends or very early in the morning. In other words they took place at a time when specialist staff would be less likely to be there. Was that a coincidence or did it indicate something more sinister? The police case against Norris judged that he was the only person who worked those specific shifts (where the incidents took place) and who had access to those patients and insulin. He was also the only nurse who worked on the two wards where the deaths took place. Much was made too of the fact that Norris had once predicted when a patient would die and been proved completely accurate in this prediction. Norris would claim this was simply some dark humour which was blown out of all proportion. What didn't help Norris though was that he confessed to this 'prediction' in a police interview but then denied it in court. That was obviously a contradiction.

During the police investigation into Norris he was suspended from work on full pay. He even went abroad a few times during this period and enjoyed some holidays. Those who were close to Norris said he was scared though at the thought that he might end up in prison. The police conducted a number of interviews with Norris and one particular detail struck them as a big red flag. Norris claimed that the insulin which was taken from the fridge in the hospital without permission and then used on the patients must have been stolen by an intruder while the nurses were busy or taking a break. Presumably then this alleged intruder, according to Colin Norris, must have injected the patients too. This all struck the police as pure fiction. It was rather implausible to think that someone would sneak into a hospital somehow unobserved and then - for reasons best known to themselves - attempt to kill elderly patients with overdoses of insulin. Added to this was the fact that the insulin fridge was locked with a key code which was only known to the medical staff. The police believed that Colin Norris was simply making this up. They didn't believe he was telling the truth in his interviews.

The police also found Colin Norris to be something of a cold fish in that he showed no sorrow whatsoever for the deaths of these old people on the wards. Norris told the police he couldn't even remember these patients. Norris was combative and arrogant in his dealings with the police. He treated them with disdain and said they had no case against him.

Norris became quite obstreperous at times during his trial at Newcastle. Those who believe he is innocent might argue that this was perfectly natural in the circumstances. If you were charged with awful crimes you didn't commit then anger and frustration would be understandable.

Norris was found guilty of four murders on an 11-1 majority verdict. One member of the jury was clearly not convinced that Norris was a killer. Norris got life with a minimum of 30 years. Usually with medical killers they are found to be highly disturbed individuals with dark pasts who become addicted to the power they wield as medical professions. They like to play God with the lives of their patients. A number of other medical killers in history did their crimes for financial reasons in that they wanted to get their grubby mitts on the money and valuables of their patients. Colin Norris didn't really fit these patterns though. He was a reasonably normal sort of person whose main motive seemed to be that these elderly patients got on his nerves.

Colin Norris was called 'evil' by the police and judge. He was (inevitably) compared to Harold Shipman in the media. In the years since the conviction of Colin Norris though there has been a concerted campaign to overturn his conviction. Some scientific experts believe his conviction was unsafe and that the evidence against him was circumstantial. Those that convicted Norris though remain convinced that he was a ruthless medical killer. In 2021 his case was referred to the court of appeals. It remains to be seen if Norris will ever prove his innocence or whether he was guilty all along. Colin Norris and his family still believe that one day he will be free again and his convictions will be quashed.

At the start of February 2016, Dr Stephen Brearey sent a review of the deaths in the neonatal unit at the Countess of Chester Hospital to the medical director Ian Harvey. Brearey was now explicitly pointing out that Lucy Letby was on shift during all of these deaths. If foul play was the explanation for the spike in deaths then the culprit could only have been Lucy Letby. Brearey wanted a meeting with executives to discuss Letby but no one wanted to meet with him. The general line of the hospital at this point was that the deaths were most likely a result of staffing problems and not having enough senior staff on call. This explanation was of course hopelessly wide of the mark. The real explanation for the tragedies was beyond comprehension and too awful for words.

On the 9th of April, Letby attempted to kill twin boys in the unit. Baby L was given a secret dose of insulin by Letby. The insulin was injected into the baby's drip feed. it was alleged that Letby volunteered for an extra shift for the express purpose of carrying out this murder - which thankfully was not successful. Letby would later say that the insulin must have already been in one of the bags but this was not deemed to be a credible defence. Baby M, the other twin, came close to death after being injected with air. the baby survived but suffered brain damage. Lucy Letby made diary entries after these incidents but her mood, given the circumstances, was what you might describe as surprisingly carefree. In the aftermath of these worrying emergencies at the unit, Letby was more concerned about a house-warming party she was arranging and celebrating winning £135 on the Grand National.

Dr Stephen Brearey met with colleagues in May to raise his concerns about Lucy Letby. There was however an 'assurance' document doing the rounds of the hospital which stated - 'There is no evidence whatsoever against LL [Letby] other than coincidence.' Brearey was, as you might imagine, becoming rather frustrated by this point. He felt as if no one was listening to him. It was as if the hospital bigwigs had their heads buried in the sand. In June, it was later alleged that Lucy Letby attempted to kill Baby N. Baby N was a male baby born premature. The baby had haemophilia - though it was apparently a mild form of the condition. Haemophilia is a rare genetic disorder that impairs the body's ability to form blood clots, leading to excessive bleeding. Letby is alleged to have thought that the baby's condition would make it less likely that any foul play would be detected. Letby allegedly made three attempts to kill Baby N by adjusting his breathing tube but the baby thankfully survived and was transferred to a special medical unit in Liverpool. The jury could reach no verdict of whether Letby attempted to kill Baby N.

Lucy Letby went on holiday to Ibiza around this time but - sadly - soon returned to her old ways when she went back to work at the hospital. Letby killed two of three triplets by injecting them with air. The male babies were not considered to be in a critical condition until they were unfortunate enough to encounter Letby. Letby's last attack was on Baby Q. Letby once again injected air into the baby but in this case - thankfully - the baby survived. Incredibly, the authorities had still not come to the conclusion that Lucy Letby was the link in these deaths. The inquest into the death of one of the triplets actually cited the fact the baby was born premature as the cause of death. This was plainly not accurate. Dr Stephen Brearey demanded that Letby be taken off duty in June. This request was ignored by the hospital management. In fact, the management even made it clear that they would tolerate no whispers about Letby.

The fact that Lucy Letby was the most plausible common denominator in the baby deaths and medical emergencies at the hospital was something that hadn't escaped Letby herself. Her texts at this time clearly show that she anticipated that some scrutiny from the hospital was on the cards. She was now in communication with a doctor (we shall be hearing more of this doctor - it was alleged that Letby was having an affair with this married doctor) online and seeking reassurance. The doctor told Letby that there was going to be an inquest into the recent deaths (the doctor obviously shouldn't have been telling Letby this because it was confidential information) but she had nothing to worry about. The doctor even offered to provide a statement for Letby should she fall under any suspicion.

Clearly, this doctor had no idea that Letby was involved in these deaths. He simply assumed it was a coincidence that these things had happened during Letby's shifts. Letby is believed to have been love with this married doctor from the same hospital. She burst into tears during the trial when this doctor gave evidence. There is a theory that Letby's crimes at the hospital were designed to get attention from this doctor. She hoped that he would be the person called to the scene. This theory is interesting remains exactly that, just a theory. The problem with this theory is that it has since been established that this doctor only arrived at the hospital when Letby had already begun killing infants. This doctor was therefore not the motivation for Letby's crimes - at least not from the outset.

It was established at the trial that this married doctor, who was never named because he applied for anonymity, went on a trip to London with Lucy Letby and made plans to do this again (though this second trip never happened). The doctor and Letby would use affectionate heart emojis when they texted. Letby denied though that that this relationship was anything more than platonic and denied too that she had an infatuation with this man. Letby said he was just a trusted friend she confided in at a difficult time.

Theories for why Letby did what she did are difficult to pin down on any one thing. Among the theories we haven't mentioned yet, there is a possibility that Letby had a sadistic disorder. Sadistic Personality Disorder is a psychiatric disorder characterised by an individual's persistent and pervasive pattern of deriving pleasure, satisfaction, or gratification from inflicting physical or psychological pain, suffering, or humiliation on others. People with this disorder tend to exhibit aggressive and cruel behaviours towards others without feeling remorse or guilt.

Although she was destined to become of Britain's most infamous female serial killers, Lucy Letby was atypical in many ways when it comes to the general profile of other female killers. Letby was not married or beset with relationship problems. There was no violence or alcoholism in her life. She didn't take drugs. She suffered no abuse as a child. She had loving parents. She had no previous criminal convictions for anything. Letby also had no history or diagnosis of mental illness. Letby was a blank when it comes to serial killer indicators. Just about the only thing she had in common with a lot of previous female killers is that she worked in the health profession.

Serial killers are often said to have a superficial charm and one could probably attribute this quality to Letby because she was clearly well liked at the hospital and had friends in the outside world. Many killers are highly manipulative and while one wouldn't say Letby showed any signs of being some Machiavellian mastermind her texts do show that she was constantly fishing for sympathy and support from colleagues and running what you might describe as a rather ghoulish (given the circumstances) public relations campaign for herself.

Sadly, true crime history is not bereft of medical killers and the Countess of Chester Hospital in Chester was certainly not the first hospital to face criticism for the way it handled a killer employee. The case of Genene Jones, like that of Letby, raised many serious questions about why it took so long to deduce that a nurse was a killer. The Genene Jones also highlighted the lengths hospitals will sometimes go to simply to avoid scandal and bad publicity. Genene Jones was born in Texas in 1950. She was adopted as a child and worked as a beautician before deciding to go to nursing school. Jones also got married and had children of her own. She eventually worked as a licensed vocational nurse (LVN) at the Bexar County Hospital (now University Hospital of San Antonio) in the pediatric intensive care unit.

However, an unusually large number of children seemed to die during her shifts. Jones would inject digoxin, heparin, and other drugs into patients to induce a medical emergency. She would then swoop in to revive them. Tragically a number of children died because of this. A motive for these murders was never established but Genene Jones, like all 'Angel of Death' medical killers, apparently developed a God complex. She was exhilarated by the power that she had over life and death and had become addicted to the practice of taking a child to the brink of death and then resuscitating them. Nurses who worked with her later recalled that Jones seemed to get strangely excited when a patient fell ill and even used to offer predictions on when the patient in question might expire.

It is impossible to say how many children Genene Jones killed through her activities. Though she was convicted of just two murders, fresh charges arrive to this day and a conservative estimate would put the number of victims around forty at the very least. The Bexar County Hospital was aware of the high number of deaths and feared a lawsuit so they simply dismissed all the licensed vocational nurses and replaced them with registered nurses. They also shredded medical records to protect themselves. The loss of these records later made prosecuting Genene Jones more complicated than it should have been.

After the Bexar County Hospital dismissed their nurses, Genene Jones soon got a job at a pediatrician's clinic in Kerrville,

Texas. Once again though she was soon up to her old tricks. A doctor there found a puncture in a bottle of succinylcholine which only Jones had access to out of all the nurses. Succinylcholine is a medication used to cause short-term paralysis as part of general anesthesia. People under the influence of this drug can't breathe. Chelsea McClellan, a baby at the clinic, had died after Jones gave her some shots. Jones is believed to have killed around six children at this clinic.

Jones tried to use an insanity defence as her trial loomed but this didn't wash. The prosecution proved that she was perfectly sane and knew exactly what she was doing when she killed those patients. In 1985, Jones was sentenced to 99 years in prison for killing 15-month-old Chelsea McClellan with succinylcholine. In the second trial (for another hospital), she received 60 years. Genene Jones was indicted on new charges in recent years - which ended any lingering hopes she might have had of parole or freedom one day. In 2020, Jones pleaded guilty to causing the death of an eleven month old baby who had been under her care in 1981.

After the near death of Baby Q, Lucy Letby worked three more nursing shifts before being moved to clerical duties at the hospital's risk and patient safety office in July. 'Bloody hell fuming,' Letby texted a colleague. 'I'm on email and makes it sound like my choice.' It what can only be described as darkly ironic, Letby's new duties involved raising serious incident investigation reports to NHS England. This actually gave her access to sensitive medical documents. Although this was only the beginning of the long drawn out case to come, the pressure applied by Dr Stephen Brearey was at least starting to have effect and, mercifully, Letby was no longer working in the baby unit.

Dr Ravi Jayaram later said that in June he had done some research on air embolism because it had been floated (in private) as a theory pertaining to the tragedies in the baby unit. Dr Jayaram said that when he read up on the subject his blood ran cold because it fitted with what had happened to many of the babies. Dr Brearey was exceptionally suspicious of Letby by now. This suspicion was heightened by the fact that the nursing staff seemed understandably traumatised by the recent tragedies and emergencies and yet Letby seemed unphased. On the contrary, Letby had continued to ask for extra right up the end of her time in the baby unit. The lack of emotion displayed by Letby was certainly in keeping with killers past.

In a text to a colleague in July, Letby was clearly bracing herself for the reviews and investigations to come. Letby knows that all the staff are going to be spoken to. 'Hoping to get as much info together as I can,' texted Letby. 'If they have nothing or minimal on me they'll look silly.' In July, 2016, the Countess of Chester Hospital decided to no longer accommodate premature births before the 32-week mark. This was an obvious consequence of what had happened at the neonatal unit - with deaths now well above the national average. Senior consultants at the hospital were now privately debating whether or not to ask the police to conduct an investigation. The medical director Ian Harvey poured cold water on this plan of action by telling colleagues that 'action' was being taken. The head of corporate affairs and legal services, Stephen Cross, had told Harvey that it would be a disaster for the hospital if the police were involved.

Senior staff were advised to drop the subject in their communications. Staff were also told not to discuss Lucy Letby. Rather than involve the police, the Royal College of Paediatrics and Child Heath (RCPCH) were asked to review the level of service on the neonatal unit. During this time Lucy Letby continued to email colleagues seeking assurance, support, and sympathy. This was still in ample supply as colleagues continued to tell Letby she was a good nurse who had done nothing wrong. Letby even registered a grievance procedure in complaint at her treatment. It clearly infuriated Letby that she had been taken away from her job as a nurse and placed in a clerical role. One might conjecture though that Letby's grievance procedure was actually a calculated move with an obvious subtext. Letby was letting it be known that she was 'innocent' and wasn't willing to be singled out by the hospital authorities or made a 'scapegoat'. It was a pre-emptive strike.

Dr Jane Hawdon, a premature baby specialist in London, was also asked to compile a report on infant deaths at the Countess of Chester Hospital. Hawdon's report was compromised by the fact she didn't have much spare time and it certainly didn't yield any conclusions which would point in the direction of foul play. The review by the RCPCH arrived in November. They could find no clear answer for the spike in deaths at the unit but suggested it could have been a consequence of not having enough senior staff covering shifts. The upshot of all of this is that Lucy Letby, at this point, was not under any official suspicion. There were certainly whispers though.

Letby met the chief executive in December and brought her parents along for support as if she was a little kid. Doctors at the hospital were told that Letby's parents had threatened to refer Dr Brearey and Dr Ravi Jayaram to the General Medical Council in protest at their daughter's treatment. Incredibly, senior doctors were ordered to write a letter of apology to Letby on 26 January 2017 for repeatedly raising concerns about her. It appears that the hospital management were under the impression that the two reviews had cleared Lucy Letby and that she was now owed some sort of apology. This was assuredly not the case though. The reviews had not come to any definitive conclusion and had also recommended further investigation should be undertaken. A crucial point too is that neither review was instructed to investigate Lucy Letby - nor indeed the possibility of foul play. Dr Stephen Brearey felt that all of the bureaucratic gymnastics were designed to stave off the inevitable. The inevitable in this specific instance was obviously a police investigation.

CHAPTER THREE

Amazingly, in January 2017, the Countess of Chester Hospital began seriously considering putting Lucy Letby back on the neonatal unit. The parents of the babies who had died in the unit were told by the hospital that there were no suspicious circumstances. The hospital's CEO Tony Chambers was the person who had told staff to apologise to Letby. Chambers had spent many hours talking to Letby and was convinced that she was innocent. It was inconceivable to Chambers that this pleasant and well liked young woman would have been capable of harming an infant. There were much later stories that staff had asked for CCTV cameras to be installed in the unit when they learned Letby might be coming back. Though it might seem strange, there were no cameras in the unit because it is up to each NHS Trust whether or want to do this and many choose not to on the grounds that patients and relatives of patients have a right to privacy.

Paediatric consultant Dr John Gibbs, who would be a witness at the trial, later said that doctors were starting to 'think the unthinkable' and believe that foul play was the (hitherto) unknown factor in these deaths. However, the management at the hospital clearly didn't want to 'think the unthinkable'. Gibbs was rather appalled when Stephen Cross had complained that a police investigation would 'disrupt' the hospital. A police investigation was clearly the right thing to do. The police didn't care about hospital politics or the reputation of the hospital. They would conduct an impartial independent investigation to deduce if any crimes had taken place. That's exactly what was needed. Tony Chambers, to the surprise of few one would imagine, later left the hospital trust shortly after Lucy Letby was arrested.

At this point Lucy Letby must have felt as if she was in a strange limbo. Different forces in the hospital were pulling in different directions and this created a sort of stalemate where reviews were commissioned but simply advised further investigation. Letby's texts in the middle of this drama spoke of being in 'meltdown' but at the start of 2017 she appeared to have not exactly got away with it but at the very least pulled the wool over the management's eyes. Letby was constantly told by the hospital bigwigs that she wasn't suspected of anything or being blamed. The possibility of Letby returning to the neonatal unit was ample evidence that the management did not think she was a suspect in the infant deaths. Lucy Letby wasn't out of the woods yet but she must have felt like she now had some breathing space. Letby would have been alarmed though if she'd known what was about to happen behind the scenes.

Dr Brearey and Dr Ravi Jayaram were trying to work out a way to stop Lucy Letby from going back to work. They consulted with retired detective chief superintendent Nigel Wenham. Wenham told them the police would have to get involved. Lucy Letby had been less than a week away from returning to work but now she would never go on that unit again. This was March 2017. The regional neonatal lead advised the hospital they must consult the police and so - finally - this happened. Tony Chambers penned a letter to the Chief Constable of the Cheshire force, Simon Byrne, requesting that the police to 'put their minds at rest.' Lucy Letby was due to return to work only days after this happened. Chesire Police now had to decide if the case merited an extensive investigation. The fact that the baby deaths were unexplained was the deciding factor. A police investigation named Operation Hummingbird officially began. The man asked to investigate the hospital was Detective inspector Paul Hughes. Hughes was the head of the major investigation team at Cheshire police's western syndicate.

It was obviously a complex and difficult task facing the police. They would have to rely on a number of medical experts and they would also have to investigate each death and incident. The police quickly learned from independent medical experts that it is not normal for babies on a neonatal unit to suddenly start dying at the rate they did at the Countess of Chester Hospital. Babies in a neonatal unit are not, contrary to presumption, all desperately ill. In fact, most of them are perfectly stable. They simply require specialist medical supervision in these early stages of life before they can go home. If babies die in a neonatal unit it is usually either expected or explainable. In the case of the tragic deaths at the Countess of Chester Hospital though this wasn't the case. The deaths were not expected and they had yet to be explained. This was a clear red flag to the police - though they were at pains not to jump to any early conclusions.

The police team of detectives were each assigned a baby death to investigate and did this independently without necessarily knowing what other detectives had or hadn't uncovered. This was a shrewd tactic because it gave each detective 'ownership' of a deceased infant. Anyone assigned a sensitive and tragic case of this nature would leave no stone unturned in their determination to get the truth for the parents and the memory of the child. The fact that detectives were investigating the cases independently also allowed the team leader to see if any patterns emerged in the conclusions coming in from the team. "I wanted to allow people to come to a determination of what they were finding on their own," said Hughes. Detectives worked independently on their cases for six months before there was a team meeting.

In order to help them with the case, the police turned to Dr Dewi Evans. Dr Evans was a retired consultant paediatrician with three decades of experience in his field. He studied all the clinical reports of the deaths at the hospital and came to a chilling conclusion. Evans felt that fifteen of the incidents of death or non-fatal collapse defied any conventional medical explanation. The only explanation in these cases was air embolism or insulin poisoning. Evans therefore felt the only explanation for the spike in deaths was someone deliberately harming the infants. When he studied the duty rosters of the neonatal unit, Evans deduced that Lucy Letby was the only nurse who was on shift when ALL of these incidents took place.

Evans was appalled at the way the hospital management had handled the case. Their response had not been good enough. They should have deduced more of these things for themselves much sooner, taken Letby off duty, and called in the police. There was certainly evidence of a cover-up too in the way the hospital had ignored warnings about Letby from senior doctors. Dr Evans believed that many of these tragic deaths should have prevented. Dr Evans was impressed by Lucy Letby's medical notes (nurses obviously have to write a lot of medical notes as part of their job) and felt this was someone who was intelligent and knew their job. The fact that Letby was intelligent and knew her 'stuff' was probably one of the reasons why she had got away with it for so long.

The police investigation did not begin with a suspect. The first task was to decide whether or not the deaths were natural or a result of foul play. When the evidence began to heavily lean towards someone deliberately causing these deaths then it wasn't too difficult to isolate the one nurse who had been on the unit when all of theses tragic and near tragic events occurred.

There were some nurses who were on shift for six or seven of the incidents but Letby was the only nurse on duty for ALL of them. It obviously didn't escape the notice of the police too that the unusually high spate of infant deaths and emergencies in the neonatal unit had stopped when Lucy Letby was taken off nurse duty and put in a clerical job at a desk.

Early in 2018, Dr Brearey had been asked by detectives to review some of the tragic incidents which happened in the neonatal unit. Brearey noticed that Baby F's insulin level was 4,657 when a normal insulin level was between 200 and 300. The C-peptide level in Baby F though was low. C-peptide level refers to the measurement of the amount of C-peptide in the blood. C-peptide is a molecule that is cleaved from proinsulin during the production of insulin in the pancreas. Therefore, the level of C-peptide in the blood can be used as an indicator of insulin production in the body. What this all meant was that Baby F had been poisoned. There was no other explanation. "I just had this gut-wrenching moment," said Brearey. "It was a smoking gun. You saw it there, in plain sight. If there was any iota of doubt [about Letby's guilt], it was removed then." The police were informed of Dr Brearey's discovery and the net began to tighten even more around Lucy Letby.

"At the beginning we hoped we wouldn't find a criminal offence because that meant that we were going to go and tell parents that their children had been murdered," said Detective Chief Inspector Nicola Evans. "We never anticipated the experts would come back and tell us there was inflicted harm, so when we realised that a crime had been committed it was really hard for everybody to believe, that somebody would do this. It was a milestone because it was shocking, and we also knew what we were about to embark on and take the families through."

The police now faced the delicate and unenviable task of informing the families of the babies that a criminal investigation into the deaths was now underway. The parents of the victims had to be told that this was now essentially a murder investigation. The loss of a child is the worst thing that can happen to anyone. That grief and sorrow is something that never goes away. There was now another awful burden on the affected parents because they were being told that the deaths were most likely not an accident. The families were assigned family liaison officers. This was certainly a difficult and sad time for everyone - both the grieving parents and the police detectives (many of whom had children themselves so couldn't help but fell empathy and sadness at this dreadful case they were working on). What the police now had to do was make a decision on whether to arrest Lucy Letby.

On 3 July 2018, Lucy Letby was arrested by police on suspicion of eight counts of murder and six counts of attempted murder. The arrest took place early in the morning. Letby was wearing blue tracksuit gear. She later complained about being dragged from her house in pyjamas but this was not the case because the police filmed the arrest. It was certainly sedate as far as arrests go. Letby was subdued and co-operative and it was all done with a minimum of fuss. It was obvious that Letby was not exactly shocked or outraged to find the police on the doorstep. She had been expecting this moment to arrive sooner or later. Whether or not she realised how much trouble she was in is another question. Letby certainly didn't seem distressed or unduly worried. It was actually quite difficult for Letby to get in the police car because she had just had knee surgery and so had limited mobility.

Only a few months before her arrest, Lucy Letby had attended the leaving party for Karen Rees. Rees had been head of nursing for urgent care at the Countess of Chester Hospital. Rees had a lot of contact with Lucy Letby and was convinced that Letby was innocent. "She was very convincing," said Rees. "I now know that this was a calculated and successful attempt to make me believe her story, and I was deceived, as were so many others. I did not attend the trial so I had an incomplete picture until the verdicts were announced, and more detail provided." There were four searches of Letby's house by the police and they also dug up her garden. The police were astonished by how much evidence they found. There were thousands of digital documents, plus diaries, post it notes, medical reports, and text messages which would all have to be studied. This was going to take many months. Letby was also found to have 247 pieces of paper with patient names and confidential hospital information. It was a grim treasure trove of information but would it be enough to build a case?

Letby was interviewed thirteen times in police custody in Blacon, Chester. Letby would later be interviewed a further fourteen times by the police in June 2019 and then three more times in November 2020. The reason why Letby was released and re-bailed during this period is that the police and CPS wanted more time to get enough evidence together. If this case was going to go to trial it needed to as strong as possible and that was obviously going to take some time. Lucy Letby was described by the police as 'controlled' during the interviews. Letby seemed to have the ability to 'disengage' from the circumstances she found herself in. She remained calm and composed throughout the custody interviews. In fact, Letby came across as something of a tabula rasa. She displayed no emotion whatsoever.

The police certainly found it strange that here was a woman being accused of murdering infants and yet not once did she get emotional, tearful, or angry. Not once did Letby protest her innocence (though of course she denied the charges) or show any distress at hearing the awful details of what she was being charged with. It was as if Lucy Letby had completely shut down all human emotions. Letby was questioned about all the infant deaths and emergencies which had occurred at the hospital during her time there on the neonatal unit. In regard to Baby A, Letby said that another nurse attended to the TPN bag and then they probably both checked it together. A TPN bag, also known as a Total Parenteral Nutrition bag, is a medical device used to administer nutrients, fluids, and medications directly into a person's bloodstream. Letby suggested to the police that there might have been a problem with the line or contents of the bag. Letby denied having much solo contact with the baby.

Letby was told by the police that Dr Dewi Evans had concluded that Baby A had been injected with air. The police told Letby that Dr Owen Arthurs had also detected air in radiographs (radiographs, also known as X-rays, are diagnostic imaging tests that use a small amount of ionizing radiation to create images of the inside of the body). In response to this Letby said that she had not given the child any air and had no explanation for how it might have 'got there'. Letby was questioned about Baby B - the twin sister of Baby A. Letby was accused of attempting to murder Baby B. Letby said her memory of this infant was vague because she had not been that child's designated nurse. Letby said she couldn't remember much about Baby B besides seeing a rash on the infant and couldn't recall if she had any contact with this child. In answer to the specific accusation in this charge, Letby denied that she had tried to murder Baby B. Letby said she didn't know why the infant suddenly fell ill.

Lucy Letby was questioned by the police next about the circumstances surrounding the death of Baby C - a boy who died after air was inserted into his stomach through a tube. The police told Letby that the infant's designated nurse Sophie Ellis had heard Baby C's alarm go off and found Letby standing over him. Furthermore, this was in nursery one. Letby was working in nursery three that shift so why was she in nursery one? Letby said she couldn't remember why she was in nursery one but might have had to go there to check something on a computer. Letby then added that she may even have heard the alarm and gone to check on the infant.

Letby's texts revealed that shortly before the baby's collapse Letby had texted someone and expressed frustration at not being in nursery one because it would be 'cathartic' to see a live baby in a place where a tragedy had recently occurred. Letby told the police in response to this that she had been frustrated by not working in nursery one that night but had nothing to do with Banby C's death. Letby also denied murdering Baby D - a girl who died June 2015. Letby had texted after this death that an 'element of fate' was involved. Asked what she had meant by that by detectives, Letby replied that she hadn't really meant anything. It was just a casual observation about how some things are just impossible to explain.

Letby also denied murdering Baby E - who died early in August 2015. Letby was asked about Baby F - the twin brother of Baby E. Baby F had insulin poisoning but was saved by doctors. Letby said she was not aware of anything being added to the nutrient bag and asked if the bags had been kept so they could be analysed. The police said they had not been kept by the hospital. It was evident that Letby liked using the word 'team' a lot when discussing her time on the neonatal unit. The subtext of this was rather obvious.

Letby was asked why she carried out Facebook searches on the families of Baby E and Baby F for months after these incidents. Letby said she simply wanted to know how Baby F was doing and denied an obsession with the family. It transpired that Letby had done these searches on victim anniversaries, birthdays, and even Christmas Day. This was, one might argue, deeply weird and sinister. It suggested a voyeuristic fascination with others' suffering.

Letby was questioned about Baby G and Baby H and denied having harmed these babies. The police asked Letby if she had any explanation for why there was a spike in baby deaths at the hospital at this time. Did she think it was just bad luck? Yes, said Letby. It was just bad luck. Letby was questioned at length about the death of Baby I. This was a girl who Letby was charged with making three medical attacks on before murdering her. Letby told the police she didn't remember much about the night Baby I died but did remember the girl's parents because she spoke to them quite a bit and they were kind to her. Letby said she had wanted to attend the funeral but couldn't get off work. Letby had sent the parents a sympathy card and kept a picture of the card on her phone. Asked why she had done this, Letby said she did it as a sort of memory of the parents. Letby said she often took pictures of cards she sent people.

Letby was asked about an incident where another nurse saw Letby standing near Baby I and said Letby looked nervous and worried. Letby brushed this off and said she hadn't attacked Baby I. Asked why she had done Facebook searches on Baby I's family in the months that followed, Letby replied that she had no memory of doing any online searches about the family. In response to questions about Baby K (this was the baby who had dangerously low oxygen levels when Dr Ravi Jayaram found Letby standing over her), Letby said she could remember little about this child. Letby said if she had noticed the low oxygen levels she would have called for help.

Letby had also been accused of attempting to murder Baby L with insulin. She was asked to explain the protocols for the use of insulin in the unit. Letby said the insulin was locked in a fridge and had to be prescribed. The nurses 'shared' the keys. Letby told the police that if this baby had been given insulin it wasn't by her. Letby conceded though that it was unlikely the child could have been given the insulin by mistake. Letby also denied attempting to kill Baby M - the twin brother of Baby L. Letby gave similar sorts of answers here to previous police interviews. She said she didn't know why this baby had collapsed and couldn't remember much about that shift. Letby was asked about a paper towel found in her house which was used as an impromptu drugs chart for Baby M when doctors were trying to save him. Letby said she must have taken the paper towel home by mistake.

Letby denied attempting to harm Baby N and denied murdering Baby O. Once again Letby could offer no medical explanation for why these babies had collapsed (and in one case tragically died). Letby also denied murdering Baby P - the brother of Baby O. All Letby could offer by way of explanation for this death was that it hadn't been expected. Letby was asked about a comment by another nurse - who claimed Letby had said she found feeding babies in the nursery boring and wanted to be in intensive care. Letby denied that she had ever said this. Letby said she loved all facets of her job.

Letby was asked, finally, about Baby Q. Letby was accused of injecting air into this baby in an act of attempted murder. Letby seemed to have more recall on this baby than others. Letby also seemed desperate to bring other nurses into this specific case - consistently pointing out she wasn't the only nurse who attended to this child. Letby said Baby Q was stable the last time she left him. Letby was also asked about texts she had shared with a doctor where she seemed to be aware that she was attracting gossip - perhaps even suspicion. Letby told the police she was concerned that she might be singled out as incompetent or something like that and was seeking some support and reassurance.

Letby was asked about the notes found in her house. She

had written what seemed like, on the face of it, self-incriminating things like 'I didn't kill them on purpose' and 'I AM EVIL I DID THIS'. Letby denied these notes were confessions. She said she tended to get feelings out on paper and the notes were not an admission of guilt but a sense that she hadn't been good enough as a nurse. Letby said the meaning of the notes were rooted in her fear that people might think the worst of her because of medical mistakes. Letby said the notes were an outpouring of guilt that she hadn't been able to save the babies. Letby then added that she had later reviewed her time in the unit and come to the conclusion that she hadn't made any mistakes. It's probably safe to say that the detectives interviewing Lucy Letby were not buying all of this.

Lucy Letby didn't have much to say about her views on the spike in deaths when questioned on the individual babies but now that the interview had moved onto more general matters she seemed more willing to offer her own theory. Letby told the police that the unit had poor morale because it was understaffed and had too many people 'pulling sickies'. Letby said the management at the hospital was poor and there were too many new members of staff who had to learn on the job. Letby also said that equipment on the unit was in short supply due to budget cuts.

Letby said she respected Dr Ravi Jayaram and Dr Stephen Brearey and had a good relationship with them. Letby said though that she felt as if she was being made a scapegoat just because she had volunteered for more shifts than anyone else. It is remarkable really how medical killers don't seem to realise that rota shifts will most likely be the cause of their downfall. If several of these deaths had occurred when Lucy Letby was not on shift then it obviously would have been impossible to build a case against her. Letby was always there though. She was on duty in the unit when all of these tragedies and emergencies happened. The defence would try to argue that this wasn't necessarily the case but the prosecution had the shift rotas and they were pretty damning.

Letby was asked why she had a large number of hospital handover sheets in her house. These sheets are usually disposed of in the hospital after a shift. Letby said she didn't really know why she had ended up with these and had probably forget they were in her pocket. She was asked why she hadn't thrown them in the bin or destroyed them and Letby said she hadn't got around to it. Letby was asked why she had written 'HATE' in bold in one of her notes and said this was done when she'd been taken off the unit and effectively demoted to a desk job so it just expressed her foul mood at the time. Letby said she was annoyed that she was no longer able to work with her nurse friends and felt isolated in a clerical job.

Letby was asked about her training as a nurse and said she had never failed any courses. She confirmed that she had done resuscitation training and was also trained to administer medication (a doctor was present for safety reasons if a nurse did this on the unit). Letby was asked if any of her training had involved learning about air embolisms. Letby said it had not - which wasn't entirely true. Lucy Letby's HR file at the Countess of Chester Hospital showed that she had answered a question in relation to air embolisms in a nursing exam once.

Letby told the police that she didn't really know much about air embolisms. Letby was asked if air embolisms had ever been a problem in the neonatal unit. In response to this Letby said she was not aware of any air embolisms during her time in the neonatal unit at Chester. Letby was asked why the names of the babies who died or suffered emergencies were listed prominently in her diary. Letby said she had done this because she tended to write down the names of babies to whom she served as the designated nurse. Letby said there was no particular significance to this. Letby was also asked about a note in which she written 'kill me'. Letby said this was written at the time she had been moved to the office in a clerical position. Letby told the police that 'kill me' was just a silly doodle related to the fact that she loathed working in an office and found it tedious.

The notes found in Letby's house were certainly alarming. They were full of phrases like 'I don't know if I killed them maybe I did maybe this is all down to me', 'I want someone to help me but they can't', 'I can't do this any more', 'I can't recover from this'. These notes in and of themselves, due to their ambiguous nature, were obviously a long way from proof of guilt but they were were the sort of thing that might be useful in a trial allied to the inexplicable collapse of the babies and Letby's presence in the unit during all of the incidents. There was a strange detail in that Letby said she hadn't destroyed any hospital notes at home because she didn't have a shredder. And yet the police found a shredder in her house. Was this a deliberate lie? Did she simply forget she had a shredder?

Lucy Letby's house was very neat and tidy - save for the bedroom. The bedroom was the only room which suffered from any clutter. There were bags on the floor and an unmade bed. The house had an open plan ground floor with a dining room and bright living room. Perhaps as a consequence of the fact that Lucy Letby was single, had no kids, and worked long shifts at the hospital, the house seemed unlived in save for the bedroom. The bathroom and kitchen were both modern and tidy. Letby had a reasonably large back garden but there was absolutely nothing in it apart from some turf and paving slabs. There were no flowers or trees. In what could be described as a bleakly ironic coincidence, Letby's house backed out on Blacon Crematorium - which had a memorial garden for babies. Although some of the media tried to portray Letby's interior decor as weird or childlike it wasn't really. It was just a normal house much like any other semi-detached house. The only childlike touch was a couple of teddy bears on the bed and some sparkle lights. The fact that Letby's bedroom was a bit untidy and teenagerish was the only detail which betrayed her immaturity.

At the trial, Lucy Letby said, in response to questions about the doctor she texted with and seemed close to, that she actually had a boyfriend already. However, this boyfriend has never been identified or pictured in the media. The alleged boyfriend has never done any interviews and was never seen at Letby's house. Lucy Letby's friends said that in all the time they knew her there was never once a boyfriend. It is possible then that this boyfriend was a figment of Lucy Letby's imagination. It was just something she made up. After her first arrest though, a neighbour told one of the tabloids that they sometimes saw Lucy Letby going in and out of her house with a man. Was this the boyfriend? A friend? A work colleague? This mystery was, it seems, solved at the trial. Letby said that a male doctor and four or five nurses from work were her social circle and would sometimes come round her house.

What is unusual about the Lucy Letby case is that even in the wake of the trial, when reporting restrictions had been lifted, the tabloids could find absolutely nothing in Lucy Letby's private life. There were no ex-lovers, no tales of weird, dark, or worrying things she had done as a youngster, no history of crimes prior to her medical career, no sign of mental illness or alcoholism. Lucy Letby was called the 'beige killer' in the media because her life up until her awful crimes had been so uneventful. There is a theory that this was some sort of motivation for her crimes and descent into what can only be described as a controlled madness. Could it be that Letby was saddened and mentally troubled by the lack of any love life and the possibility that she would never have a family? Were her crimes a twisted sort of revenge on people who had something yearned for herself? It's just a theory but it may yet have some grains of truth.

One of history's most famous medical killers is Jane Toppan. Toppan's motivation for her crimes is said to have been unhappiness at her lack of a love life. This wasn't mere idle speculation - Toppan actually said this herself. Toppan was born in Boston in 1854. She was (predictably) known as the Angel of Death. Toppan murdered at least 31 people with lethal injections in her duties as a nurse. Her parents were Irish immigrants and life was not exactly plain sailing for Jane Toppan as a child. Her mother died of tuberculosis and Jane Toppan's father was said to be so crazy that he once tried to sew up one of his eyelids. Jane Toppan was a bright girl though and entered medical school in 1885. She was known as Jolly Jane to her colleagues because she was always laughing and smiling. Everyone seemed to like her. She worked at Cambridge Hospital in Massachusetts and developed a fondness for working with patients who were sick or elderly.

Jane Toppan first attracted mild suspicion in her medical duties because she was completely obsessed with autopsies. She was absolutely fascinated with death and loved going to the morgue. Jane Toppan used her patients at the hospital to experiment with the drugs morphine and atropine. She would vary the doses to see what reaction occurred in the patient. Naturally, she created bogus medical charts for her patients to disguise what she was actually doing. Jane Toppan is said to have got a sexual thrill from her murders. She said she even climbed into bed with one patient she had just killed. In 1889, she worked at the Massachusetts General Hospital and continued to murder patients with overdoses. However, her murders were not just confined to the medical world. In 1895 she killed her landlord by poisoning and also murdered his wife. Jane Toppan then killed her sister Elizabeth with strychnine. You didn't have to be in hospital to be at risk from Jane Toppan. She would murder people anywhere given half a chance.

In 1901, Jane Toppan was hired as a private nurse to look after an elderly man named Alden Davis. You can probably guess what happened next. Yes, she murdered this man. But she didn't stop there. She also murdered his sister and two daughters. The relatives of the victims were understandably suspicious of Jane Toppan after these tragic sudden deaths. They arranged for a medical test on the youngest daughter and the tests concluded the reason for death was poison. After she was taken into custody, Jane Toppan confessed to many murders. Toppan told the police that she was perfectly sane and always knew exactly what she was doing. She said to the police - "That is my ambition, to have killed more people — more helpless people — than any man or woman who has ever lived." Toppan told the police that she experienced a thrill from having absolute power over patients and enjoyed taking them to the brink of death and then reviving them - and so on.

Despite her claim that she was perfectly sane, it was clearly obvious that Jane Toppan was not sane in the least. Jane Toppan was so disturbed she had even poisoned herself once to appear ill and attract sympathy from a prospective boyfriend. We will never know exactly how many people she actually killed. By any standards, Jane Toppan was completely ruthless. She once poisoned her best friend so that she could have her friend's job as a matron. Jane Toppan would kill literally anyone given the chance. As for explanations for why this woman became a compulsive killer, Jane Toppan was once jilted at the alter when she was supposed to get married. This is speculated to have been one of the sources of her anger and mental instability. "If I had been a married woman, I probably would not have killed all of those people," she said. "I would have had my husband, my children and my home to take up my mind." Jane Toppan was found not guilty of her crimes by reasons of insanity and committed for life in the Taunton Insane Hospital. She died in 1938 at the age of 84. There was a rather dark irony when Jane Toppan was sent to the Taunton Insane Hospital. At one point, she refused to eat anything at the hospital and complained that someone was trying to poison her.

In the face of all the police scrutiny and the real possibility of a trial, Lucy Letby retreated back into childhood and moved in with her parents (Letby didn't really have much choice because the police told her not to go back to her house - which was basically now an active crime scene). Her parents were very supportive and thought the charges against their daughter were preposterous. Like any loving parents, their daughter was the apple of their eye and could do no wrong. Lucy Letby had, especially as an only child, always been mollycuddled and indulged by her parents. She was used to being the centre of attention. One can understand why Letby's parents refused to believe she was capable of the crimes she was alleged to have done and were now determined to clear her name. Any parent would have had the same reaction in that situation. Lucy Letby's ability to go under the radar was maybe not surprising in hindsight. Lucy Letby was dorky and wholesome looking. She was soft-spoken and likeable. She was literally the last person in the world you'd suspect of being a serial killer.

CHAPTER FOUR

Lucy Letby was prescribed anti-depressants after becoming the centre of the (eventual) suspicion surrounding the tragedies at the hospital. Letby would later claim to have suffered PTSD as a result of her arrests. She said she was a nervous person who hated noise and was easily frightened. Letby was hypothyroid (hypothyroidism is a condition where the thyroid gland does not produce enough thyroid hormone) and said she had been diagnosed with optic neuritis (an inflammation of the optic nerve which can cause blurry vision and discomfort). There was no mental health diagnosis though which might help explain (not that anything really could) why Letby had done the things she was accused of.

On the 11th of November 2020, Letby was charged with eight counts of murder and 10 counts of attempted murder. This time there would be no bail. The Crown Prosecution Service were convinced to approve all of the charges Cheshire Constabulary requested against Letby. For the police team who had investigated Letby this was an emotional moment. It was not a cause for celebration but quiet reflection and sadness. For the third and final arrest of Lucy Letby in November 2020, Mr Letby answered the door. Mrs Letby was very distressed and told the police to take her instead of her daughter. Letby was eventually moved to HMP Bronzefield. HMP Bronzefield is a women's prison located in Ashford, Surrey. HMP Bronzefield houses adult female prisoners, including those on remand.

The news that a nurse had been arrested on charges of killing babies and attempting to murder others made national headlines. When the first pictures of Lucy Letby emerged in the public sphere it probably wasn't what people were expecting. Letby didn't look like a monster. She looked like a smiling, caring, happy young nurse. Those who had been neighbours to Lucy Letby described her as an 'enigma' She kept herself to herself at home and didn't form friendships with any neighbours. The trial of Lucy Letby was, due to its sensitive and complex nature, a long drawn out affair. It was also complicated by the Covid pandemic (which slowed the police investigation and therefore delayed the trial).

In October, 2021, Letby pleaded not guilty to murdering eight babies and attempting to murder another 10. She was 31 years-old at the time. Letby made two court appearances by videolink. Shortly before the actual trial, Letby was moved to HM

Prison New Hall in Yorkshire. HM Prison New Hall was the home of the infamous Rose West. Letby was annoyed at being moved because she now had to get used to a new prison. Though she hadn't been found guilty of anything yet there were stringent security measures for Letby in prison. The nature of the crimes she was connected to made her a target.

The barrister who would be defending Lucy Letby in court was Benjamin Myers KC. Myers was an experienced barrister considered to be very good at his job. He was probably most famous for successfully defending David Duckenfield. David Duckenfield was the Police Chief Superintendent in charge of the 1989 FA Cup semi-final between Liverpool and Nottingham Forest. This was the tragic Hillsborough disaster match. Duckenfield was found not guilty of the gross negligence manslaughter of 95 Liverpool fans who died in the crush caused by them being trapped in one end of the ground. The man in the opposite corner to Myers would be the equally experienced and sought after Nick Johnson KC. Johnson would be leading the prosecution.

There was certainly a lot of public fascination with this grim case. Lucy Letby was being charged with being Britain's worst modern day child killer. The police were confident in the case against her but there were precedents for making mistakes when it came to accusing and convicting people for medical murders. Lucia de Berk is a Dutch nurse who was wrongfully convicted of multiple murders and attempted murders of patients under her care. She worked as a paediatric nurse at various hospitals in the Netherlands from 1997 to 2001. In 2001, she was arrested and charged with the murder of several patients based on statistical analysis of deaths on her shifts. During her trial, the prosecution argued that De Berk administered lethal doses of medication, causing the deaths of seven patients and the near deaths of three others. There was no direct evidence linking De Berk to the crimes, only statistical data, as well as testimonies from colleagues who found her behaviour suspicious.

In 2003, De Berk was found guilty and sentenced to life imprisonment. However, doubts about her guilt emerged after the trial, and a reinvestigation of the case was initiated. Independent experts reviewed the statistical evidence and concluded that there was no proof of criminal behaviour by De Berk. In 2010, De Berk's case was reopened, and in 2013, the Dutch Supreme Court acquitted her of all charges, ruling that there was no scientific evidence to support her conviction. She was released from prison after spending almost seven years behind bars. The case of Lucia de Berk sparked a public debate about the reliability of statistical evidence in criminal cases and the potential for miscarriages of justice. It also led to reforms in the Dutch legal system to prevent similar wrongful convictions from occurring in the future.

There was also the case of Rebecca Leighton. Rebecca Leighton is a former nurse from Stepping Hill Hospital in Stockport. In July 2011, she was arrested and charged with the murder of patients in her care. It was alleged that she tampered with medication, leading to the deaths of several patients. However, the charges against Rebecca Leighton were dropped in September 2011 when it was revealed that the evidence against her was insufficient. The tampering of medication was later discovered to have been carried out by another nurse, Victorino Chua, who was subsequently convicted of murder and poisoning in 2015.

Some wondered if Lucy Letby might be another Lucia de Berk or Rebecca Leighton. Was this all a big mistake? Not from where the CPS and police were standing. The big problem for Letby and any defence of her in court was the workshift patterns in relation to the attacks on babies. It was established that Letby had been on shift in all of these incidents. This was all clearly not an idle coincidence. If these babies had collapsed through natural causes only at times when the unwitting Lucy Letby was on shift then that would make Letby the unluckiest person in the history of the universe. Suffice to say then, no one could actually believe that was the case. Foul play was the most logical explanation and the prosecution believed they had the evidence to back that up.

Letby's trial began at Manchester Crown Court on the 10th of October 2022 before Mr Justice Goss. Mr Justice Goss had presided over a number of high profile cases - including the fairly recent Carl Beech affair. Carl Beech got a lot of attention and sympathy (and even some financial compensation) when he made claims about a child killing paedophile ring that included politicians, celebrities, and even army generals. However, in 2019, after a huge police investigation, Beech was jailed after being proven to be a liar and fantasist. Lucy Letby cut a ruined figure in court. Her blonde hair was now lank and its more natural brown (Letby had worn a large hat during her visits to the police station - the brown hair was evidently part of the disguise and now she was stuck with it what with being in prison). She looked pale and thin. In court she clutched comfort scarfs - like Linus and his blanket in the Peanuts comic strips. This once happy young nurse who goofed around with her friends and was profiled in the local paper now was at the centre of the most high profile murder trial for years and being compared to monsters like Beverly Allitt. Letby had actually led a fairly normal life while on police bail. The local paper in Chester later reported that during this time she had attended yoga classes at Holmer Park Spa and Health Club.

Relatives of the hospital victims and survivors in this case were present in court - as too were Lucy Letby's parents. The twelve person jury (made up of eight women and four men) were given evidence on iPads to save paperwork. This trial was going to have a LOT of evidence. The jury had to be taught how to use the iPads - as too did Mr Justice Goss. It was certainly an unenviable task faced by the jury. Not only was the trial expected to last for months but it also involved, even by the standards of trials, a desperately sad, incomparably distressing, and grim case. In his opening statement, Nicholas Johnson KC spoke about the city of Chester and the hospital where Letby had worked. He then spoke about the neonatal unit in the hospital. Mr Johnson told the court about the significant rise in baby deaths at the unit and said the rise defied any medical explanation. Babies do not just collapse for no reason and it made no medical sense that most of the resuscitations failed.

Johnson told the court that these babies had been perfectly stable before their sudden collapses. The prosecutor then told the court that there was only one common denominator in these tragic cases - the presence of Lucy Letby. Mr Johnson told the court that the baby collapses began during the night shift - which

Lucy Letby worked. However, when Lucy Letby was taken off nights and moved to a day shift the baby collapses now happened during the day rather than the night. It was surely not a coincidence, argued Mr Johnson, that the deaths and emergencies were only happening on Letby's shifts. The prosecution told the court that some of the babies had been poisoned with insulin or had air injected into them. Mr Johnson pointed out that neonatal unit was a very secure place which few people had access to. It was therefore not complex to do a process of elimination through the staff rota shifts and that process left only one name standing - Lucy Letby.

Mr Johnson spoke about the internal hospital politics and disagreements over which course of action to take and the delay this had on the need to involve the police. "No doubt they were acutely aware that making such an allegation against a nurse was as serious as it gets. They, at the time, did not have the benefit of the evidence that you will hear and the decision was taken by the hospital took the decision to remove Lucy Letby from a hands-on role. She was moved to clerical duties where she would not come into contact with children. The police were contacted and began a very lengthy and complex enquiry." Johnson also spoke of the written evidence found in Letby's house - where she had written notes which contained the lines "'I am a horrible evil person' and 'I AM EVIL I DID THIS'.

In his opening statement for the defence, Benjamin Myers KC told the jury that just because Lucy Letby was on shift during the incidents she was now charged with this was not proof of guilt. Mr Myers said that it could not be proven that Letby was with all of the babies in question before their condition worsened. Myers also cast doubt on the claim that Letby had injected babies with air - pointing out that this science was highly speculative and debatable and air can occur naturally in post-mortem. Most of all, Mr Myers sought to cast doubt on the overall quality of care in the hospital unit and cite this as a factor in these tragedies. Myers said these hospital failings could not be blamed on Lucy Lety - who Mr Myers portrayed as a kind and caring nurse who was simply doing her job as part of a team. "We do not suggest for one moment the doctors and nurses did anything other than the best they could. What they do is admirable and crucial. We say there were problems with the way the unit performed which had nothing to do with Lucy Letby."

Mr Myers also argued out that many of the babies in the unit were born premature so their collapses were not, as the prosecution claimed, unexplained or completely unexpected. "We are dealing with some of the most medically fragile babies under the most intense medical care. All of them, bar one, are premature to varying degrees. Some had considerable problems. These babies are already at risk of deterioration and this can happen unexpectedly and it can be rapid." Mr Myers told the court that tragedies and emergencies involving babies at the hospital were a result of many factors - including the fragility of the infants, existing medical conditions, less than stellar care at the hospital, and - in some cases - unexplained deterioration. He cited the case of Child D - who the defence claimed had died because of a lack of swift antibiotics. Mr Myers said that to take all of these elements and come to a conclusion of 'deliberate harm' by one solitary person as a single explanation was simply wrong.

Mr Myers suggested that to convict Lucy Letby on the grounds of hospital gossip, coincidence, and ambiguous notes found in her house would be like relying on amateur psychology rather than medical science and facts. In relation to the claims that some babies were heard screaming before they died, Myers said it would be wrong to jump to conclusions that Letby was responsible for this. Mr Myers argued that babies crying or screaming was not exactly uncommon and that babies often do this when they are hungry. Myers spoke of the 'suspicion' Letby had attracted in the hospital but asked why - if this was the case - she had not been taken off duty sooner. Mr Myers also pointed out that babies had died in the hospital before Lucy Letby worked there. It would be wrong, argued Myers, to attribute every tragedy in a hospital related to infants to Lucy Letby. Mr Myers warned the jury of 'confirmation bias'. He said that just because the police and prosecution had pointed the finger at Lucy Letby it didn't mean that the jury had to follow in this direction. "If someone looks for something, and has something in mind, they will look for that," said Myers.

The court heard how the mother of Baby E had apparently interrupted Letby attacking her child. The mother could see blood on the baby's mouth but was told by Letby not to worry and ushered away. The court heard that the mother was alarmed by this and telephoned her husband. The woman in question was the mother of twin boys Baby E and Baby F. The prosecution told the court that in her nursing notes for that evening Letby failed to mention that Baby E had been bleeding from the mouth. Letby also wrote in her notes that the mother of Baby E had a meeting with a doctor to discuss the child. However, both the mother of Baby E and the doctor named by Letby both said they had no recollection of such a meeting because it never took place. Letby's nursing notes were therefore, argued the prosecution, deliberate misdirection.

In the opening statement for the prosecution, Mr Johnson had told the court that Letby had, according to another nurse, aspirated the stomach (draining the contents of the stomach for medical reasons) of Baby Q and yet Letby made no mention of this in her notes. Johnson's basic point was that Letby was an unreliable narrator in this grim tale. The prosecution told the court there was no post-mortem for Baby E because the parents did not want one. In hindsight this was obviously a mistake. Nick Johnson KC told the court that Letby had attempted to kill Baby E's brother Baby F by adding insulin to his nutrient bag. "You know who was in the room, and you know from the records who hung the [feed] bag," the jury were told. The prosecution also told the court that Letby seemed to develop an odd fascination with the parents of these twins and did repeated Facebook searches on them in the months to come. Letby had also made a point of doing a Facebook search on Christmas Day when she must have known full well that days like Christmas and birthdays were the most painful of all for parents who have lost a child.

The prosecution also told the court about Letby's attempted murder of the girl Baby G. Mr Johnson told the court that the baby was perfectly fine in the care of another hospital and only showed signs of ill health when being cared for by Letby in Chester. "Putting it simply the milk in her vomit did not come from nowhere. That doesn't happen by accident," Mr Johnson said. Mr Johnson also spoke of the alleged murders of Baby C and Baby D. Johnson told the court that Letby was the only person working the night shift when Child C died. Mr Johnson then told the court that this pattern was evident in the earlier cases of babies collapsing. All of these things happened during Letby's shifts.

The prosecution also noted that the alleged methods of murder were varied. They argued that Letby was calculating and shrewd and had deduced there was less chance of being caught or a pattern emerging if she avoided using the same methods for each attack. The defence obviously begged to differ. In his opening statement Benjamin Myers KC had gone through each of the alleged murders and attempted murders and outlined medical problems which (he argued) provided a plausible alternative to the outlandish claim that Letby was a serial killer. Mr Myers told the court that 'presence' and 'coincidence' was neither guilt nor murder.

As part of his days long opening statement, Nick Johnson KC told the court how Lucy Letby had asked the mother of Baby I if she wanted to bathe the child after their death. The mother said that while she was doing this Letby came in smiling and was inappropriately upbeat - talking about how she had given the baby its first bath. The court also heard how Dr Ravi Jayaram had become suspicious of Letby at the hospital. Mr Johnson went through all of the deaths and baby emergencies at the hospital during Letby's time there and noted how, in the case of latter, babies always made a recovery when they were transferred to another hospital far away from Lucy Letby. This, the prosecution argued, was far from a coincidence. Mr Johnson also spoke of the notes found in Letby's house where she called herself 'evil'. The prosecution said these notes were by a troubled person who had done awful things. In his opening statement for the defence, Benjamin Myers KC, disagreed with this view. Mr Myers said the notes were a stream of consciousness by a person suffering a lot of stress and anguish. In no way, argued Myers, were the notes confessions or proof of guilt.

Nick Johnson KC told the court of how Lucy Letby predicted in the hospital that Baby P was 'not getting out of here alive'. Mr Johnson said a doctor had found this comment odd because the prognosis for the baby was considered to be fine. Sure enough, Letby's prediction came true - by her own hand claimed the prosecution. The first witness in court after the opening statements had finally been completed was Dr Dewi Evans. Dr Evans had been brought in by the police as an independent expert as part of their investigation.

The court heard about the expertise and experience of Dr Evans and were told that he had designed a neonatal unit in Wales in the 1980s. Dr Evans told the court he had given up his medical practice in 2009 and now dedicated himself to doing reports for baby care. He was involved in clinical negligence reports but didn't do that anymore. The court were told that Dr Evans had no connections to the Countess of Chester Hospital and was simply brought in to investigate the spike in baby deaths in an impartial and objective fashion.

There was a lot of medical information for the jury to take in. It had to be explained to them how a neonatal unit works. They were told about neopuff machines, baby alarm systems, and the general structure of a baby care unit in a hospital. They were told about oxygen levels, air embolisms, apnoea, blood gases, and how babies are cared for. Given his vast experience in this field there seemed few better to explain all of this than Dr Dewi Evans. Nonetheless, Letby's defence barrister Benjamin Myers KC questioned the expertise of Dr Evans when he got his chance to cross-examine. Mr Myers said that Dr Evans was not a consultant neonatologist and suggested (in polite court language) that Dr Evans was a bit out of touch with the modern medical world because he hadn't had 'day-to-day' experience for a number of years. "Because there were so few consultants around, you had greater contact with babies than with 10 neonatologists," replied Dr Evans of his background. "The other consultants deferred to my interests in neonatalogy development. My experience was huge. My hands-on experience of developing neonatal experience is, I am more than happy to say, is as extensive as anybody's."

Mr Myers continued with his theme of portraying Dr Evans

as someone who was out of touch with the modern medical world. He suggested Dr Evans wasn't familiar with modern baby alarm machines and asked Dr Evans if he wasn't at a disadvantage being an expert on this case because he was no longer in practice. Mr Myers was basically trying to depict Dr Evans as some retired old fossil who hadn't been in a hospital for years. "I have kept fully up to speed with neonatal practice," replied Dr Evans. "You develop your professionalism through the whole of your career. You don't simply forget, the day you finish. If you can tell me of any new approach, then do so, but babies do not change in the approach of their conditions, and that has not changed in the past 10 years."

When the trial resumed again after the weekend the was focus on Baby A and Baby B. Letby was charged with the murder of the former and the attempted murder of the latter. Baby A was a boy and Baby B was his twin sister. This was a very distressing and unbearably sad day of evidence because the court heard from the mother, father, and grandmother of the babies as they recounted what happened from their perspective. The mother of these babies said she was very angry when a consultant at the hospital suggested that a blood condition she had might have been a factor in what happened to the babies. Claire Hocknell, an intelligence analyst for Cheshire Police, was also in court. Hocknell had extensive electronic records of Letby's neonatal unit access and phone messages during this time. What the prosecution were doing were showing how these (in their view) dovetailed with the cases of Baby A and Baby B. At the specific time of these incidents Letby had been asked to work extra shifts at the hospital and had agreed to this.

The court heard that Lucy Letby had done a Facebook search for Baby A's parents only two hours after her shift (during which the child died) had ended. Messages showed that Letby told colleagues she couldn't face dealing with the parents - though she would have to as Baby B was still under her care. Letby's text messages at this time, suggested the prosecution, were somewhat suspicious. When a colleague said it was "weird" that there had been so many worrying incidents in the unit lately, Letby responded by saying "What do you mean?" - a response which could be construed as defensive. Letby informed one nursing colleague about the death of Baby A by text and the nurse responded by saying - "Oh god, he was doing really well when I left." A subtext of the prosecution's outline of this information was that Letby was enjoying all of this drama - the drama they (the prosecution) believed she had manufactured. The court also heard more details about how Lucy Letby had made further repeated Facebook searches concerning the family of Baby A.

The court then heard how Baby B, according to nursing and medical notes was considered to be stable just before Lucy Letby began her shift at midnight and became the child's designated nurse. Soon after this the baby changed colour and had to have emergency care by doctors. The prosecution argued that there were too many incidents like this which dovetailed in neatly with Letby's shift patterns. The prosecution believed that none of this was coincidence. In their view there was a clear link between babies collapsing in the unit and Lucy Letby.

CHAPTER FIVE

The court heard from Dr Sally Ogden, who was a registrar on duty when Baby A died. "This came as a surprise, it came completely out of the blue and was very upsetting," said Dr Ogden of Baby A's death. The court also heard from Melanie Taylor, who was a nurse on the unit and worked with Lucy Letby at the time. Taylor told the court that she was on a computer when Baby A fell ill and found Lucy Letby standing over the child's incubator when she investigated. Melanie Taylor told the court that she'd had no major concerns about Baby A previously because the baby was stable and seemed to be doing well. The court heard that Baby A had a symptom of newborn respiratory distress syndrome but this was not considered unusual or life threatening. Newborn Respiratory Distress Syndrome (NRDS) is a condition that affects newborn babies, specifically premature infants. It is characterised by difficulty in breathing due to underdeveloped lungs and insufficient production of surfactant, a substance that helps the lungs expand and stay inflated.

The next day the court heard from Paediatric registrar Dr David Harkness - who was on duty at the hospital when Baby A died. "This was a completely stable, well baby, who had no reason to suddenly deteriorate, so I was very surprised to be called back," said Dr Harkness. "He had very unusual patching of his skin, which I have never seen before. The patches were blue, purple, red and white. I've never seen it before or since. It didn't come and go - it came and then he went into cardiac arrest." In his his cross-examination of Dr Harkness for the defence, Benjamin Myers KC pointed out that Harkness had made no mention of the change in colour in his medical notes written afterwards. Dr Harkness said this was because he was distressed and upset due to the fact this was the first baby death he had experienced in the unit.

Mr Myers was also able to cross examine Nurse Melanie Taylor about the fact that staff had had difficulty putting an IV line into Baby A. Melanie Taylor conceded that this was true. Mr Myers had made great play of this 'long line' but Dr Harkness, in his cross-examination, said it was not a factor in the baby's declining health. Mr Myers argued that because of this Baby A had not had access to sufficient fluids. The defence told the court that Nurse Taylor's notes for that day read - "UVC in wrong position, reinserted...again in wrong position. Cannula tissued. Doctors busy on ward 30. Aware no fluids running for a couple of hours. Long line inserted by Reg Harkness. awaiting X-ray. Remains settled on NCPAP. Enteral feeds of donor expressed breast milk started at 1ml/2hourly."

Mr Myers also discussed the staffing levels on the unit and suggested they were inadequate. The job of Mr Myers in court, when boiled down, was basically to shift the perception of blame from Lucy Letby and make the case that a combination of hospital failings and natural illness was the most logical explanation for what had happened. Mr Myers also made a point of reminding the court that the mother of Baby A and Baby B had a difficult pregnancy because she was suffering from high blood pressure which had to be controlled.

Mr Myers told Melanie Taylor that in an investigation interview in February, 2018, she had expressed the view that babies sometimes collapse with no explanation. "That is what I believed, that was my opinion at the time," replied Taylor in court. "I tried to rationalise what happened at the time. Whether that's true - I'm not medical - but that was my opinion at the time. I feel like I shouldn't have said that - I tried to rationalise that, because as a nurse, that is what I tried to do."

The prosecution sought to counter what gains Benjamin Myers might have won with his cross-examinations. They produced intensive care charts which they argued was proof that, contrary to what the defence might claim, Baby A had sufficient feeds and fluids. They also returned to the evidence of staff in the hospital at the time - doctors and nurses - who expressed surprise at Baby A's death because the baby was considered to be stable. The prosecution argued that there was no medical explanation for why Baby A would suddenly collapse without warning. The court heard from the neonatal nurse assistant Lisa Walker - who was working with Letby and other staff in the hospital. "I remember thinking, 'what on earth is happening?'" said Walker in relation to the spike in deaths and emergencies. Walker said there had only been a 'couple' of baby deaths in the previous ten years at the hospital.

On the 21st of October the court heard from Dr Owen Arthurs. Arthurs was the consultant paediatric radiologist at Great Ormond Street Hospital. He had studied the X-rays of the babies at the Chester hospital as part of the police investigation. Dr Arthers said that the X-rays of Baby A showed a line of gas in front of the spine - which was highly unusual. "In my opinion this was an unusual appearance. In the absence of any other explanation this appearance is consistent with, but not diagnostic, of air having been administered." Dr Arthurs told the court that gas is not found in front of the spine in cases of natural death. The prosecution asked Dr Arthurs if he had ever seen an example of gas in a child like this before. Arthurs said that he had but only in one. That was in the X-rays of another baby alleged to have been a victim of Lucy Letby in the same hospital.

Benjamin Myers KC for the defence asked Dr Arthurs if radiographic evidence of air embolus was rare. Dr Arthurs had to concede that it was very rare. The defence reminded the court that the baby had two failed attempts to correctly insert a catheter in the belly button and this happened before Letby's shift began. Dr Arthurs said it was possible the air could have come from these devices. Prompted by the defence, Dr Arthurs also said there was no evidence of air embolus in Baby B. Mr Myers attempted to cast doubt on the claim that gas was not found in this fashion in other baby deaths and said that Dr Arthurs own research found 38 cases of internal gas at Great Ormond Street. Dr Arthurs refuted this and said no gas was found in front of the spine in any deaths which had no medical explanation.

The court heard from senior neonatal practitioner Caroline Bennion - who spent a lot of time in the unit and knew Lucy Letby. Bennion told the court that babies in a unit like this are vulnerable and can rapidly deteriorate at any time. Bennion added though that she had never experienced anything quite so rapid and unexpected as the incidents in the unit in Chester. Benjamin Myers KC, in his questioning, often probed away at the levels of staffing in the hospital. His strategy was obviously to depict the hospital as a place where not everything was perfect and therefore mistakes were possible. Caroline Bennion gave a diplomatic answer to this line of questioning and said - "We were always very fortunate to have a lot of senior staff. There were occasions where we had busier periods, but that is the nature of a neonatal unit."

The next day, a nursing colleague of Letby who could not be named (witnesses can apply for the right to give evidence anonymously) gave evidence. The evidence related to Baby A and Baby B. The nurse, as with other members of staff at the hospital, conceded that babies can get poorly very quickly sometimes without much warning but said what happened on the unit during that time was unprecedented and unusual. The nurse said she and other nurses spoke at the time about the discolouration they had noticed in the babies who died or had non-fatal collapses. The nurse said that she had been a friend and mentor to Lucy Letby at the hospital. The nurse, under questioning from Benjamin Myers KC, said that Letby was a professional and dedicated nurse. This nurse had not noticed Lucy Letby doing anything suspicious.

The following day, Dr Dewi Evans was called to give more evidence. Benjamin Myers KC asked him how he got involved in this case and inquired (in not so many words) whether his contact with the police and National Crime Agency might possibly render his contribution impartial. "My state of mind was very clear - let's find a diagnosis," said Dr Evans. "Nothing to do with crime. Let's identify any specific collapse and see if I can explain it. There were occasions where I couldn't explain it, and occasions where I found something deeply suspicious. The name Lucy Letby meant nothing to me. I didn't know the staff. I was a blank sheet of paper. I had no idea and relied entirely on the evidence I could see from the clinical notes and applying my clinical experience and forming an opinion to the cause."

Dr Evans was asked about the reports of Baby A before the collapse. "He was as well as could be expected. All the markers of well-being were very satisfactory. He was in air, not needing additional oxygen, heart rate in normal limits, oxygen saturation normal - it had been in the 90s...respiratory rate slightly above normal rate but that was the only marker outside normal rate. Somehow air had got into the circulation...I found this opinion without knowing about the rash and without anybody suggesting expressing concern of air embolus." Benjamin Myers KC, for the defence, suggested to Dr Evans that the air embolus diagnosis was one of 'exclusion' which ruled out other possibilities. Dr Evans disagreed with this and also said he wasn't even told about the skin discolouration when he made the diagnosis (this was an effective counter to Mr Myers making the point that air embolus can often occur without skin discolouration).

Dr Evans said he was perfectly willing to consider all possibilities but his diagnosis was obviously directed by the evidence he found as he investigated. Mr Myers wanted to know if the term 'air embolus' was in the case file Dr Evans was given when he began his investigation. "No," insisted Dr Evans. "The first person to use air embolus, as far as I was concerned, was me. I need to give the NCA a compliment, they never gave me a steer. They are good, professional people." Mr Myers sought to challenge the perception that Baby A was perfectly stable and had no problems by presenting a chart of things which may have been a factor. These included an increase in respiratory rate readings.

Dr Evans disagreed with the chart and said the list of alleged problems the defence had presented were either marginal or stable readings. Dr Evans also refuted the claims of the defence that Baby A had not being given fluids for four hours and this might have been a factor. Dr Evans said this was not ideal but it sometimes happens in busy neonatal units and a baby that hasn't had fluids for four hours will assuredly not collapse and die as a consequence. Dr Evans also poured cold water on suggestions by the defence that an infection might have caused Baby A's death. Dr Evans said this was a ridiculous claim because it would have been easy to verify.

Interestingly, Dr Evans said he had completed nearly all of his preliminary reports by November 2017 and at that time had no idea that a nurse in the neonatal unit was a potential suspect in this case. He said he only became aware of Lucy Letby when she was arrested for the first time. It was after this happened that he saw the shift patterns were decidedly not in her favour. Dr Evans told the court that, in his view, air embolus was also the reason why Baby B collapsed. Mr Myers said this contradicted the theory of Dr Evans because Baby B was saved and recovered. If it was air embolus in both cases why not the same result? Dr Evans replied -"We cannot do studies where we inject air into babies and see what happens." Dr Evans suggested that resuscitations can vary in effectiveness and this was probably a factor in the differing outcomes.

Dr Sandie Bohin, another expert who helped the police with the investigation, told the court that it very unlikely that air was administered to a baby by mistake as medical protocols on this are very strict and the staff are all trained to avoid this happening. Modern hospital equipment is designed to prevent air emboli. Asked by Nick Johnson KC what she thought the cause of death for Baby A was, Dr Bohin answered "[Child A] was killed by an air embolus." This evidence was understandably distressing for the mother of Baby A, who was in court that day. Dr Sandie Bohin was back in court the next day to give more evidence. Dr Bohin described Baby B's collapse as 'concerning' because there was nothing in the hospital's medical files and charts to suggest the child was in danger. Bohin was asked by the prosecution if misplaced nasal prongs could be an explanation for the baby's collapse. In response to this Dr Bohin said that this wasn't a factor. Dr Bohin said that a process of elimination could rule out a variety of possible explanations until one was left only with air embolus.

Benjamin Myers KC, in his questioning, once again returned to the theme of whether experts no longer involved in day to day practice were qualified to make decisions on what had really happened in that hospital. Dr Bohin, much like Dr Evans, replied by saying that just because you are no longer involved in day to day practice it doesn't mean you've forgotten all the medical knowledge you built up over the years. Bohin also said that you can be a medical expert without working a shift in a hospital or practice - although the latter is obviously useful. Bohin was asked about her relationship with the other independent expert in the investigation - Dr Evans. Bohin said she had only spoken to Evans for the first time by telephone earlier in the year. Dr Bohin said that she and Dr Evans had both come to their conclusions independently and alone.

Mr Myers, in his questioning, attempted again to cast doubt on the opinion of the experts that Baby A was in a stable condition before the collapse. Myers produced charts of a rise in heart-rate and also (again) returned to the long line which was inserted incorrectly and the lack of fluids the child had received at one point. Dr Bohin disagreed with Mr Myers on all of these points and said that none of these factors would have caused the child to collapse and die. In the view of Dr Bohin there had to have been something else - something more serious. Mr Myers now cited a paper published by the International Journal of Critical Illness and Injury Services which said air can enter through the UVC (umbilical venous catheter) into vessels. Dr Bohin said she was aware of this possibility with adults but had never known it to happen in any neonatal case of her experience.

Mr Myers had slightly more success with a change of approach. He once again went through the circumstances of Baby A and Baby B's conditions and treatment and asked Dr Bohin if the care and condition of the respective child was "sub-optimal" on occasions. Dr Bohin had to concede that this term was applicable to certain circumstances in relation to the babies. Mr Myers then returned to another theme which he was attempting to use in Letby's favour. This was the fact that Baby B had (mercifully) recovered and gone home to her parents. The point Myers was making was that if this baby was a victim of air embolus, as Dr Bohin and Dr Evans claimed, why was she still alive given that air embolus is supposed to be deadly? Dr Bohin said that volume and speed can be a factor in air embolus - which was basically to say that the cases of Baby A and Baby B were not identical and it was a simplification to say that they were.

Dr Bohin was then questioned by Nick Johnson KC for the prosecution. Mr Johnson ran through the medical charts of the Baby A and Baby B and asked Dr Bohin if any of the charts were worrying, unusual, or a sign of imminent danger. Dr Bohin said there was nothing in the charts and reports which indicated the babies were in danger. Dr Bohin also repeated her statement that she'd never heard of air embolus in a neonatal unit from as a result of negative air pressure (this part of the questioning was essentially Mr Johnson pouring cold water on the academic paper that Benjamin Myers had cited earlier in the morning).

In the afternoon, the court heard moving testimony from the parents of Baby C - a boy who died in the unit allegedly at the hands of Lucy Letby. This was an unbearably sad afternoon of evidence as the parents spoke of how their child had become ill and passed away - much to their shock. This was a very eventful day of evidence because the jury also heard more details of Letby's text messages at this time and the prosecution also read out Letby's police interviews in relation to Baby A and Baby B. It was certainly a grim and difficult case to be in court for. Not only was the case desperately tragic and sad but there was an awful lot of medical jargon and information to process. At this stage it was difficult to say how the trial was going for Letby. It was too early for that. Armchair detectives following the case were still split and neither Benjamin Myers KC nor Nick Johnson KC had yet to land any knockout blows.

When the trial resumed again, early in the morning the

court were read the text messages that Lucy Letby had sent following the death of Baby C. Letby had texted her mother about this death and also two colleagues. Letby said in the texts that she had persuaded the parents to get hand and footprints of the baby despite their reluctance. The court then heard that at just after 3-30 in the afternoon, that tragic day, Letby had done done a Facebook search for the parents of Baby C. Dr Sally Ogden was then called to give evidence. Dr Ogden was a paediatric registrar at the Countess of Chester Hospital and present at the birth of Baby C. Dr Ogden, in answer to questions, said that the baby was stable and seemed to be suffering from no concerning medical conditions. The child was screened for sepsis and placed on antibiotics as a precaution. Dr Ogden said there was a worry at one point the child had a problem in its abdomen but this proved to be a false alarm.

In his questions to Dr Ogden, Benjamin Myers KC pointed out that the weight of Baby C was cited as 'borderline' and clearly a concern. He also wanted to know why the baby had not been transferred to a unit 3 equipped hospital in Liverpool. Dr Ogden said this was a decision that had to be made by both hospitals and it also depended on availability.

Dr Ogden did concede that she had wanted some 'communication' on the possibility of a transfer. In the afternoon, Mr Myers continued to question Dr Ogden and pointed out there were concerns about Baby C's breathing at birth. He also showed Dr Ogden an X-ray of Baby C's lung taken at the hospital which indicated a possibility of infection. Dr Ogden had to admit that she had not seen this X-ray and that it could indicate a possible infection. The strategy of Mr Myers was to consistently suggest that these babies had not been as stable and healthy as the prosecution claimed. Myers had some success in this.

Dr Gail Beech, who was working at the Countess of Chester Hospital as a registrar in 2015, was called to give evidence next. Dr Beech was asked to look through Baby C's charts and files and said there were no alarming signs in the baby. Dr Beech said that the baby was even allowed out of the incubator to have contact with its mother. The court also heard from Yvonne Griffiths, who was the Countess of Chester Hospital neonatal unit deputy manager in 2015 and a senior nursing practitioner. Benjamin Myers KC told the court that, in a police statement, Yvonne Griffiths had said that the hospital in Chester didn't usually care for babies of Baby C's weight. Griffiths told the court that it is sometimes risky to transfer a baby and a decision on that still required more consultation at the time. Mr Myers also noted that Griffiths had told the police that the outcome for Baby C had been uncertain and her nursing notes noted 'dark bile' coming from the child. Yvonne Griffiths told the court that the bile was a concern but she had asked a senior doctor to look into this and nothing of great alarm was found as a consequence.

The next morning Nurse Joanne Williams was called again to give evidence. Williams was the designated nurse for Baby C. The barrister Philip Astbury questioned Williams in the morning for the prosecution. By use of the nursing notes of Williams from the time, the prosecution painted a picture of a child who was fragile (as all premature newborns unavoidably are) but had no life threatening conditions and was not felt to be in any grave danger. In her nursing notes from the time, Williams had written at one point - 'Mummy and daddy on the unit during the day, both have had skin-to-skin with [Child C]. Pleased to see him more settled this afternoon. Appear happy with plan of care.' When it was his turn to question Nurse Williams for the defence, Benjamin Myers returned to the baby's weight and the dark bile, pointing out that these were cause for concern.

Sophie Ellis, who was working as a neonatal unit nurse in the hospital at the time, was the next to give evidence. Ellis was the nurse who saw Lucy Letby standing over Baby C's incubator for reasons which seemed unexplained. Letby had actually volunteered to take over Baby's C's care from Ellis. Mr Myers, for the defence, suggested that Lucy Letby was not even there when the baby's condition deteriorated but Sophie Ellis disagreed with this claim. Ellis had only been working there for a few months and Mr Myers questioned her inexperience for such a key role in the unit. In response, Ellis pointed out that she was supported by highly experienced nurses who were also on the unit. And it wasn't as if Sophie Ellis was a member of the public who had just idly wandered into the unit on a whim and been given a job! She

WAS actually a fully qualified nurse.

Another nurse, Melanie Taylor, gave evidence in the afternoon. Taylor told the court that she saw Lucy Letby at Baby C's incubator after the child deteriorated. Mr Myers pointed out that Melanie Taylor had not said this in her police statement but now, in court, was suddenly making Letby (in the words of Myers) the 'front and centre' of her evidence. in response to this, Melanie Taylor said - "I'm just saying what I remembered. I tell you now, when I approached the incubator, she [Lucy Letby] was there on the other side." Mr Myers was attempting to give the impression that Melanie Taylor's memory was unreliable. It was a busy shift and a traumatic day so it would understandable if she didn't remember everything correctly. Melanie Taylor would not concede though that she could have been mistaken. Taylor said that Letby was very 'calm' in the midst of this drama and sadness.

When the trial resumed again on Monday the 31st of October, the court heard from the nursing shift leader who was on duty when Baby C died. Due to reporting restrictions this nurse was not named at the trial. The witness said there were no concerns about Baby C at the start of her shift and the child's designated nurse was Sophie Ellis. The witness said that she later had some concerns over a 'grunting' noise the baby made and remembered asking Lucy Letby, who was on duty that night, to do some observation. By the time that Baby C had sadly passed away, Melane Taylor had taken over as the designated nurse. The witness said that Lucy Letby kept going into the family room where the grieving parents were and had to be repeatedly told to attend to her duties and leave Melanie Taylor to deal with the family.

Benjamin Myers KC asked the witness about official complaints made about the ratio of staff to babies in the hospital and suggested to it was inadequate. The witness agreed there had been staffing problems but said this did not mean staff were negligent in their care. Under questioning the witness agreed with Mr Myers that Baby C was fragile and with a fragile newborn baby there is always risk. The witness was also asked questions by Simon Driver for the prosecution. These questions were about the care given to Baby C and also the movements of Lucy

Letby. The witness repeated what she had previously told the defence. In reply to a question by Driver, the witness was adamant that the quality and level of care in the unit was in no way diminished by staffing levels.

The next person to give evidence was Dr Katherine Davis, who was a paediatric registrar at the Countess of Chester Hospital and responded when Baby C collapsed. Dr Davis said it was unusual to get no response from the desperate attempt to resuscitate Baby C. This was very distressing evidence. The child had suffered brain and kidney damage and had to be given morphine to ease the pain. A baptism and blessing was performed. It was every parent's worst nightmare. Mr Myers, for the prosecution, once again returned to the child's 'borderline' weight when he questioned Dr Davis. Dr Davis conceded that the baby had a lot of 'challenges' but felt that overall it was doing well. Davis also said that 'dark bile', while worrying, is not uncommon in newborn babies. Dr Davis was asked by the prosecution if she had ever seen a baby collapse as suddenly and unexpectedly as Baby C. "Absolutely not," replied Davis.

The day ended with evidence by Dr John Gibbs, who was working at the Countess of Chester Hospital as a consultant paediatric in 2015. Dr Gibbs offered more harrowing testimony in regard to Baby C's fatal collapse. Dr Gibbs echoed previous witnesses by saying that the baby had seemed fairly normal and wasn't thought to be in danger. Gibbs said that no specific cause of death was apparent at the time so they contacted the coroner. Dr Gibbs said that pulmonary embolus was deemed a possibility.

CHAPTER SIX

The next morning Dr Gibbs was questioned by Benjamin Myers KC for the prosecution. Mr Myers returned to his favourite theme - the staffing levels in the hospital. The defence strategy was obviously to depict this hospital as understaffed - to the point where mistakes happened. Mr Myers also returned to another recurring theme of the defence - Baby C's weight. Myers asked Dr Gibbs if Baby C should have been in a tertiary centre with specialist care rather than the hospital in Chester. "No," replied Dr Gibbs. The defence attempted to link the dark bile produced by Baby C to intestinal blockage. Dr Gibbs did not concur with this theory. He said the symptom of a blockage would be repeated vomiting. The baby's abdomen was also deemed normal. Mr Myers asked if it was not unusual that the child had not 'opened its bowels'. Dr Gibbs said it wasn't unusual at all because the baby hadn't been fed and had nothing to get rid of. Mr Myers asked Dr Gibbs why he had made no mention of 'dark bile aspirates' in his notes at the time and was this because the hospital feared legal action. Dr Gibbs didn't have too much time for this question. He said his medical notes were aimed at the welfare of patients not lawyers.

Philip Astbury for the prosecution asked Dr Gibbs about the work hours of the staff. Dr Gibbs said that long hours were a problem for all hospitals in the country but it had no impact on the quality and quantity of care provided by the hospital in Chester. A statement was then read to the court by a nurse named Bernadette Butterworth in which she appeared, in her notes from the time, to express some concern at Baby C's condition and breathing before his collapse. After this statement had been read, Dr Dewi Evans returned to the court to give more evidence. In response to questions by Nick Johnson KC, Dr Evans listed the possible risks Baby C faced upon birth but said all the markers for the baby were good and pointed out that the child had been allowed contact with its mother. Dr Evans said you can't do that if a child is unstable. Dr Evans also said that the 'dark bile aspirate' readings in Baby C were tiny and there was no sign of persistent vomiting. The blood gas readings were also acceptable. Dr Evans described Baby C as a "stable little baby". Dr Evans said the baby had a lung infection but this was being treated with antibiotics.

Dr Evans said there was nothing in the baby's medical records which would cause a sudden collapse. The prosecution ran through all the 'challenges' faced by Baby C which the defence had highlighted and in response to each one Dr Evans said it would not have caused a sudden collapse and death. Dr Evans said that in his medical opinion the baby had died through an injection of air - which caused a splintering of the diaphragm. Benjamin Myers KC now questioned Dr Evans for the defence. This exchange produced the most drama the court had seen so far in what had understandably been a sombre and almost hushed case. Mr Myers pointed out that Dr Evans had not cited splintering of the diaphragm as the cause of death in any of his reports before today. Dr Evans had suggested possible infection in one of his early reports, according to Mr Myers. Myers accused Dr Evans of changing his diagnosis to support the allegations against Lucy Letby. He told Dr Evans that he wasn't an independent witness.

Dr Evans was, as you might imagine, not too happy about these accusations. "I'm completely independent," said Dr Evans." I have been giving evidence in court for a long time. I know about impartiality; I know about the rules. I'm not here for the prosecution. I'm not here for the defence. I'm here for the court." Dr Evans called Mr Myers' accusations 'insulting' and said he had altered his opinion on this case because he now had more information and had read new reports. He told Mr Myers that that's what doctors do. They find as much clinical evidence as they can and sometimes this means they come to a slightly different conclusion. The exchanges between Myers and Evans got quite bad tempered and testy in the end. The strategy of Myers in this instance was perfectly clear. Dr Evans was the main medical expert the police turned to when they were asked to investigate the baby deaths at the hospital. It was Dr Evans who came to a conclusion which suggested foul play - which led to this trial. The prosecution strategy then was clearly to discredit Dr Evans as much as they could.

Dr Sandie Bohin returned to give evidence late in the afternoon. In response to questions by the prosecution, she said that her own investigation was not a case of 'rubber stamping' what Dr Evans had said and she came to independent conclusions. Her task had basically been to sort of peer review the investigation. The police investigation needed a 'second opinion' to see if their medical experts came to a consensus. If there had been no consensus between Evans and Bohin there probably would have been no case. In response to questions about Baby C, Dr Bohin said this was a baby who seemed to be in a good state of recovery at the time of its collapse. Dr Bohin said the child died "with his pneumonia, not because of his pneumonia."

The next morning the court heard evidence from the mother of Baby D - a girl alleged to have been killed by Lucy Letby. The mother (who couldn't be named obviously) recounted her pregnancy - which was something of an ordeal and eventually done by c-section. The witness was not tremendously impressed by the care she got from the Chester hospital during the pregnancy. The baby seemed quite poorly at first but seemed to be fine once it was moved to the neonatal unit. Then came the first collapse. The mother said that a Dr Bruton was involved in the resuscitation and she remembered a nurse, who she believed was Lucy Letby, holding a phone to his ear. The day before the baby died the mother found Lucy Letby 'hovering' over the baby constantly for no apparent reason. The witness told the court that she wished Letby would just go away and give them privacy. The prosecution asked if Lucy Letby was there when the baby died and the witness said yes, Letby was there.

Benjamin Myers asked the witness if she could be mistaken and have confused Letby for another nurse. The witness said no. Although she had no idea who what Letby's name was at the time the subsequent arrest and publicity of Letby meant that she knew for sure it was her now. The court then heard from the father of Baby D. He gave similar evidence to the mother - although he differed in that he had no memory of Lucy Letby at the hospital. This was understandable because he had far more important things to worry about at the time than the names of nurses. After this evidence the court heard details of Lucy Letby's shift patterns and how these related to the babies that had been discussed so far during the trial. The court were given more background on Baby D's treatment and condition and then in the afternoon heard that Lucy Letby was one of two nurses who signed for a saline dose prescription. Five minutes later the child collapsed.

A further neonatal infusion prescription was made in the middle of the night, with Lucy Letby being one of the signatories.

About fifteen minutes later the baby had its third and final collapse. The court heard that at 8-30 in the morning, Letby texted a colleague to inform them of what had happened. "Our job is just far too sad sometimes," was how Letby began the text conversation. Letby suggested that sepsis was the cause of the collapse. It was during this conversation that Letby made her comment about fate and the random nature of life and death. The next evening Letby had another text conversation with her colleague. The court heard that Letby was now saying that Baby D might have had meningitis - according to a theory she heard. At 9-15 that evening, Letby had searched for the parents of Baby D on Facebook. Letby told the colleague that the deaths had suddenly hit her but that work was her 'priority'.

The next day heard evidence from Caroline Oakley. Oakley was a nurse who helped care for Baby D. Oakley outlined her memories and notes of Baby D. The short version is that there were some concerns, as there usually are with newborns in a neonatal unit, but the baby seemed to be doing quite well. Caroline Oakley said she was called back from a break when Baby D became poorly. Oakley said she was surprised by this because the baby was fine when she went to her break. Oakley said the baby had a reddish brown rash which she had never seen before in all her years of nursing. This rash was resolved though by doctors and the baby became stable.

Oakley told the court that Lucy Letby was involved in tasks related to the baby at this specific time. The baby had two more collapses that night. In the final one Oakley was involved in the resuscitation. The witness said that Lucy Letby was also there. Benjamin Myers asked Caroline Oakley if the increase in poorly babies at the unit could be attributed to the fact that they were dealing with more babies than usual. Oakley said she didn't really know. Myers then returned (once again) to staffing levels. Oakley responded by saying they had the staff they needed, but she didn't know what the actual staffing levels were. Myers said that babies require 'one to one' care but Oakley and other nurses were looking after more than one baby that night. In response to this Oakley said it wasn't ideal but it does happen. Mr Myers said there had been a delay in getting antibiotics to Baby D. He then argued that the condition of Baby D was not as 'stable' as the court had been led to believe. He cited the baby's heart rate and breathing as 'warning signs'.

Dr Andrew Brunton, the doctor who tried to save Baby D also gave evidence. Dr Brunton said he was puzzled by the rash on the baby and had never seen this before on an infant. He also said that it made no sense to him why the baby suddenly collapsed and died. Mr Myers, for the defence, argued the inadequate care in the hospital and an infection was considerably more plausible for Baby D's tragic death than the allegations against Lucy Letby. Nursing assistant Lisa Walker also gave evidence and said she was shocked by an incident in the unit where Lucy Letby got cross and short with another nurse who asked for assistance when a baby's oxygen level dropped. Walker said it was strange that Letby should react like that to a colleague simply requesting a little bit of help. Under questioning by Mr Myers though, Lisa Walker conceded that she couldn't remember who the nurse was or which baby they were attending to.

The next morning began with evidence by Dr Sarah Rylance, a former registrar at the hospital in Chester. Rylance gave evidence from Switzerland via a videolink. Rylance refereed to her notes from the time and said they suggested Baby D was stable but did have some problems. Mr Myers, in his questioning, made Dr Rylance concede that the baby was quite poorly at times and should have been given antibiotics sooner. Dr Rylance also conceded that the level of care at the unit sometimes fell below the standards one would expect. The court also heard that there was a rather unfortunate and embarrassing mistake in the hospital when Dr Brunton, who was trying to save Baby D, was trying to talk to a consultant on the phone and was put through to the mother of Baby A by mistake. Little details like this were not exactly evidence but they were of some use to the defence because it depicted a hospital where people were fallible and capable of making mistakes. Simon Driver also questioned Dr Rylance for the prosecution. Driver asked Dr Rylance what her last assessment of Baby D had been. Dr Rylance replied that the baby was not out of the woods yet (so to speak) but was making good progress.

The next person to give evidence was a nurse who could not be named due to reporting restrictions. The nurse had been working in the unit when Baby D died. The nurse spoke of the unusual rash found on the child and also gave evidence about the failed resuscitation. The nurse said that the chart used for guidelines about the drug levels to be used in an emergency had actually gone missing when the baby collapsed the final time. This chart later turned up. The nurse remembered talking to Lucy Letby after the tragedy. Letby asked her questions about the resuscitation. Mr Myers questioned the nurse for the defence and was able to extract an agreement that one to one care for babies was impossible on the unit due to the ratio of babies to staff. Mr Myers was consistently making this point in the trial and trying to use it to the advantage of the defence.

The court then heard from Dr Emily Thomas, who was working at the hospital in Chester at the time of these events. Dr Thomas said that it was Lucy Letby who called for help when Baby D had a third collapse. Dr Thomas said that Letby seemed upset. Elizabeth Marsh, who was doing the night shift in the unit, also gave evidence and recalled seeing Lucy Letby giving chest compressions to Baby D after the third collapse. Chest compressions, also known as cardiopulmonary resuscitation (CPR), are a lifesaving technique used in emergency situations when someone's heart has stopped working effectively. Chest compressions involve applying pressure to the chest to manually pump blood to the body's vital organs.

The next session of the trial saw evidence by consultant paediatrician Dr Elizabeth Newby. Dr Newby had been involved in treating Baby D. She said she was shocked when she was called back for the final collapse because the baby had seemed stable when she was last there. "I admit these things can happen," said Dr Newby, "but it was not what we expected that night to happen." Kathryn Percival-Calderbank, a nurse at the hospital, also gave evidence. Percival-Calderbank said she was surprised by the collapses of Baby D because the baby wasn't considered to be in extreme danger. The trial was postponed the next day because a member of the jury was ill. You obviously can't have a day of evidence if one of the jury is missing. The trial resumed again the day after. In the morning paediatric radiologist Dr Owen Arthurs returned to court to give more evidence. Dr Athurs was asked to discuss X-rays of Baby D. He noted an unusually high amount of gas which he said could have a number of explanations. However an X-ray taken after death was judged by Dr Arthurs to be indicative of deliberate injection of air. The only other explanations were sepsis and a traumatic accident - neither of which were applicable.

Mr Myers questioned Dr Arthurs in court and suggested that Baby C (who was discussed in depth earlier in the trial) had a bowel blockage according to medical evidence. Dr Arthurs did not agree with this theory and said such a blockage would have been identified. Mr Myers had more success with a line of questioning in which Dr Arthurs agreed that Baby C did show signs of an infection. Dr Sandie Bohin was called to give more evidence in the afternoon. Dr Bohin told the court there was nothing to indicate that Baby D was in danger of imminent death and that therefore the tragic loss of the child was unexpected. Dr Bohin said she had ruled out infection as the cause of death (though Dr Bohin did agree the child had an infection, in her view it was treated and under control) in her review and believed that an injection of air was the most plausible explanation.

Dr Bohin said that a danger with infants is that that their parents can unwittingly damage them when they hold them for the first time as babies are very fragile. Dr Bohin did not believe though that this was a factor with Baby D. Mr Myers for the defence asked Dr Bohin if she was not just trying to find anything that supported her theory of air embolus. Dr Bohin strongly denied this. Mr Myers spent some time questioning Bohin on the rash found on Baby D and argued there was no consistent pattern of rashes in cases of air embolus recorded in medical studies. He was basically seeking to argue that this field of study was vague and not completely understood. The subtext of Myers was that, as such, it would be dangerous and difficult to jump to conclusions about alleged incidents of air embolus. Dr Bohin didn't really agree with this and argued there was enough evidence and other markers to make accurate medical conclusions.

Mr Myers and Dr Bohin also disagreed on the health of

Baby D prior to the collapse. Mr Myers listed some issues the baby had and the mother's evidence and asked if the baby had been 'poorly' but Dr Bohin said if the baby was really as bad as Mr Myers was making out it wouldn't have been in the neonatal unit. It would have been moved to somewhere with even more specialist care. Mr Myers asked Dr Bohin if she wasn't trying to minimise the condition of the baby because this didn't support her theory of foul play in its death. "I'd like to make it clear my duty is to the court, to present my findings in an impartial way," replied Dr Bohin. The court then heard details of Letby's police interviews about Baby D from intelligence analyst Kate Tyndall. In her police interviews, Letby had said she had no strong memory of Baby D and couldn't really remember much about this baby. Letby was asked by the police about her Facebook searches for Baby D's parents but said she had no memory of doing this. Letby was also asked why she had suggested sepsis as a cause of death for Baby D to a colleague. Letby told the police she didn't recall saying this.

When the trial resumed the following Monday the evidence had moved to twins Baby E and Baby F. As we have discussed earlier in the book, Letby was accused of murdering Baby E and attempting to murder Baby F (by means of insulin poisoning). The mother of these babies gave evidence to the court in the morning. She said the babies seemed to be in 'good' condition when they were born. The witness said that there was never any indication from staff that the babies had any medical issues and she had some contact with the twins. She was waiting for the babies to be moved to a hospital closer to where the family lived.

The mother said the two babies were doing 'great' - until that is Child E began screaming. The mother investigated and found blood coming from the baby's mouth. Lucy Letby was the only nurse on the scene and told the mother the blood was due to a tube that needed adjusting. Letby told the mother not to worry and to go and wait somewhere. The witness said she did this because she obviously presumed the nurse knew what she was doing. The witness said she phoned her husband and they both had a creeping sense that something was not quite right about this situation. The witness was later at the failed attempt to save her infant after the collapse. She said Lucy Letby had bathed her son afterwards and prepared a memory box. The mother said that Lucy Letby gave her a picture of Baby F cuddling Baby E's teddy bear and she was touched by this and wrote a thank you card to the staff on the unit. Nick Johnson KC asked the witness about the post-mortem. The mother said that a doctor told them a post-mortem wouldn't reveal much that was new and would delay the transfer of the deceased child home.

Mr Myers obviously had a delicate task interviewing this witness - who everyone naturally had the greatest sympathy for. Myers began by offering his condolences for her loss and said that his questioning would in no way seek to minimise the care and love she had afforded her child in his short life. Mr Myers then sought to establish if the mother was mistaken when it came to the exact timing of these events but she disagreed with this and said she wasn't mistaken. The witness revealed that at one point Lucy Letby had said a registrar would be down to talk to her but this never happened. Mr Myers suggested that the screams of Baby E were not as 'horrendous' as described but the witness disagreed with this. The father of the twins also gave evidence and echoed what the mother had said. The father said the progress of the babies had been 'good' and he wasn't as distressed as his wife because he presumed (as one would) that the hospital staff knew what they were doing.

The court heard that, in text messages, Lucy Letby had said of this latest tragedy in the unit - "Not a lot I can do really, he had a massive haemorrhage, could have happened to any baby". The court heard that Letby had later done a Facebook search for the mother of the twins on Christmas Day. In all, Letby would make nine Facebook searches on the family. The trial that day heard a lot of detail from the nursing notes of Lucy Letby in relation to Baby E and Baby F. The notes recorded the treatments of the babies and the collapses (one of which was sadly fatal). The court heard that Letby was the designated nurse for both of these babies. Mr Myers pointed out that Letby's nursing notes were extracts from a much larger journal. This was Mr Myers essentially telling the jury not to draw any conclusions, one way or the other, from such a small sample.

The next morning the court heard from Dr Christopher Wood. He was on a four-month trainee placement at the Countess of Chester Hospital and there when Baby E collapsed. Wood was also present at the birth of both of the twins. Dr Wood said there were six people on the scene where Baby E collapsed and Lucy Letby was one of them. Benjamin Myers established through his questioning that Dr Wood was the only senior health officer covering paediatrics and the neonatal unit at that specific. This obviously wasn't great because Dr Wood was a trainee and didn't have much experience of neonatal care.

A nurse who had previously given evidence, was also in court that day to give more evidence. The nurse (who could not be named) was the designated nurse for Baby E and Baby F during the day shift. The questioning by Mr Myers of this nurse soon settled into a by now familiar pattern. The witness said the baby had been stable (though its blood glucose readings were, said the nurse, a cause for slight concern) while Mr Myers did his best to argue that the baby had been hovering between life and death all the time. Mr Myers must have felt like a qualified doctor by the time this trial was over, such was the battery of medical terms and files he had to use in court each day. One of the tactics of Mr Myers was to frequently ask witnesses if they felt there was always an inherent risk when it came to newborn babies - especially those born premature. The witnesses could only give one answer to this question. Yes, of course there were risks with premature newborns. Both the prosecution and defence asked questions about the method of prescribing insulin to a baby. Was it one continuous dose? The nurse said that it would be a fresh dose each time.

CHAPTER SEVEN

By now it was the middle of November, 2022. Lucy Letby had turned 32 years-old. Lucy Letby's parents were in court day after day. One of her friends was seen in court occasionally but Letby had told other friends and relatives not to come to the trial. She didn't want them to see her in the dock and she didn't want them to hear the distressing evidence the trial was going to examine and accuse HER of. The trial, already a marathon, continued on as Christmas loomed on the horizon. Letby, as of yet, had shown no emotion in court. She was a blank and had listened to all of this distressing evidence without displaying any visible reaction to anything.

The court heard next from the on-call consultant at the time of Baby E's death. This doctor could not be named in the media. After the death of Baby E this doctor had not asked for a post-mortem examination and cited enterocolitis as the cause of death. Enterocolitis is inflammation of the small intestine (enteritis) and colon (colitis). It is typically caused by infections, particularly bacterial or viral infections. However, this doctor had changed her mind on that because she saw an X-ray of the child shortly before it died and it did not indicate enterocolitis. What had happened was that the hospital hadn't pressed for a post-mortem because they wanted to spare the parents - who at this awful and terrible moment needed some space and time alone. The doctor said she deeply regretted that decision now and should have insisted on a post-mortem. The parents of Baby E were in court and the doctor offered them an apology.

Mr Driver, for the prosecution, asked for details about why the baby's death, in the doctor's considered opinion, was not enterocolitis. This evidence was clearly in favour of the prosecution so they were happy to let the doctor expand on this. In his own questions, Mr Myers suggested a blood transfusion for the child was done too late but the witness disagreed with this. Myers proposed that a gastro-intestinal bleed through stress might be an explanation. The witness begged to differ and said the baby was perfectly stable before its collapse. The consultant said she wished she had gone on the neonatal unit sooner that night and perhaps could have prevented this. It was a very poignant moment in the trial because this consultant, though the death was not her fault and unexpected, was clearly full of remorse and regret and still bore the mental scars of that tragic and difficult night.

The next day, Dr Harkness, a paediatric registrar on the night shift when Baby E died, was called again to give evidence. Dr Harkness was questioned by the prosecution first and ran through his notes and memories of Baby E's health. His general view was that the baby was stable and not in any danger. Dr Harkness was also asked to provide details about Lucy Letby's movements and shifts. He confirmed that Letby was tasked with observing Baby E on the night shift. Dr Harkness then spoke about the strange purple patches the baby developed. The only time he had seen something like this was with Baby A - in the same unit. Dr Harkness said he was standing over the baby's incubator discussing the treatment plan when it suddenly collapsed without warning. The blood produced by the baby was something he had never seen before.

When he questioned Dr Harkness, Benjamin Myers wanted to know why a baby that had lost a 'quarter' of its blood was not given a blood transfusion. Dr Harkness said this was discussed but it wasn't deemed a life or death situation at this point. Mr Myers said that the notes of Dr Harkness made no mention of discussing a blood transfusion. He then suggested that not getting a blood transfusion earlier was a mistake. "I disagree," said Dr Harkness. Mr Myers, pulling no punches by this point, suggested that Dr Harkness was 'out of his depth' that night and should have got help from someone. "I disagree," said Dr Harkness, "That is wrong and disrespectful to my ability."

Mr Myers and Dr Harkness had what could be described as a spirited exchange. Mr Myers asked Dr Harkness if he would admit if he was too slow in taking any action. Dr Harkness said yes, he would admit if he had made mistakes, but he hadn't. Mr Myers then argued that the descriptions of the rash on the baby by Dr Harkness were inconsistent and he may have been influenced by subsequent reports and witnesses. Mr Myers also claimed that the evidence of Dr Harkness in court in regard of the discolouration seen on the baby did not match his police statement. Dr Harkness did not agree with this and said they were 'similar' enough. It was obviously difficult in court for the medical witnesses who had worked at the Chester hospital with Letby. They were being asked very precise and detailed questions about the chronology of a specific medical treatment which happened seven years ago. Even with their notes from the time this was not easy.

The next day Dr Dewi Evans was back in court and had another spirited exchange with Benjamin Myers. Dr Evans said the bleeding in Baby E could have been the result of a medical instrument used incorrectly but he stuck to his verdict that an injection of air was the cause of death. Mr Myers accused Dr Evans of selecting 'items' which supported his conclusion but ignoring the big picture - which offered other explanations. Dr Evans obviously did not agree this was the case. Dr Bohin also gave more evidence and expressed regret that a post-mortem was not carried out. Dr Bohin said the only 'natural' thing which could account for the bleeding in Baby E was Dieulafoy's lesion. Dieulafoy's lesion, is a rare and potentially life-threatening condition involving a pathologic artery within the gastrointestinal tract. The symptoms of Dieulafoy's lesion include sudden, severe gastrointestinal bleeding, which may present as hematemesis (vomiting of blood) or melena (dark, tarry stools). The bleeding can be massive and life-threatening, requiring urgent medical intervention. Dr Bohin said she had never seen a bleed like this and that it was very difficult to explain.

When the trial resumed again after the weekend, the focus turned to Baby F. This was the brother of Baby E. Letby was accused of trying to poison Baby F by insulin a day after his brother died. The court heard that Letby was in the unit the night Baby F collapsed. Earlier she had signed a 48 hour prescription for the baby's nutrient bag. Baby F took a turn for the worse when the nutrient bag was administered at 12-25 am. Blood tests were immediately ordered. The blood glucose level, as pointed out by the prosecutor Mr Johnson in court, for the baby had become dangerously low by the next morning. Blood glucose level refers to the concentration of glucose (sugar) in the blood. Low blood glucose levels, known as hypoglycemia, can cause symptoms such as shakiness, sweating, confusion, and dizziness.

The court heard that Letby exchanged text messages with another nurse about the worrying blood glucose levels. It was

Letby who apparently initiated this exchange. At 6pm, Letby texted a friend to ask if 'salsa' (dancing) was still on tonight. Letby signed off with "Hasta luego" (see you later). That afternoon Letby was also engaged in arranging to view a house in Chester (this is the house she lived in when she was arrested). What is remarkable about this is that, if guilty, Lucy Letby was chatting about salsa classes and arranging to view a house merely hours after trying to murder two infant twins. It was like she had a split personality.

Perhaps this is why Letby didn't seem to compute as an evil serial killer when this awful case first became a story in the media. Beverley Allitt, who Letby is most often compared to, was found to have a history of weird and disturbing behaviour before her medical crimes. There was also something 'off' about Allitt in her pictures. She LOOKS scary and unhinged. There was none of that with Lucy Letby though. Nothing in her past. Nothing in her appearance. It was as if she came out of nowhere. It was only in a police mugshot of Letby where she finally started to look the part of the role history had in store for her. Sullen, dead eyed. It was only then that smiling, goofy, ordinary Lucy Letby looked a little bit chilling for the first time.

The court in Manchester heard how Letby had texted Baby F's designated nurse through the day to get updates on the baby's condition. As was her custom, Letby also did Facebook searches for the parents of Baby E and Baby F. At 1-52 am, Lucy sent a text message saying she had said goodbye to the parents of Baby E and Baby F and that they hugged and thanked her. Letby said the parents said 'they could never thank me enough for the precious memories I've given them. It's heartbreaking. I just feel sad that they are thanking me when they have lost him and for something that any of us would have done. But it's really nice to know that I got it right for them. That's all I want.'

The prosecution called Dr Gail Beech to give evidence. Dr Beech went into great detail on the condition and treatments of Baby F. Aside from the low blood glucose levels, which were successfully rectified in the end, Dr Beech said the baby was considered to be quite healthy. The next day three nurses, Shelley Tomlins, Sophie Ellis and Belinda Williamson, who worked in the unit with Lucy Letby while Baby F was there all, had to give evidence. The nurses were asked a simple and important question. Did they give Baby F any insulin? All three nurses gave a firm no to this question. They did not give the baby insulin.

The next morning a doctor, who could not be named, was called back to give more evidence. He said that Baby F had not been prescribed insulin and no baby on the unit was receiving insulin at the time. This, in his view, ruled out the possibility that the insulin was administered by mistake. In light of this he said the insulin readings in the baby were very confusing at the time. The doctor said the baby was given 'rapid acting insulin' but this would have been gone by the time of the hypoglycemic episode so couldn't be a factor. Rapid-acting insulin (as the name suggests) is a type of insulin that is designed to quickly lower blood sugar levels. The prosecution asked the doctor if any investigation was prompted by this confusing state of affairs. The doctor said that no 'action' was taken.

The next witness was Dr John Gibbs, who was a consultant paediatrician in August 2015. Dr Gibbs said that his notes at the time in relation to Baby F suggested infection but he had changed his mind about that after reviewing the case. He now believed the baby was given a large dose of insulin. This was synthetic drug insulin - not natural insulin produced by the body. Natural insulin is a hormone produced by the pancreas to regulate blood sugar levels. It helps to transport glucose from the bloodstream into cells, where it can be used for energy. Natural insulin is distinguished from synthetic insulin, which is produced in a laboratory and used as a medication to manage diabetes.

Dr Gibbs said the reason why no one suspected insulin poisoning at the time was because there was no reason why this baby should be given a large dose of insulin so it didn't occur to them. It didn't make sense that anyone should do that. The afternoon session that day was taken up with evidence from a nurse (who could not be named) and involved a lot of information about nutrient bags and the protocols and guidelines for feeding. There was an awful lot of information for the jury to take in - so much so that one of them even got to ask a question about something they were slightly confused about.

The next morning the court heard from Anna Milan, a clinical biochemist at Liverpool Royal Hospital. Milan explained to the court the method behind analysing blood tests. The insulin reading for Baby F from a blood sample was confirmed by Milan for the court. The court heard next from Professor Peter Hindmarsh - professor of paediatric endocrinology at University College London and consultant in paediatric endocrinology and diabetes at University College London Hospitals. Professor Hindmarsh told the court that he had helped Cheshire Police in their investigation in this case - specially the case of Baby F. Hindmarsh spoke at length about the low blood sugar readings in the baby and how these readings were dangerous because they risked permanent damage. He agreed with the prosecutor Mr Johnson that the low readings were a 'paradox' because the baby was given treatments for low blood sugar.

The jury were shown what a hospital insulin bottle looks like and it was explained to them that a syringe has to be used to extract a dose of insulin. The insulin bottle then seals itself after the syringe is withdrawn. Professor Hindmarsh discussed the most plausible way that insulin had been administered to Baby F. He believed that infusion by use of the nutrient bags was the most likely and the method which most matched the chronology of the hypoglycaemia. Mr Johnson asked if the conclusion of Professor Hindmarsh was that the fluid Baby F was receiving had been contaminated with insulin. Professor Hindmarsh said yes - that was the only explanation. In his questioning of Professor Hindmarsh, Mr Myers for the defence asked why, if this baby was being given high doses of insulin, it displayed only low blood sugar. Wouldn't there be other obvious effects if this baby was being poisoned? Professor Hindmarsh responded by saying that babies being given too much insulin often show no great effect until the point of collapse.

A key piece of evidence from this juncture in the trial is that there was no system for signing in and out of the fridge used to store insulin. The keys were shared by the nurses. This detail was obviously not brilliant for the defence. The next day the court heard from a nurse, who could not be named, who was working with Lucy Letby the night that Baby F was allegedly poisoned. The court was shown a document which showed that Letby and this nurse had signed to confirm the baby's nutrient bag had been changed (that is to say changed to the one which would prove to be near fatal according to the prosecution). The nurse said she had no memory of signing for the bag and couldn't remember if it was her or Letby who changed it. In answer to a direct question from the prosecution the nurse denied she had put anything in the bag and insisted she had not given this baby any insulin.

The next session of the trial began with evidence by blood expert Professor Sally Kinsey. Professor Kinsey had assisted the police in the investigation into the spike in deaths at the hospital. Professor Kinsey said that, in her view, Baby E's bleeding was not caused by an existing condition - although under questioning by Mr Myers she conceded that it was possible there might have been something that was missed. Kinsey also said that Baby A and Baby B were, in her view, killed by air embolus. Mr Myers suggested to Professor Kinsey that air embolus was not her field of expertise. In response to this, Kinsey said it wasn't and she'd never seen one herself but she had read all the medical 'literature' on this. Mr Myers countered this by saying there was very little existing literature on air emboli. Myers then said that a research paper Kinsey had mentioned was about the 'bends' in deep sea divers as much as air embolus in 'normal' people. The strategy of Mr Myers was by now familiar and logical. He was basically seeking to knock down these medical experts a peg or two and make their evidence less credible as a consequence.

In the afternoon the court heard from Ian Allen, who worked in the Countess of Chester Hospital's pharmacy department in summer 2015. Allen explained to jury how nutrient bags worked and what the process was for changing them. Mr Allen said that insulin would not be added to one of these bags - that would be done directly by syringe. The next day Dr Evans was called back to give evidence again and, in answer to questions from the prosecution, said he had never heard of insulin being administered through a nutrient bag. "No. never happens. Insulin is always given in a 50ml syringe driver." Dr Evans said the only explanation for the readings in Baby F is that the child was given insulin by an 'outside' source.

Dr Sandie Bohin also gave evidence and said she agreed with Dr Evans that this was a case of insulin poisoning. The court also heard from three more nurses who were working in the unit when Baby F took a turn for the worse. All three of these nurses were asked if they gave the baby insulin and all three said they did NOT. They all said they would never administer insulin through a nutrient bag. The defence did not always do terribly well when it came to the case of Baby F at the trial. For that they couldn't really be blamed. It was difficult for the defence to argue that the baby hadn't been given insulin. Then the court had heard all of these nurses point blank say they hadn't administered any insulin. That basically left Lucy Letby - the only nurse who could be linked to these deaths and non-fatal collapses. The same Lucy Letby who told the police she couldn't remember Baby F and didn't have much to do with him - which was patently not true.

The next day in court was the 1st of December. The trial now turned its attention to Baby G. Child G was a baby girl born premature. Letby was accused of trying to murder Baby G three times. The baby lived but is now disabled. The jury was shown Lucy Letby's shift patterns - which proved she was in the unit when Baby G suffered her first collapse.

The designated nurse for Baby G during the day was Vicky Blamire. The court were read Blamire's notes about the condition and care of the baby. The baby was putting on some weight and seemed to be doing well. The designated nurse for Baby G when the night shift began was a nurse who couldn't be named. Lucy Letby was on the night shift but working in a different room to where Baby G was. Lucy Letby was though the co-signer for medication administrations for Baby G.

According to Letby's nursing notes, Letby took over for Baby G after an 'event' which required a doctor to examine the baby. Letby's notes say the 'event' was some vomiting and a distended and discoloured abdomen (Letby appeared to have spelled 'abdomen' incorrectly in her notes - for a qualified nurse Letby was terrible at spelling). The notes of Dr Alison Ventress said the baby turned 'red and purple'. Mr Johnson, for the prosecution, noted that this was another case where a baby was found bleeding from the mouth. The court heard various medical reports on Baby G and how doctors treated the child to try and make it more stable and comfortable. A transfer of the baby was discussed. X-rays taken near noon the next morning indicated that the baby's lungs were better and that progress was slowly being made. The baby's colour improved and arrangements were made to transfer the child to Arrowe Park Hospital.

The designated nurse on the day shift wrote that Baby G still had problems but said they trying to remain positive - especially as the baby was about to turn 100 days old (which is a big milestone in neonatal terms). Letby was in text communication with the designated nurse and other colleagues during the day discussing Baby G's condition. When her night shift began, Letby helped to make a banner for Baby G's 100 day milestone. At 3am the baby was moved to Arrowe Park Hospital. Letby got a text about this during the day and said it was 'great news'. Baby G spent nine days at Arrowe Park Hospital before being moved back to Chester. The mother of Baby G now gave evidence and recalled an incident where the baby was 'freaking out' with Letby and another nurse over the incubator. The mother said she was able to calm the baby down herself.

Baby G went home in the end but was left with quadriplegic cerebral palsy and problems with her sight. Cerebral palsy is a neurological disorder that affects movement and muscle coordination, and it is caused by damage to the developing brain. In the case of quadriplegic cerebral palsy, the areas of the brain that control movement in the arms, legs, and trunk are affected, resulting in varying degrees of paralysis or impairment in these areas. Those with quadriplegic cerebral palsy may have difficulties with mobility, coordination, muscle control, and other motor functions. The mother said she had been taught to feed Baby G in the hospital by syringe and it was usually Lucy Letby who assisted in this. The father of Baby G also gave evidence. He said his daughter was tiny with underdeveloped lungs and had been given only a 5% chance of survival at birth. The father said he had never seen any of the nurses do anything suspicious or unprofessional. In his experience they were all kind and helpful. The witness said that after a bout of vomiting he noticed a change in his daughter. Whereas the baby was previously responsive and seemed to be aware of his presence this was no longer the case.

Dr Sarah Ventress gave evidence next and said the saturation levels of Baby G were often a concern. Oxygen saturation is a measure of the amount of oxygen being carried by red blood cells from the lungs to the rest of the body. Desaturation occurs when the oxygen levels in the blood are lower than the normal range, usually below 95%. The saturation levels in Baby G fell below 50% at one point - which was obviously not good at all. Mr Myers, in his questioning of Dr Ventress, was able to establish that the baby had a number of existing health problems before the near-fatal collapse. The basic accusation by the prosecution here was that Letby had deliberately overfed the child and possibility injected air. The last collapse occurred during the last of four consecutive night shifts that Letby did at this time.

Letby was clearly very interested in Baby G the next day and did a lot of texting to colleagues. Letby was in her 'amateur doctor' mode and proposing her own medical theories. What was interesting was that, if guilty, Letby had now altered her MO. First it was injected air, then insulin poisoning, then experimenting with overfeeding. Was this to muddy the trail? Or did Letby decide that injecting air was too lethal? If the latter this would suggest the White Knight/God theory in relation to medical killers. That is to say that Letby liked the idea of creating a crisis and then helping to save the patient. The next day the court heard from a nurse (who could not be named) who said she was surprised when Baby G collapsed because the baby had been fine when she fed her before taking her lunch break. "She was fed and settled when I left her and there had not been any observations on her chart which caused me any concern." Ailsa Simpson, the nursing shift leader, also gave evidence and said the mood had been 'calm' before the collapse.

CHAPTER EIGHT

There was a forced break in the trial due to a member of the jury falling ill. On the first full day of evidence after the resumption, Dr Stephen Brearey was called to give evidence in the morning. Dr Brearey said his notes at the time indicated that Baby G was doing quite well but then there was the worrying incident of projectile vomiting.

"This was not something I had witnessed before," Dr Breary said. Breary told the court the desaturation of the baby was so bewildering they even wondered if there was a malfunction with the ventilation equipment. Mr Myers questioned Dr Breary and told him that he had suspected an infection in his original notes. Breary agreed this was true.

Dr Harkness was called to give evidence and Mr Myers told him he had said in his police interview that a sudden deterioration in a child like Baby G was 'not uncommon'. In response to this, Dr Harkness said he had had seven years more experience in neonatal care now (2022) and that in his revised opinion, now that he knew a lot more, it was uncommon. It was quite a common tactic for the defence to point out contradictions in the police statements of witnesses compared to what they were now saying in court. However, it is debatable if this was of much use. The point of Dr Harkness was perfectly valid.

The court then heard from a nurse named Christopher Booth who worked on the unit when Baby G was there. Mr Booth spoke about the staff making a banner and buying a cake (for the family obviously - not the baby) to celebrate Baby G's 100 day milestone. Mr Booth told the court that he didn't have many duties in relation to Baby G but he recalled the resuscitation efforts and saw that Lucy Letby was involved in this. Letby had intensive care training but there were some nurses who didn't. As a consequence, in an emergency, Letby was more senior than some (but obviously not all) of the other nurses.

In the afternoon a by now familiar figure was called to give evidence. Dr Dewi Evans was back again. Dr Evans (who had obviously read all the medical notes on this child as part of his investigation) said that the condition of Baby G was satisfactory in early September. Evans was asked about the projectile vomiting of the baby and said he had never known of a baby to vomit this distance. Dr Evans believed Baby G's turn for the worse was a result of too much milk down the NG tube and possibly a bolus of air. Dr Evans was asked about a claim by Lucy Letby that babies can take in a lot of air when they vomit. Dr Evans said this wasn't true. Mr Myers then questioned Dr Evans for the defence and spent a lot of time arguing that Baby G's stomach was not empty at the time of the vomiting and there was already milk in her system. Dr Evans disagreed with this and cited medical readings to support this.

Dr Evans did agree with Mr Myers though that the baby was delicate and in the 'margins of viability'. Dr Evans said the bleeding on the baby was similar to that of Baby E (who was discussed earlier in the trial). Mr Myers disputed this and asked Dr Evans if he was making this link to help the prosecution. Dr Evans said this was not true and that Baby G was actually the first baby he investigated so he didn't even know about Baby E at the time. Mr Myers said gastro-oesophageal reflux can cause projectile vomiting but Dr Evans said this was not diagnosed or mentioned in either of the hospitals where Baby G was treated so can be ruled out. Myers suggested that it was plausible an infection could have occurred before the vomiting. In response to this, Dr Evans said - "There is no clinical evidence to back up that hypothesis. I don't deal with 'ifs', I deal with evidence."

Dr Sandie Bohin also gave evidence, and when questioned by the prosecution, said Baby G was considered to be stable before the first collapse. The following morning, Dr Bohin continued to give evidence. Mr Myers suggested that her evidence was somehow suspect now because she had heard a lot of evidence from Dr Evans and seemed to echo whatever he said. Dr Bohin said her evidence was independent and did not arise from dialogue with Dr Evans or anyone else. The court also heard from an engineer who confirmed there was no problem with any of the medical equipment at that time. A nurse, who could not be named, was also asked to give evidence in relation to Baby G. The nurse pointed out that the prosecution had suggested in their opening statement that Lucy Letby had turned off Baby G's monitor (this was the machine which provided readings) at one point. The nurse said this was not true and that other staff did this by mistake and actually told her and apologised at the time.

Consultant Dr John Gibbs and registrar Dr David Harkness were apparently the staff who offered the apology. This evidence, though not of huge significance, was not good for the prosecution because it made it look as if they were trying to blame Letby for literally everything which ever went wrong in this hospital - even if it wasn't her fault. The next day in court Dr Gibbs was questioned by the defence about the monitor incident. This happened during cannulation. Cannulation is a medical procedure that involves the insertion of a tube or catheter into a blood vessel, usually a vein or an artery. This is done to allow for the administration of medications, fluids, or blood products, as well as for monitoring purposes. Dr Gibbs told the court that he had no memory of this incident but accepted that it must have happened if the nurse said it did. It should be noted that the monitor was simply for readings. The monitor being briefly disconnected would not affect the baby - though it obviously isn't good because the readings are vital to observation and treatment.

The day Dr Harkness gave evidence and given a rather rough time by Mr Myers. Myers accused Dr Harkness of leaving Baby G unattended and also of forgetting to tell nurses that the monitor was switched off. Dr Harkness said he had no memory of these incidents but definitely wouldn't have done either of those things. Unlike Dr Gibbs (who was retired, Dr Harkness was not), Harkness said he had no memory of offering an apology to a nurse for the monitor incident and doubted that this actually happened. At the conclusion of this day's evidence the court adjourned for Christmas. No more evidence could be heard that week because members of the jury were absent. The fact that this trial ran into Christmas, a magical holiday for children, seemed especially cruel and poignant given the circumstances.

Over a month passed before the trial resumed. The trial of Lucy Letby began again on the 18th of January, 2023. This was day 40. The court began with the wrapping up of the Baby G evidence. Dr Evans and Dr Bohin were both back in court. Benjamin Myers for the defence concentrated on the 'projectile vomiting' of the baby prior to a collapse. This had been deemed unusual by all the experts in court. Suspicious you might say. Mr Myers offered nursing notes and evidence by Baby G's father to argue that the baby had vomited several times before the alleged attacks by Lucy Letby and on occasions when she wasn't even there. Dr Evans and Dr Bohin both countered this by saying that vomiting and projectile vomiting are not the same thing. Dr Evans told the court that none of the medical notes for Baby G constituted the volume of projectile vomiting - until the incidents the court had discussed before Christmas.

The court were also told the details of Letby's police interview in relation to Baby G. Letby said there were no major concerns with Baby G before the incidents of collapse. Letby said she had other babies to look after too at the time so couldn't remember all the details about Baby G. Letby denied switching the monitor off and said she didn't actually remember this incident. Letby denied attempting to harm this baby and told the police there must have been too much milk in a feed it was given. The trial now turned to Baby H - a girl who Letby was accused of attempting to murder twice. This baby recovered and went home to its family. The court heard evidence from both the parents in which they said it was a difficult birth but the baby seemed to be doing ok.

Meanwhile, Lucy Letby had been assigned extra shifts because the unit was busy. In a text message to a colleague, Letby jokes that work has been so 'mad' she's fallen way behind on the plotlines in Coronation Street. Letby was the designated nurse for Baby H. This baby had a difficult start in life. The baby suffered desaturation (a decrease in the saturation of oxygen in the blood) issues and had to have a blood transfusion and be resuscitated. Child H was transferred to Arrowe Park Hospital for three days before being returned to Chester. It was discharged on October the 9th, 2015. Letby's online searches, the court heard, included the parents of Baby H. The prosecution were very keen for the court to have details of Letby's online activity because they obviously believed it was highly suspicious that she often searched for the families of these babies on significant anniversaries. Letby also did online searches for many people and also patients who suffered no drama or harm in hospital. Letby seemed to be somewhat addicted to having a 'nose' about people online.

The next day the court heard distressing evidence of how the baby had collapsed twice after taking on a strange mottled appearance. The two resuscitations were successful and - thankfully - the baby suffered no lasting damage (happily, the baby in question is today a little girl and doing ok). The father said he recalled Lucy Letby assisting in one of the resuscitations. The parents said that the baby improved 'leaps and bounds' when it was moved to Arrowe Park Hospital. The next day in court was quite dramatic. The court heard that Baby H had to be treated for pneumothorax. Pneumothorax, commonly referred to as a collapsed lung, occurs when air enters the space between the chest wall and the lung, causing the lung to partially or completely collapse. Dr Alison Ventress had to insert a needle into the chest to perform thoracentesis - a medical procedure used to remove excess fluid or air. A chest drain (a tube in the chest) was then inserted.

Dr Ravi Jayaram then arrived on the scene and decided that a second chest drain should be used. Mr Myers questioned Dr Jayaram forensically and doggedly on this for some time. Myers told Dr Jayaram that he had inserted the chest drain in the wrong place because it should go in the fifth intercostal space. Dr Jayaram was forced to concede that he hadn't done this but said the focus should be on outcomes not the 'process'. Dr Jayaram had a point because the child was saved but Mr Myers had a point too. When Dr Gibbs gave evidence afterwards and said there seemed to be no reason for the baby's collapses, Mr Myers disagreed and proposed that chest drains against the heart were plausibly a factor. This was a good day for the defence. One could see that the prosecution case for Baby H was not as strong as it was for the others. Dr John Gibbs told the court that an ultrasound had ruled out the chest drains as a potential factor in the collapse but the case of Baby H certainly seemed more vague and speculative than others in this trial when it came to ascribing the blame to Lucy Letby. It would obviously be up to the jury to decide in each individual case whether they felt the prosecution had done enough to convince them of Letby's guilt.

The next day the court heard evidence from Dr Matthew Neame. Dr Neame said the second collapse of Baby H was unexplained and unexpected. He said he recalled Lucy Letby being one of the first people on the scene when the collapse happened. Baby H had two bouts of bradycardia. Bradyarrhythmia is a medical term that refers to a heart rate that is slower than normal. Thankfully, the baby recovered once it was made stable and transferred to another hospital. Nurse Shelley Tomlins, Child H's designated nurse on the nightshift beginning 26 September, gave evidence and - under questioning from Mr Myers - agreed that Baby H had been a 'poorly' baby. The nurse Christopher Booth was also called back to give evidence. He described Lucy Letby as 'hard working' and said, in response to a question by Myers, that Letby did get emotional and upset when babies got ill or died in the unit. The day next in court, Mr Myers asked Dr Sandie Bohin if leaving a needle in Baby H as a temporary chest drain was 'sub-optimal' practice and should have been removed sooner. Dr Bohin agreed with Mr Myers that this was not good practice and could have been hazardous. The defence was clearly doing an effective job in arguing that Baby H had not been given the best care in Chester. Dr Evans also gave more evidence - though he was less willing to concede this point than Dr Bohin and had some spirited exchanges with Mr Myers as a consequence.

When the trial began again the following day, the case moved to Baby I. This was a baby girl that Letby was accused of making four attempts to murder - finally doing so by means of air injection. The court heard evidence from the mother of Baby I. The baby seemed fine at birth although its weight was a slight concern and it was very small. The baby spent some time at a high dependency unit in Liverpool before going back to Chester. The mother said she was annoyed that one of the nurses in the unit in Chester clearly had a cold (this nurse wasn't Letby) and was coughing and sneezing. The mother was understandably worried about these germs being passed to her child. A bout of ill health in the baby required it to go back to Liverpool but then it was deemed well enough to go back to Chester. Just before the child took a turn for the worse again, the mother recalled Lucy Letby telling her that the baby's stomach looked swollen. The baby later had to be resuscitated.

The mother said the baby seemed to recover again and she hoped she could soon take the child home. The mother said she wasn't impressed by the hygiene in the hospital and felt staff didn't wash their hands enough. The witness said that Lucy Letby offered to take some photographs of Baby I for her and she agreed to this. The witness said that Letby, compared to the other nurses, seemed a trifle enigmatic and reserved. The mother became aware that the mood of staff in relation to her baby now seemed more pessimistic. The baby was put on antibiotics. The situation soon got a lot worse. The baby had to be resuscitated several times and doctors didn't seem to know what the problem was. The mother said she was annoyed to notice that the baby's monitor had been turned off.

The baby was taken to Arrowe Park Hospital - where the mother said the staff were 'rude' and told her there was nothing wrong with the baby. One of the nurses there went to feed the baby and had to be informed by the mother that the child was nil by mouth. Nil by mouth refers to a patient not being allowed to have anything by mouth, including food, drink, or medication. This is usually done in preparation for surgery or certain medical procedures to prevent aspiration (inhalation) of gastric contents into the lungs. The baby was eventually deemed stable and sent back to Chester. The mother told the court that in her view all this ferrying back and forth between hospitals didn't do the baby much good. At 12.30am on October 23, the mother got a call from the hospital and was told the baby was on a ventilator. Yet another resuscitation was being performed.

The mother said Lucy Letby was one of the staff involved in this effort. The mother told staff that they couldn't keep doing this and felt it was only prolonging the suffering and pain of her child. The resuscitation effort finally stopped and the child was pronounced dead. The mother was handed the baby so she could have contact and say goodbye. It was after this that Lucy Letby, as we noted earlier in the book, asked the mother if she wanted to bathe the baby. The mother said as she was doing this Letby was smiling and talking about how she had been the first person to bathe the baby. The mother, understandably given the tragic and awful circumstances, found Letby highly irritating and tactless and wished she would just go away. In a moment like that you simply want to be alone. Letby eventually got the message and left the mother.

Intelligence analyst Claire Hocknall then told the court about Letby's shift rotations in relation to Baby I. Letby was on shift when all the collapses took place. At this time Letby was working both day and night shifts and wasn't confined to any one shift pattern. Letby still lived in nearby hospital accommodation at this time and was also young, not married, and had no kids. As a consequence of all of this Letby was very flexible and available to work whatever shifts or hours the hospital wanted. Letby was also one of only three band five nurses that had done the neonatal course at that time. As such she was valuable to the unit.

The court heard from other nurses about the condition of Baby I and were then read Letby's nursing notes on the child. Shortly before one collapse Letby had written that the baby was not woken for a feed and therefore fed with a tube. Letby's text messages at this time were read out. Letby indicated in them that she did not feel supported by her colleagues. Letby also texted her mother to say that she would be home for Christmas (which was actually still quite a long way off at the time). Her mother was very happy to hear that. It was also revealed that in court Letby had done an online search for the mother of Baby I. The court heard from nurse Bernadette Butterworth. This nurse said there was a slight mix-up with Baby I not getting sufficient antibiotics at one point but this was rectified and wasn't serious.

This was an interesting day of evidence for a couple of reasons. First of all, we learned that Arrowe Park Hospital felt there was nothing wrong with Baby I. This was good for the prosecution case because it indicated that the baby only got ill in Chester. A second interesting observation was that the Lucy Letby had sent a sympathy card to Baby I's mother and said in police interviews that she did this because it was rare to get to know a parent so well. Letby had painted a picture where she got on well with Baby I's mother and had developed a bond. Baby I's mother though more or less said in court she found Letby annoying and a bit weird and didn't have much to do with her.

The next day the court heard from Dr Lucy Beebe. Dr Beebe said she remembered an incident where Lucy Letby was crying and upset about the incidents which had happened with the babies. Mr Myers for the prosecution said this was a very 'normal' reaction because who wouldn't be upset in that situation? There was an interesting piece of evidence this day from a nurse named Ashleigh Hudson. Hudson was on the unit with Letby and cared for Baby I. She said she was shocked when Baby I collapsed because the child seemed stable to her. Hudson recalled an incident where she went away to get some milk and then found Letby standing near the baby. Letby commented that Baby I looked pale - despite the fact the lights were dimmed and Letby was about six feet away.

Hudson was closer than Letby but couldn't see anything. When she did examine the baby she saw it looked poorly and Letby had been right. Nurse Hudson found it very distressing to give evidence about the baby and was often in tears. She told the court that she had to go back to the unit with police as part of the investigation into Baby I so they that they understood the geography of where this alleged incident happened. Mr Myers had said to Hudson - "It's impossible, isn't it, to recall precisely how the lighting was five years previously?" Ashleigh Hudson didn't quite agree with this though. "Not precisely. It is an image that has been imprinted on my brain for quite some time. It's quite vivid."

The next day the court heard from Dr Matthew Neame. Dr Neame discussed the strange 'mottling' on Baby I and discussed some of the theories and treatments which occurred. Mr Myers wanted to know if infection was a possibility - or perhaps low oxygen levels. Dr Neame didn't believe there was clear sign of an infection but agreed that low oxygen levels were possible. Of most interest this day was Letby's text messages at this time. Letby had asked if she could have Baby I again (that is be the baby's designated nurse) and this was agreed. An hour later though, Letby got a text saying the baby had been reallocated to another nurse. Letby then asked if something had happened. The reply said - "No. Was just asked to reallocate so no one has her for more than one night at a time. Or one shift. Not just night." The possible meaning of this is interesting. Were the hospital now suspicious? Did they want to avoid any one nurse (especially Letby) having prolonged contact with Baby I?

The next day began with evidence by Nurse Shelley Tomlins. Tomlins, distressingly, told how Baby I seemed to go into cardiac arrest right in front of them without warning and had to be resuscitated. This was actually Tomlins' last ever shift at the hospital as she was leaving her job there. It was not a nice way to go out. The court heard from Dr Harkness and also a consultant at Arrowe Park Hospital. They discussed the transfers of the baby to and from the hospitals and how its condition had seemed stable at various points. Nurse Caroline Oakley told the court that her observations for Baby I were 'unremarkable' (that is to say there was nothing of alarm) just before Lucy Letby began her shift on the 22nd of October. The court then heard, from various witnesses, a timeline of Baby I's collapses and tragic death. The court heard that Lucy Letby sent a card to Baby I's parents when the funeral took place. Letby had written - "There are no words to make this time any easier. It was a real privilege to care for [Child I] and get to know you as a family - a family who always put [Child I] first and did everything possible for her..." The court then heard from Nurse Ashleigh Hudson again. Hudson said the baby's collapse was a shock because it seemed to be doing quite well. In his questions, Mr Myers got Hudson to agree though that the baby had problems and was never 'out of the woods' completely.

Consultant paediatric radiologist Dr Owen Arthurs was back in court the next day. Dr Arthurs had done a study of air in post-mortem infants so was considered to be an expert in this field. Mr Johnson, for the prosecution, asked Dr Arthurs if, in the absence of any other explanation, it stood to reason that air was injected into Baby I. "I think that stands to reason," replied Dr Arthurs. Arthurs had cited the dilation of the stomach (which he said was highly unusual) and gas within the wall of the small or large intestine on an X-ray for his conclusion. In his questioning of Dr Arthurs, Benjamin Myers for the defence returned to his claim that Dr Ravi Jayaram had placed the chest drains on Baby I in the wrong place. Dr Arthurs said Mr Myers was mistakenly using guidelines for outside the chest not INSIDE but conceded that a neonatologist would know more about this matter than him. Dr Arthurs also had to agree with Mr Myers that X-rays alone are not a completely precise way of concluding that air is present.

Registrar Dr Rachel Chang also gave evidence. Dr Chang was involved in the last attempt to save Baby I. Dr Chang burst into tears in court at one point when she had to talk about the baby's death. It was a dreadfully sad and awful memory. Dr Chang was asked by the prosecution if she had any theories about what caused the baby's death. Dr Chang said it was a mystery to her and she didn't know. The court also heard from some nurses who spoke of the shock and devastation of the nursing team when Baby I passed away. They had grown very attached to this baby and it was shattering when she died.

The next morning Dr Sandie Bohin was back in court. Dr Bohin said that air embolus was the cause of Baby I's death. Mr Myers, for the defence, suggested that Dr Bohin had merely 'rubber stamped' the conclusions of Dr Evans. Dr Bohin got a bit annoyed at this and said Mr Myers wasn't being very polite. She said her work was independent and that she didn't agree with every single thing in the work done by Dr Evans. Myers suggested that Dr Bohin was trying to make the case match the air embolus theory rather than judge it on its own terms. Dr Bohin obviously disagreed with this. By now this was a familiar tactic by Mr Myers. Dr Bohin and Dr Evans were the two big independent medical experts in the police investigation so the defence strategy was to tarnish them as much as they could by going on the attack. Mr Myers, interestingly, pointed out that Baby I had an abdominal distension. In her own investigation notes, Dr Bohin had said this was 'suspicious' (as in possible foul play).

Around this time in the trial, Mr Myers also drew the court's attention to the fact that the evidence of Dr Evans had been called 'worthless' by a judge in another case (this case was unrelated to Letby and involved two parents seeking to get access to children cared for by grandparents). The judge in that case had said Dr Evans report "... has the hallmarks of an exercise in 'working out an explanation' that exculpates the applicants. It ends with tendentious and partisan expressions of opinion that are outside Dr Evans' professional competence and have no place in a reputable expert report." As you might imagine, Mr Myers was very keen for the jury in Manchester to hear about this. In response to this, Dr Evans said - "This is the first judgement that has gone against me in 30 years. I do object to being called partisan. If you are partisan you don't survive in the courts for long. My reports are impartial." Mr Myers wasn't finished yet and said - "The reference to 'working out an explanation', that is precisely what you are doing in this case at various points, isn't it?" Dr Evans said that wasn't true.

In questioning Dr Bohin, Mr Myers had pointed out that Lucy Letby was not actually on shift when some 'suspicious' things occurred. It was quite a good double point for Myers because it obviously suggested that Letby wasn't there when every single suspicious thing happened and also called into question the judgement of Dr Bohin - because how could this truly have been 'suspicious' (this was plainly a reference to the abdominal distension Dr Bohin described as suspicious in her report) if Lucy Letby, the person now being accused of being a medical serial killer, wasn't actually there? In isolation it was a good exchange for Mr Myers but the big picture was another matter. While there was no obvious smoking gun in the trial so far (though the insulin poisoning was certainly not far off) the persistent drip feed of information tended to sway armchair detectives, so far at least, slightly towards the view that these deaths and collapses couldn't have been some random freak coincidence - a run of tragic bad luck which always seemed to feature the same luckless nurse being on shift.

Mr Myers continued to question Dr Bohin and attempted to portray Baby I as a child who was desperately ill and could have had all manner of ailments. Dr Bohin did not agree with this and felt there was no obvious medical reason for why the child should have died. Babies, said Dr Bohin, are fragile and vulnerable but they don't go into cardiac arrest for no reason. Dr Bohin said the hospital was notoriously poor on whether naso-gastric tubes were in situ, inserted, replaced or removed. This was incompetence but Dr Bohin said it did not cause the child's death - though Mr Myers made a meal of this point. Mr Johnson, for the prosecution, obviously didn't have any cause to disagree with what Dr Bohin was saying so he merely asked her to agree on a few things - things which supported the prosecution.

It's fair to say that Mr Myers was having to do a lot more work in this trial than Mr Johnson - so far at least. Mr Johnson would become the focal point at a later time. Mr Johnson told the court about Lucy Letby's poliice interviews in relation to Baby I. Letby said she couldn't remember much about Baby I - not even the night the child died. In the interview Letby was asked about Nurse Ashleigh Hudson's evidence about Letby saying Baby I was 'pale' - despite the fact it was dark and she was six feet away. Letby told the police she couldn't remember this incident much but there was some light. Letby said that 'maybe' she had noticed something about the baby before and just repeated this.

The afternoon session moved to the case of Baby J. Letby was accused of trying to murder Baby J on November 27. Baby J's mother told the court about the birth and also informed the court that Baby J had surgery for a bowel problem. The mother said the baby faced a number of challenges and was critical of the level of care at the hospital in Chester. The mother's main complaint seemed to be a lack of communication from the staff. The mother said she got a call on the 27th of November telling her that her daughter had collapsed. This was a shock because the baby was doing well and the family had made preparations to bring her home. The baby recovered but had another collapse shortly before Christmas. The child was taken to Alder Hey to have another operation (this reversed the previous operation). The baby used stoma bags and the mother believed there was a problem with these bags not working 'as they should'. Stoma bags, also known as ostomy bags or colostomy bags, are medical devices used by individuals who have undergone certain surgical procedures. These surgeries involve creating an opening (stoma) on the abdomen, through which waste products from the digestive or urinary system are diverted. This second operation seemed to rectify the problems the child had and it was able to go home in January, 2016.

Under questioning from Mr Myers, the mother of Baby J outlined the challenges the baby had faced. The mother also spoke of an incident where she noticed her baby was wrapped in a towel which it seemed to have gone to the toilet on. The mother was naturally very annoyed at this and complained to a consultant at the Chester hospital. The court heard some of Letby's text messages from the day Baby J was taken back to the unit in Chester from Alder Hay. Letby said it was 'chaos' on the unit and said she'd had an argument with another member of staff. In the days that followed, Letby complained about the staffing levels at the unit to a colleague. Letby said that at one point there were only five nurses on duty. The court would hear from a number of doctors concerning Baby J. They said they could not explain why the baby had suffered two seizures. This grim trial had a rare happy note though when the court was told that Baby J went home and made excellent progress.

Dr Evans and Dr Bohin gave evidence during the sessions relating to Baby J. Dr Evans told the court that the seizures were caused by lack of oxygen to the brain. Evans didn't believe it was an infection because the baby recovered too quickly to suggest that diagnosis but he conceded to Mr Myers that an infection couldn't be completely ruled out. Dr Bohin disagreed with this and DID believe that infection could be excluded as a possibility. "I thought that seemed extremely unusual - the speed of the collapse, the longevity of the resuscitations and the fact that she seemed to recover quite quickly. That is not the way that infection normally plays out."

The trial now moved on to the cases of Baby L and Baby M. The court were told that the case of Baby K would not be covered at this time for reasons that would later be clear. Baby M and Baby L were twins boys which Letby was charged with attempting to murder. The court were read some of Letby's nursing notes for Baby L and also heard some of her text messages. Letby had just moved into her first house so was unpacking when at home. Letby told a colleague that there were no 'unwell' babies in the unit but it was busy. Lucy Letby's text messages at this time also seemed preoccupied with the Grand National. Letby texted her mother and asked if she could get her father to put a bet on the race for her. Letby also invites some colleagues to 'crash' at her house and says she has prosecco and vodka.

The court heard a lot of detail concerning the blood sugar levels of Baby L. This was obviously a challenging trial for the jury because they had to quickly learn and understand a lot of medical terms in order to make any sense of the complex evidence they were hearing. The timeline of this specific part of the trial was that Letby was doing day shifts in the unit when the twins were born. A blood test was ordered on Baby L and done in Liverpool. The results were astonishing. The insulin level was recorded as 1,099, and the C-peptide recorded as 264. The baby was diagnosed with hypoglacaemia - which was weird because it had been given regular doses of dextrose. Letby, meanwhile, was texting to celebrate winning £135 on the Grand National. Letby is also privately critical of staff at the unit - complaining of 'poor skills'. The text messages reveal that Letby turned down a few shifts at this time because she needed to catch up on some sleep.

The court heard from the parents of the twin boys. They spoke about the pregnancy and also the collapse of Baby M. The mother said she prayed to God that her baby would be saved. The mother recalled Lucy Letby being there when she prayed. The court actually heard from a midwife who said the twins had scored top marks on a health reading after they were were born. It was unexpected that either of them would ever be in a critical condition. Dr Sudeshna Bhowmik, who was a paediatric trainee at the time, was called to give evidence. Dr Bhowmik said she had no memory of the twins but did have her medical notes on them from the time. Her notes confirmed that the hospital were worried about the blood glucose readings for Baby L. Amy Davies, a neonatal practitioner, gave evidence and recalled changing nutrient bags with Lucy Letby. The court heard that a baby with low blood sugar is usually given glucose after some milk. That could change though depending on circumstances. Davies was asked if she gave Baby L any insulin and said no, she definitely hadn't given Baby L any insulin. Dr Anthony Ukoh was the last person to give evidence. Dr Ukoh said that there were no 'red flags' concerning the twins when they were born.

The next session was a dramatic one in court due to evidence from a doctor who worked at the Countess of Chester Hospital in 2016. Though this doctor gave evidence behind a screen to protect his identity, Lucy Letby clearly knew who he was. In fact, she burst into tears when he started speaking. Letby went to leave the court but after speaking to a dock officer and her barrister she sat down again and Mr Myers informed the judge that they could carry on. This was the first display of emotion that Letby had shown during the trial. She had sat impassive as awful details about baby deaths were forensically examined but the recognition of this doctor had produced a flood of tears. It was clear that Letby had some emotional connection to this doctor. Him giving evidence in this case was almost more than she could tolerate.

The doctor had treated Baby L after Letby was alleged to have tried to poison the baby with insulin. The doctor didn't give evidence for very long and spoke about how they had to stop the blood sugar levels from dropping. Happily, both the twin boys were eventually discharged and are now ok. Dr John Gibbs also gave evidence and said that blood test results had proved beyond doubt that Baby L was given insulin by someone. "I was not thinking at the time that someone might have administered insulin. The results showed that, but unfortunately the junior doctors who read them didn't realise the significance." When the court resumed again, Dr Anna Milan, a consultant clinical scientist at Royal Liverpool Hospital, confirmed that the blood test confirmed insulin in Baby L. Mr Myers asked Dr Milan if the handling of the sample (that is to say the way it is handled and transported from ward to lab) could affect the findings. This question (which you'd imagine Dr Milan would have been justified in rolling her eyes at) was a clear sign of how weak the defence case was with Baby L. Mr Myers was now trying to cobble together some dubious theory for how the blood test sample might have been wrong. It was desperate stuff.

It should be noted that Baby L was alleged to have been poisoned with insulin while Baby M was alleged to have been injected with air. Letby was accused of attempting to murder the twins both around the same time but by different methods. All of this evidence obviously did not paint the Countess of Chester Hospital in a very good light. It begged a rather obvious question. If the tests showed someone had given Baby L unprescribed insulin why was there no investigation at the time? Why was nothing done about this? It painted a bleak picture of bureaucratic incompetence and apathy. The court heard about Letby's police interviews concerning Baby L. Letby had told the police that no one had prescribed insulin and if anyone had administered it then it hadn't been her. Letby said she didn't believe someone had given the baby insulin by mistake.

The following day the court was told that a blood gas report on Baby M and a paper towel which was used to scribble down drug doses during the resuscitation was found in a Morrisons carrier bag under Lucy Letby's bed in her house by the police. Letby had told the police she must have taken this home by mistake and not got around to destroying it. Staff taking home medical documents by mistake does happen but it did seem rather suspicious that Letby had these specific items - one of which related directly to the moment where Baby M's life was in danger and he had to be saved. A nurse named Mary Griffith gave evidence that day and was asked by Mr Driver for the prosecution if she'd ever taken home documents like the ones found in Letby's house. "No," replied the nurse. Mr Myers, now on the back foot, suggested that Letby had written the notes on the paper towel (so presumably had put it in her pocket at some point and forgotten about it). In response to this Mary Griffith said she didn't know if Letby had written anything on the paper towel at the time of the emergency.

The next session of court was notable for evidence from Dr Ravi Jayaram. Dr Jayaram spoke of the 30 minute effort to save Baby M's life after the child crashed. Dr Jayaram said at one point they were going to stop but - thankfully - they carried on and managed to save the child. This incident, said Dr Jayaram, and the others which preceded it, led consultants to have a meeting in which they discussed what was happening in the neonatal unit. The rise in deaths and incidents was clearly not normal. Dr

Jayaram said that air embolus was something which came up this meeting. He also conducted some research of his own and said he was 'chilled' to the bone when he saw the air embolus seemed to fit all the symptoms he had seem when Baby M crashed - including discolouration.

Mr Myers pointed out to Dr Jayaram that he had not mentioned any discolouration in his medical notes at the time. "At that time I had no knowledge or suspicion that the discolouration could have been related to something else that could have caused cardio-respiratory arrest, which is probably why I didn't specifically put it in the notes," replied Dr Jayaram. "At the time it was not the priority. I wish I had and we would not be sitting here years later having this rather academic discussion." Mr Myers responded by saying this was not an 'academic' discussion. Dr Jayaram, under questions by the defence, said that he and Dr Brearey had suspicions about Letby by now as she seemed to always be on shift when these events happened. The defence pointed out though that Letby continued to work on the unit for another eleven months. Mr Myers also used the term 'all eyes on Letby' - his way of suggesting that she was being watched with suspicion (which would have presumably made it more difficult for her to do anything wrong).

CHAPTER NINE

Day 60 of the trial saw more courtroom sparring between Dr Evans and Benjamin Myers. Dr Evans told the prosecution that in his view Baby M had been injected with air. Evans said that all other explanations could be ruled out by logic when you went through them. Mr Myers for the defence said that Dr Evans had no empirical evidence for this theory. Dr Evans replied by saying that of course there is no empirical evidence because you can't inject babies with air as part of a research study! Dr Evans added that injection of air by mistake was all but impossible with the modern equipment in hospitals.

Dr Bohin also gave evidence and agreed with Dr Evans that

Baby M had been injected with air. Mr Myers said she had no evidence to back this up but Dr Bohin obviously disagreed with that. The robust exchanges between Mr Myers and Dr Evans were interesting but as of yet they hadn't really provided any major breakthroughs for the defence. Although he did quite well at times and managed to ruffle a few feathers on Dr Evans, the main problem Mr Myers faced was that he was a barrister trying to cross-examine a doctor who had 30 years of pediatric experience. However well briefed and clever Mr Myers was, an inescapable fact was that Dr Evans knew a lot more about this stuff than he did. Mr Myers, despite his efforts, was never going to score a clear points victory over Dr Evans in court. The same was true of Dr Bohin.

The next day Professor Peter Hindmarsh (professor of paediatric endocrinology at University College London) was back to give more evidence. This was not good news for the defence because Dr Hindmarsh said the blood readings of Baby L could only be explained by insulin poisoning. Dr Hindmarsh explained that insulin bottles are very small and the liquid is clear. It could be added to a nutrient bag without any obvious visual sign of its appearance. Dr Hindmarsh estimated that up to three or four nutrients bags had been contaminated in his view. The evidence this day was very complex - so much so that even the judge (half in jest) said he was finding it difficult to keep up with all the medical readings and charts. This was in response to a comment by Mr Johnson for the prosecution about how the jury must be finding this case quite difficult with the endless medical notes. Benjamin Myers didn't have much to work on with Dr Hindmarsh. The defence couldn't credibly dispute that Baby L had been given unprescribed insulin so this left them in a very difficult position at this juncture in the trial.

The next session of the trial saw the court move to the case of Baby K. This was the baby where Dr Jayaram had found Lucy Letby standing over the incubator when the baby's oxygen levels had fallen. Letby was charged with attempting to murder the girl (who tragically died three days after the alleged murder attempt). The court was told by the prosecution that Baby K was not covered earlier in the trial due to witness availability. The court heard evidence from Baby K's mother. The child had been deemed stable at birth and it was arranged for it to be moved to Arrowe Park. The prosecution claim was that Letby had attempted to murder the child when Baby K's designated nurse Joanne Williams left nursery room one at 3.47am to go to the labour ward. At around 3.50am there was a sudden deterioration and the baby had to be given emergency treatment. Lucy Letby was one of the nurses who signed the medications the baby required. Baby K was stabilised and transferred to Arrowe Park Hospital. Life support for Baby K was withdrawn on February 20. The cause of death was cited as 'severe respiratory distress syndrome' and being born premature.

The court heard that two months later, on April the 20th, Letby did an online search for the family of Baby K. Dr James Smith gave evidence to the court and said that the baby's sudden deterioration was thought to be at the time due to a problem with the breathing tubes. This was the basic thrust of the prosecution case with Baby K. They alleged that Letby had tampered with the breathing tube deliberately. The defence felt there was no evidence for this and argued that the child could easily have dislodged the tube herself. The prosecution believed that the incident where Dr Ravi Jayaram found Letby by the incubator but she hadn't yet raised an alarm for low oxygen levels was Letby literally being caught in the act. The prosecution alleged this incident happened in the aftermath of Letby dislodging the tube. Dr Smith said that the tube wasn't blocked because they would have noticed that. Benjamin Myers had a reasonably productive afternoon when he questioned Dr Smith. Myers was able to get the doctor to concede on a number of points where it was pointed out there Baby K was a very small and fragile child who had some obvious respiratory problems.

The following day, Nurse Joanne Williams finished giving evidence which she had started the previous afternoon. One of the main things Williams was asked about was notes at the time which spoke of a ventilation leak in Baby K's equipment. Williams said this didn't actually happen and there was no problem. She said that she didn't ask any specific nurse to look after Baby K when she left the room (Williams was the designated nurse). Williams was asked detailed questions about the breathing tube, the alarm, and medications for Baby K. There was nothing in her evidence which was especially significant for either the prosecution or the defence. The moment everyone had been anticipating that day was the evidence by Dr Ravi Jayaram. Dr Jayaram began giving evidence shortly after noon. Dr Jayaram told the court that he was fairly happy with Baby K and the transfer of the child was imminent. He described Baby K as 'very settled'. Dr Jayaram said that he became aware that Letby was 'babysitting' Baby K while the designated nurse was out the room. The unit did actually use the term 'babysitting' in these situations.

Dr Jayaram said that he was uneasy when he heard this because by now there was speculation about foul play in the unit and Letby was the only person who was on all the shifts when these terrible tragedies and non-fatal collapses had happened. "You can call me hysterical, completely irrational, but because of this association this thought kept coming into my head. After two, two and a half minutes I went to prove to myself that I was being ridiculous and irrational and got up. I think it was 2.5, 3 minutes after Jo had gone to the labour ward. I had not been called to review [Baby K], I had not been called because alarms had gone off - I would have heard an alarm. I got up and walked through to see [Baby K]. I saw Lucy Letby standing by the incubator. I saw her, and looked up at the monitor, and K's saturations were dropping, in the 80s and continued to drop. The ventilator was not giving out an alarm. I recall looking up and saying 'what's going on?' and Lucy said something along the lines of 'She's having a desaturation'."

Dr Jayaram said Letby was doing nothing to help until he walked in. The tube was dislodged so Dr Jayaram used a breathing face mask on the baby. Mr Myers wanted to know if Dr Jayaram had confronted Letby about this incident. Dr Jayaram said he didn't because he was too busy trying to save the child. He added - "There was no evidence to prove it. That is not our job, we are doctors. We, as a group of consultants by this stage, had experience of an unusual event, and there was one particular nurse. All of these events were unusual. Yes, if we put in Datix [incident forms] we could have investigated sooner and been here [in court] sooner." Mr Myers pointed out that there was no record of doctors charting this 'suspicious behaviour' and, in not so many words, asked Dr Jayaram why they didn't act if they thought a nurse was harming children.

Dr Jayaram said concerns had been raised. He also said that no one had written reports on this because they hadn't anticipated sitting in a court seven years later being asked detailed questions about it for a murder case. Dr Jayaram said concerns were raised by consultants in autumn 2015 but the management didn't want to listen. Jayaram said that in hindsight they should have gone straight to the police. "We by no means had played judge and jury, but the association was becoming clearer and clearer. This is an unprecedented situation for us - we play by a certain rulebook, and you don't start from a position of deliberate harm. It is very easy to see things that aren't there - in confirmation bias. But these episodes were becoming more and more and more frequent by association." Dr Jayaram said, in hindsight, they should have documented all of this at the time.

Mr Myers asked Dr Jayaram if Baby K's tube could have been dislodged by the child. Dr Jayaram said it was possible but unlikely because the baby wasn't very active. Mr Myers tried to trip up Dr Jayaram by saying that doctor's recollection of timings in relation to Baby K was a lot more precise in court today than it had been during his police interview. Dr Jayaram replied by saying he'd had more time to think about since the police interview. Mr Myers asked Dr Jayaram if the focus on Letby was a tactic to distract from the poor level of care in the hospital. Dr Jayaram obviously denied that in the strongest terms. Myers asked if the baby's mother could have been taken a tertiary centre before the birth. Dr Jayaram said he wasn't in charge of decisions like that so he wouldn't really know.

Dr Jayaram was asked about the competence of Dr Smith (Dr Jayaram said Smith was perfectly competent) and also some contradictions in his notes - which Dr Jayaram said was an honest mistake rather than a deliberate error. Dr Jayaram conceded that care in the unit wasn't always perfect but didn't feel that any mistakes had been responsible for Baby K's sad death. Mr Myers suggested that Dr Jayaram had added to his 'account' of this incident over the years. Dr Jayaram had a very quotable response to that. He simply said - "I would disagree with that - you would be questioning my brevity and honesty." The prosecution, when they got their turn, asked Dr Jayaram if he had seen the hospital electronic swipe card data for the night Baby K collapsed. Dr Jayaram said that he hadn't. This was a shrewd way for the prosecution to undercut Mr Myers implying that Dr Jayaram's recollections of timings were so precise as to be suspicious and researched.

The next day in court wrapped up the prosecution case for Baby K. Mr Johnson read out some of Letby's police interviews in relation to this baby. Letby told the police she only remembered Baby K because it was unusually small. Letby said the incident where she was found by the incubator by Dr Jayaram may have been her waiting for the baby to 'self-correct' itself. She said she would have raised the alarm if Dr Jayaram hadn't arrived. Letby said that the designated nurse wouldn't have left the baby if there was something wrong with the tube. Despite the startling evidence of Dr Jayaram, the prosecution (attempted murder) charges in relation to Baby K were not terribly strong because the baby had actually died in another hospital. Mr Johnson made it plain they were not accusing Letby of actually causing the baby's death.

The next day the trial moved onto the case of Baby N. Baby N was a boy born premature who Letby was accused of trying to kill. Letby obviously denied this charge - as she did all the charges she was now in court facing. The court heard from the mother of Baby N - who spoke about the birth and the distressing incidents where her baby had two collapses. Happily, the child was then transferred to Alder Hey and made a good recovery. The father of Baby N recalled an awful incident where he was called to the hospital and saw blood around the baby's mouth. He was given no indication that the baby was unwell by staff but then after going to get something to eat was asked if he wanted a priest (they obviously only call for a priest if they think the baby might be in danger of passing away). The father said Lucy Letby seemed to be the main nurse they dealt with.

Letby's text messages at this time were read to the court.

Letby said she didn't know much about haemophilia (which Baby N) had. Letby was also preoccupied with discussing a doctor - who was 'flirty' (this was clearly the same doctor who reduced Letby to tears when he gave evidence in court - it seems highly plausible to propose that Letby had some sort of crush on this doctor). The court heard details of Baby N's condition and treatment from some of the staff who worked at the hospital at the time. Dr Sudeshna Bhowmik said the child suffered from prematurity, jaundice and respiratory distress. By now it was familiar to the jury how each case broadly panned out in court. The prosecution cited collapses which they attributed to Letby while the defence cited existing medical challenges the babies faced and 'sub-optimal' (to use a favourite phrase of Mr Myers) care in the unit. It was up to the jury to decide to what extent it was any of the former or latter.

Dr Jennifer Loughnane, a consultant paediatrician at the Countess of Chester Hospital, was called to give evidence. Dr Loughnane was working a night shift when Baby M was on the unit. Under questioning by the defence, Dr Loughnane agreed that it was unusual for the unit to be caring for a baby with haemophilia. The nurses who gave evidence didn't seem to have much memory of Baby N's medical details. An exception was Christopher Booth. Booth said he checked the baby before taking his meal break on the night shift and it seemed fine. It was while Mr Booth was on his break that baby suffered a desaturation and seemed to be unwell. Booth said he was surprised by this because the baby had been stable when he left it.

The court heard that Lucy Letby, at this time, was the designated nurse for Baby N on the night shift. Leybny's texts are quite mundane for this day. She says she has had a 'lovely' run of shifts and discusses a trip to Torquay she plans to take with her parents. Early the next morning, Letby was texted by a colleague who said - 'Baby [N] screened, looks like s**t'. Letby swiped into the unit at 7.10 am and Baby N had a destauration not long afterwards. The father of Baby N also gave evidence in court that Lucy Letby hugged and kissed Baby N's mother when the child was due to be moved to Alder Hay.

In the next session of the trial, nurse Jennifer Jones-Key

said that Letby had become 'agitated' when a team of specialists arrived from Alder Hay to transfer Baby N. Letby was not happy about these people arriving in the unit. Was this suspicious? Was she scared they might uncover what she had done? Or was she innocent and simply worried about Baby N? It was up to the jury to make these decisions. The court also heard a series of (rather cloying and lovey dovey at times) text messages between Letby and the doctor who couldn't be named. At one point Letby asked the doctor what she thought caused the bleeding in Baby N's mouth. This once again was something that could be interpreted as sinister or innocent depending on how you looked at it.

There were evidently some problems with the intubation (the medical procedure where a flexible plastic tube, called an endotracheal tube, is inserted into a person's airway to assist with breathing) of Baby N and the defence obviously tried to use this detail to propose 'sub-optimal' care - though there was of course the prosecution theory that Letby had done this herself. While the evidence in some of the individual baby cases was circumstantial the main problem the defence faced was that what happened in that unit was not normal. It is rare for neonatal units to lose a baby and a single death is very notable and significant. For there to be a spate of deaths and collapses in such a short space of time is almost unprecedented. It is something that is not supposed to happen. It would be a remarkable combination of medical incompetence and bad luck to explain this if one excluded foul play. To give some context, in the whole of 2013 two babies died the Countess of Chester hospital. In 2015 and the start of 2016, thirteen babies died at the Countess of Chester hospital.

Day 67 of the trial saw evidence from a variety of doctors who were involved in treating Baby N. It was apparent (again) from this day of evidence that there were problems with the intubation of Baby N due to bleeding and swelling. Making repeated attempts to put a tube in obviously doesn't do the poor baby any favours. One doctor, Dr Huw Mayberry, gave evidence from Australia by videolink and recalled working on Baby N in Chester. Dr Mayberrry proposed a few explanations for medical conditions which might explain why there was swelling and blood in the back of the child's mouth. All in all, the prosecution case in regard to Baby N did not seem very strong. It was difficult to see how one could conclusively say Letby had attempted to harm this child.

When the trial began again, Professor Sally Kinsey gave evidence about Baby N's blood reports. Kinsey said that Baby N did have some medical issues but didn't think there was anything which explained what happened. Dr Dewi Evans was also back in court and this (predictably) led to some more testy exchanges with Mr Myers. Dr Evans said that it was unusual for a baby to scream in the fashion Baby N did and argued that this fit the pattern of air embolus which (the prosecution argued) was prevalent in many of the cases covered by the trial. Mr Myers accused Dr Evans of juggling the facts to support his thesis rather than approaching this in an open way.

Mr Myers then said that Dr Evans had touted for this expert witness job and produced an email Evans had sent to the National Crime Agency in which he had written - 'Incidentally I've read about the high rate of babies in Chester and that the police are investigating. Do they have a paediatric/neonatal contact? I was involved in neonatal medicine for 30 years including leading the intensive care set-up in Swansea. I've also prepared numerous neonatal cases where clinical negligence was alleged. If the Chester police had no-one in mind I'd be interested to help. Sounds like my kind of case. I understand that the Royal College (of Paediatrics and Child Health) has been involved but from my experience the police are far better at investigating this sort of problem.'

In response to this, Dr Evans told the court - "I was offering my professional opinion if that was in their interest." Asked if he was biased, Dr Evans said - "No, no. I have dealt with several police cases where I have said 'this case doesn't cross the threshold of suspicious death or injury', or whatever. My opinions are impartial and independent." Dr Evans denied that he had heard the air embolus theory from the police or someone else and insisted he had come to his conclusions independently. Dr Bohin also gave evidence and said that, in her view, the consistent screaming of Baby N was unusual and not explained by anything in the medical notes on the child.

On the 6th of March, the trial moved onto the case of Baby O. Baby O was the first of two triplets Letby was charged with murdering. X-rays had shown an unusually high amount of gas in his body. The alleged murder of Baby O happened on the 23rd of June 2016. The court heard a statement from the mother of Baby O. The mother said that the triplets were considered to be stable and healthy after birth but on the 23rd there was 'chaos' in the unit when Baby O became poorly. The mother recalled frantic attempts to treat the baby, who looked 'swollen' and red. The mother remembered Lucy Letby as one of the staff who were present. Baby O passed away at 5pm. The mother said it was a 'bolt from the blue' and made her understandably concerned about the other triplets and the standard of care in this hospital.

The next morning this nightmare happened again when Baby P collapsed and had to have emergency treatment. The mother said that once again it was chaos. She said she was highly alarmed to see a young looking doctor appearing to use google to look up how to insert a long line in the baby (this detail seemed, one would hope, highly unlikely and was probably a misinterpretation - a qualified doctor surely isn't going to be googling basic medical procedures during an emergency situation). The baby was due to be moved to Liverpool and the transport team had arrived. The mother said the Liverpool transport team seemed much more professional and competent than the staff in Chester and tried to save the child but - alas - it was too late.

The mother said that she and her partner begged the transport team to take their remaining son to Liverpool. They just wanted to get him out of Chester. The mother said they told the team they would take the baby there themselves if nothing was done. The grandmother of the triplets also gave evidence. The family painted a terrible picture of the hospital in Chester. The grandmother said that during an attempt to save Baby O one of the doctors asked Lucy Letby how many shots of adrenaline they'd used and Letby couldn't answer him. The doctor in question was apparently not very impressed with this. The baby was eventually moved to Liverpool where it was fine. The mother said the hospitals in Liverpool and Chester were far removed - with the one in Liverpool being much more professional.

The mother said she recalled Lucy Letby being upset and tearful when Baby P died. The father of the triplets also gave evidence. He recalled seeing a weird 'pot belly' on Baby O. The father said doctors at the hospital failed to give him a clear explanation for what was going on or what the explanation for anything was. Letby had come back from holiday around this time. The doctor that she seemed to be in frequent communication with told Letby that the unit always felt safer when she was there. Lucy Letby clearly saw herself as some sort of leader in the unit. Interestingly, there seems to be some evidence that when Letby first got wind of the fact she was going to be moved in the hospital (this happened later in the timeline) she actually presumed it was some sort of promotion. In reality it was a demotion to a desk job.

The day shift rotas for this time were mentioned again in court. Letby was the designated nurse for Baby O and Baby P. In her text messages Letby had said some the readings for Baby O were normal (Letby had also grumbled in this block of texts about having a student nurse in the unit who she was having to explain everything to). The court heard that a post-mortem blood test on Baby O did not reveal anything of significance. Letby got a text that day from the doctor asking if she was going to vote in the referendum on Britain's membership of the European Union. Letby she wasn't going to vote because it had been a busy day and she just wanted to go home.

The doctor told Letby that a 'debrief' into Baby O's death didn't really find anything. Letby told the doctor she had cried at work. After the death of Baby P, Letby had a Facebook conversation (in private of course) where she was asked about the care for this child. By this stage the amount of incidents and deaths in the unit was what you might describe as tragically preposterous. Those who worked with Letby clearly had no suspicions but, as we have noted, some doctors and consultants were now desperate to get her away from patients. Datix forms had to be completed after Baby P's death. Datix is a Risk Management Information System designed to collect and manage data on adverse events (as well as data on complaints, claims and risk). In her Datix form, Letby said that a piece of equipment for resuscitations was not available. The court heard that Letby did online searches for the baby triplets on the 23rd. Lucy Letby continued to be inscrutable as she sat in court listening to all of this. She was wearing a scarf that day. It was so chilly in court that morning that the judge had to apologise. Snow was falling outside and would slightly disrupt the trial because of transport problems.

The next sessions of evidence were notable for a couple of reasons. Dr Kataryna Cooke gave evidence and noted a hematoma in Baby O's liver was found post-mortem. The defence conceded that this had not been present when Dr Cooke previously examined the child. The post-mortem had actually suggested that the CPR was a factor in the death. Dr Dewi Evans had said in his report though that the liver damage was done by Letby and a factor in the death. The court also heard from Nurse Melanie Taylor. Taylor said she had noticed Baby O looking worse than before when she began her shift. She said she suggested to Letby they move the child into nursery one (where there was more room) but Letby said no. Taylor said she was a bit annoyed at Letby disagreeing with her. The child subsequently collapsed and was moved to nursery one.

When the trial resumed again on the 14th of March it was notable for the evidence given by Dr Stephen Brearey. Dr Brearey said he was baffled by the collapse of Baby O because the child had seemed fine to him. When the child became poorly, Dr Brearey noticed a strange purple rash on the baby which later disappeared. After the latest tragedy, Dr Brearey said they had a 'debrief' meeting in which Lucy Letby was present. She didn't seem to be upset or emotional - unlike some other members of staff. Dr Brearey had by now expressed private concerns about Letby - though the hospital didn't seem to want to hear this. Dr Brearey said he'd suggested to Letby that she take the weekend off but she didn't seem to want to do this and said she was booked in for Saturday.

Dr Brearey said he telephoned Karen Rees, senior nurse in the urgent care division, and asked for Letby to be taken off duty until an investigation had been done. Rees refused to do this and said there was no evidence that Lucy Letby had done anything wrong. Dr Brearey asked Rees if she would take 'responsibility' for anything that happened as a consequence of this decision. Karen Rees, according to Brearey, said yes. She would take responsibility. Mr Myers asked Dr Brearey why, if he was so suspicious of Letby, he had not called the police. "I think you are making it a bit more simplistic than it was," said Dr Brearey. "It was not something that anyone wanted to consider, that a member of staff is harming babies. Actually, the senior nursing staff on the unit didn't believe this could be true up until the point and beyond when the triplets (Child O and P) died. None of us (the consultants) wanted to believe it either. This all became very exceptional and it took a step back to think about it. The nature of these collapses, the unexpected nature of them, the lack of response to resuscitation, the unusual rash noted on a number of occasions and each time the association with Nurse Letby. I needed executive support and that was what we were after."

Dr Brearey made a salient point when he reminded the court that the mysterious deaths and non-fatal collapses in the unit stopped when Letby was given a desk job in the office answering emails. One might add too that there were no tragedies or collapses in the unit while Lucy Letby was on holiday in Ibiza. Mr Myers suggested that Dr Brearey was swayed by confirmation bias (Brearey obviously disagreed with this). Confirmation bias is a cognitive bias that refers to the tendency of individuals to favour information that confirms their preexisting beliefs or hypotheses, while neglecting or selectively interpreting evidence that contradicts their beliefs. In other words, people often only hear what they WANT to hear.

Day 72 of the trial saw the familiar figure of Dr Dewi Evans back in court. Dr Evans looked like the late comedy actor John Inman and sounded a bit like a Welsh version of Tony Benn. He had a very calming manner and voice and remained largely unflappable - despite the numerous attacks on his expertise and impartiality by Benjamin Myers. Dr Evans told the court that air embolus was the cause of death for Baby O. He pointed out the purple rash - a sure sign of air embolus according to Evans. Mr Myers for the defence said there was no evidence for air embolus and accused Dr Evans of making his evidence up as he went along. Dr Sandie Bohin also gave evidence and had the same conclusion. The court heard that Letby had told the police she was shocked by Baby O's death. On the anniversary of the death of this child in 2017, Letby had done a Facebook search for the parents.

Dr Owen Arthurs was back in court on day 73. A post-mortem for Baby P had found 'gas filled loops throughout the abdomen. Dr Arthurs said this was unusual. Arthurs believe air embolus was possible but said that infection or necrotising enterocolitis (NEC) were also possibilities. Necrotising enterocolitis is basically a bowel problem. Dr Arthurs agreed with Mr Myers that it could also be the case that Baby P suffered from something which was never identified. The next session of court heard evidence from a doctor (who could not be named) who said he was perplexed by Baby P's death because there was no indication that anything was wrong. The court heard about Letby's text messages at this time (which were, as usual, to the mystery doctor). Letby said she placed the two deceased baby boys in a cot together and they looked 'lovely'. "Life is too sad," offered Letby as they discussed the latest tragedies to befall the unit. That was the understatement of the century when it came to the Chester neonatal unit. Letby went on to discuss how her parents worried about her and said she found them 'suffocating' at times.

The next day senior nurse Kathryn Percival-Calderbank told the court that Lucy Letby found it 'boring' if she wasn't assigned to intensive care and hated being put in one of the outside nurseries. Percival-Calderbank told the court that even if Letby was put in one of the outside nurseries she tended to gravitate back to intensive care. The nurses were moved around the nursery room to vary their duties because it was deemed not good for a nurse's mental health if they spent all their time in a critical care environment.

Kathryn Percival-Calderbank said she recalled an incident where Letby got upset because she wasn't allocated to nursery one.

Mr Myers pressed Percival-Calderbank on Letby prefering

to be in nursery one where the most vulnerable babies were. He had an ulterior motive for this. Myers was happy for the court to hear that Letby liked being in nursery one and always did extra shifts because, he presumably deduced, this made the statistical fact of Letby's inevitable presence during emergencies less remarkable. There was always the risk though that Letby's reported eagerness to be in intensive care could be seen as sinister. It was true to say that the trial had established that Letby had opportunity and probably (though this was more contested and difficult to judge) means too for these alleged crimes. Motive was another matter entirely though. The police didn't even mention a motive because they genuinely had no idea why this wallflowerish young woman would kill babies.

The most dramatic evidence this day came from a doctor who could not be named. The doctor said she was angry when Letby said "He's not leaving here alive is he?" about Baby P. The doctor said that Letby was inappropriately animated and excited when she was asked if she could make a memory box for the deceased child. "I remember thinking," said the doctor, "this is not a new baby, this is a dead baby. Why are you so excited about this?" The doctor then helped get the surving triplet transferred because she feared for the baby's life in the Countess hospital. Mr Myers asked if this 'fear' was because of failings in the neonatal unit or suspicion of Lucy Letby. The doctor said it was because of Letby. Under questioning, the doctor said she had heard whispers at the time from other doctors about Letby.

Mr Myers accused the doctor of dramatising her evidence and said that Letby's comments about the baby not getting out of here 'alive' were taken out of context. The doctor disagreed. Mr Myers tactic with witnesses like this was to ask them why they didn't call the police if they suspected someone of harming babies. It was a fair enough question but it seems that hospital bureaucracy and lack of firm evidence prevented this from happening. The doctor told the court she did talk to colleagues and also warn a superior about Letby. It wasn't as if she just went home and forgot all about it.

Day 76 of this marathon trial saw evidence by Dr John Gibbs. Gibbs said - "I'd become increasingly concerned, and my consultant colleagues shared the concerns, at the accumulating number of unusual, unexpected and inexplicable collapses and deaths happening on the neonatal unit and the fact that staff nurse Letby had been involved in all of them. The deaths of the two triplets was a tipping point for realising something abnormal and wrong was happening on our unit." Dr Gibbs said that consultants insisted Letby be taken off duty. When the management tried to put her back on duty a month later Dr Gibbs said they told the management they would only let Letby back if CCTV was installed in each room of the neonatal unit. "TV cameras never came and neither did Nurse Letby."

Mr Myers, in a familiar tactic, asked Dr Gibbs why he didn't call the police. "That was difficult," said Dr Gibbs. "Nurse Letby seemed to be involved in all of the cases that involved me. Other consultants were involved with other babies. None of us regrettably realised two babies had been poisoned by insulin, so we didn't have the full picture. After the deaths of the triplets – very regrettably too late for them – because the concerns had reached a tipping point, safety measures were introduced and one of the key safety measures which the consultants were insistent on was Lucy Letby be removed from the neonatal unit and that was not a simple, straightforward decision." Dr Gibbs described Baby O and Baby P as two 'healthy boys' who shouldn't have died.

The court also heard from Dr Rackham, who was head of the transfer team from Arrowe Park Hospital. Dr Rackham and his team came to transport Baby P and ended up trying to save his life. Dr Rackham said he saw no medical reason for Baby P's collapse. Mr Myers asked Dr Rackham about the adrenaline charts for Baby P and asked if excessive adrenaline can have side effects. Dr Rackham said that it could. Mr Myers was presumably attempting to blame the adrenaline for Baby P's death - though it was the alleged attack of Letby which necessitated the adrenaline according to the prosecution. As far as anyone could make out the strategy of Mr Myers here was to mitigate Letby's involvement and perhaps get manslaughter on this charge.

The next day Dr Dewi Evans was back to give evidence. Mr Myers pointed out that Dr Evans, in his original report, had cited pneumothorax as the most likely cause of death for Baby P. Dr

Evans said that was his view at the time because there was no natural explanation for why the resuscitation had not been successful. He said he know had a better clinical understanding of events and said the baby had been given two doses of air. Mr Myers said that Dr Evans had now invented another 'dollop' (Dr Evans had used this term himself earlier) of air and also accused Evans of juggling Letby's shifts around to make it seem like something happened whenever she was on duty. Dr Evans denied this was the case.

Dr Bohin had broadly the same view as Dr Evans. She said the X-rays were unusual when it came to air. Dr Bohin said the adrenaline for the child was not calculated correctly but this wasn't a cause of death. Under questioning from Mr Myers, Dr Bohin said that pneumothorax could have 'contributed' to the collapse of Baby P but did not cause the collapse. As ever, Mr Myers threw a lot of punches in the sessions with the two main experts but not much landed on Dr Evans and Dr Bohin. Mr Myers was too often in these exchanges reduced to accusing the two experts of being biased in favour of the prosecution. Dr Bohin, in as polite and tactful way as she could, did seem to agree with Mr Myers though that the hospital in Chester seemed to make a lot of mistakes - although Dr Bohin stressed that none of these were a factor in the tragedies.

Day 77 saw evidence from Dr Marnerides, leader of the forensic children's pathology service at Guy's and St Thomas' Hospitals. This was not a good day for the defence. The prosecution asked Dr Marnerides what he believed was the cause of death for Baby O. "In my view," he replied, "the cause of death was inflicted traumatic injury to the liver, profound gastric and intestinal distension following acute excessive injection/infusion of air via a naso-gastric tube and air embolism due to administration into a venous line." Dr Marnerides then said that Baby P was killed by 'excessive injection of air into the stomach'. This was a nightmare for Mr Myers on the face of it because here was a respected medical expert coming to exactly the same conclusions as Dr Evans.

Mr Myers asked Dr Marnerides if CPR could be a possibility for the injuries to Baby P. "We are not discussing possibilities here, we are discussing probabilities," replied Dr Marnerides. "When you refer to possibilities, I am thinking for example of somebody walking in the middle of the Sahara desert found dead with a pot and head trauma. It is possible the pot fell from the air from a helicopter. The question is 'is it probable?' and I don't think we can say it is probable." It got even worse for the defence because Dr Marnerides had been asked to review all the cases in this investigation and had come to the conclusion that an injection of air was also apparent in Baby A, C, D and I. Mr Myers still had something up his sleeve. He said Dr Marnerides had used the reports of Dr Evans and Dr Bohin as part of his report. Dr Marnerides had a good answer for this though. He said ignoring clinical evidence was like asking someone to explain physics without using mathematics.

On Friday, March the 31st, 2023, the trial moved on to the case of Baby Q. Letby was accused of trying to kill Baby Q, who was born eight weeks premature, on June 25, 2016.

After this alleged incident, Letby would work only three more shifts as a nurse before being moved to a clerical position. The court heard statements from Baby Q's mother and father. They spoke of a difficult pregnancy and then suggested a lack of communication from hospital staff when Baby Q wasn't very well. The baby was later taken to Alder Hey where it had a bowel operation and recovered. The child has cerebral palsy and a weak immune system now but is doing ok.

The court heard that Baby Q's Apgar score ten minutes after birth was 9/10. The Apgar score is a test given to newborns soon after birth. This test checks a baby's heart rate, muscle tone, and other signs. Anything below 7/10 is considered below average and indicates some treatment is required. Lucy Letby was a designated nurse for Baby Q. The court heard how the baby seemed perfectly 'normal' until it had a collapse. It was at this time, after Baby Q had a collapse, that Letby asked her doctor friend by text if she needed to be worried about anything. Dr John Gibbs had gone to the neonatal unit and told nurses that they must make sure 'normal' procedures were being carried out. We know that, privately, Dr Gibbs had worries and suspicions concerning Letby at this time and wanted her removed from the unit. He was clearly then having a look to make sure everything was ok and sort of warning the staff in the neonatal unit that he was keeping an eye on them.

The doctor told Lucy Letby by text she had nothing to worry about. 'All he was doing was checking there was not a delay and that a room had been left empty...there is nothing to worry about. No more doubt - it's not you, it's the babies.' The doctor would later text Lucy Letby again and say - 'You are one of a few nurses across the region...that I would trust with my own children.' It was during these exchanges that Letby had said she was worried she had missed something or wasn't a good enough nurse and the doctor said if she ever needed a statement he would provide one. Plainly, Letby seems to be anticipating some sort of scrutiny is heading her way and the doctor was able to deduce her concern. Heaven knows what this doctor must have felt like later when he learned that Lucy Letby had been arrested and charged with murdering babies. That must have an awful bombshell.

On the 26th of June, Letby texted a nursing colleague and they discussed the staffing levels and problems the neonatal unit had faced lately. Letby said she was worried that there might be a bug or virus in the unit - adding that this would 'explain' all the recent tragedies. Letby then texted her doctor friend to ask about Baby Q. The doctor said Baby Q was stable but had a few issues. Letby then texted a nurse to say Baby Q was 'unwell'. The nurse later texted Letby back and said they think the baby might be 'volvulous' (this means suffering from a bowel obstruction). The next session of the trial saw evidence by Nurse Mary Griffith. Griffith was Baby Q's designated nurse. She said that she asked Letby to watch over the baby while she went to another and only minutes elapsed between Letby leaving the baby and the baby taking a turn for the worse. The implication here was that Letby's MO was to harm a child, leave the room, and then return as again as part of the resuscitation team.

This theory, if true, led to all manner of other theories. Was this Letby's way of trying to cover her tracks? Did she like to engineer these collapses to play the hero? Did she love the drama of an emergency? One thing that is important to note about the trial is that the jury got a lot of information that was rarely reported by the media. For example, the jury got highly detailed information about the unit's swipe card data (which logged staff entering and exiting) and also information about who was on what computer at what time. This built up an accurate chronology of where each staff member was when the collapses happened. The pattern in all of this intricate and lengthy data was that if a member of staff was harming the babies it could only have been Lucy Letby. She could be geographically connected to these incidents in a way that no one else could. The jury also heard how Lucy Letby's nursing notes on babies frequently failed to dovetail with the notes of the other nurses. This was of course highly suspicious because it implied deliberate misdirection.

The trial was adjourned for a day when a member of the jury was ill but resumed again on the 5th of April. A doctor who couldn't be named (this was presumed to the doctor who texted Letby a lot) said that another doctor had expressed concern that her chest compressions during Baby Q's resuscitation may have caused the liver injury found in post-mortem. The witness said he didn't believe this was the case but he admitted that he didn't have a full memory of the resuscitation and what everyone was doing because his focus was on helping the child breathe. Dr John Gibbs also gave evidence and was asked about his visit to the unit to check on the nurses. "I remember wanting to know who had been looking after [Child Q] at time he had desaturated," he said. "I wouldn't normally want to know who was looking after patients. I was worried about what was happening on the unit."

Dr Evans was also in court. Dr Evans was now saying that, in addition to an injection of air, he believed water or saline had been put down Child Q's stomach via a nasogastric tube. "I am going to suggest that fluid is something you have added at a late stage," said Mr Myers. "Now you have reached this point where you have added fluid now to keep the mechanism going, keep the allegation going, rather than reflect the facts?" Dr Evans begged to differ. "No, no, no. You have got it wrong again. We are here now and we have heard the evidence from the people who were looking after him. So going on about what I wrote in 2017 and 2018 is rather missing the point." Dr Sandie Bohin also gave evidence. in these last days before the Easter break. Dr Bohin said that clear liquid was aspirated by Baby Q but she could not explain where this came from.

The prosecution read out Lucy Letby's police interview in relation to Baby Q. Letby said it was merely a coincidence that the baby became ill when she began a shift. Letby said the baby had always seemed quite stable to her. The last day before Easter was a fascinating session of the trial because we heard information about Letby's text messages and emails at the point where her time on the neonatal came to an end. Letby was told not to come in for her next shift and immediately became concerned that something was wrong. She was then given a three month position in an office answering emails - which she was not happy about. 'Feel a bit like I'm being shoved in a corner and forgotten about by the trust. It's my life and career.'

Letby's doctor friend told her there was a debrief on the recent incidents but that she shouldn't worry. Dr Stephen Brearey then sent staff an email saying there was going to be an inquest into the deaths of Baby O and Baby P. In Letby's last days on the unit they were told that a period of 'clinical supervision' would be put in place. This was the hospital, far too late, finally taking some action. Lucy Letby was now going to be removed from the neonatal unit. Letby's was clearly worried in her private communications at this time. This was when Letby made her comment about getting her 'information' together and how the hospital would look 'silly' if they had nothing on her. But were these the words of a nurse worried she might be blamed for a medical mistake or the words of a serial killer worried that their crimes might be uncovered? The jury would have to make that distinction. One interesting detail was the private texts revealed Letby had talked about air embolism as a possible factor in the incidents at the hospital. And yet, when she was interviewed by the police, Letby claimed to know nothing at all about air embolisms.

When the trial began again on the 17th of April, the day began with evidence by police officer DC Collin Johnson. The police officer was asked by the prosecution to discuss what was found in Lucy Letby's house after her arrest. The court were told about notes where Letby had written things like 'help me' and also told she had written the names of the babies who collapsed in the neonatal unit in her diary. Among the things Letby had written were - 'I am evil I did this', 'Slander discrimination', 'I haven't done anything wrong', 'I can't breathe', 'All getting too much', 'I killed them on purpose because I'm not good enough' and 'I am a horrible evil person'. One of the words Letby had written was 'sterility' - which has (unavoidably) led to theories that she couldn't have children and somehow became twisted about this.

On one note Letby had crossed out 'I don't know if I killed them maybe I did maybe this is all down to me'. The court heard how Letby had a number of medical handover sheets in her house. There were also medical chart readings for some of the babies who had died and collapsed. In Letby's place of work, notes were found in her desk which read - 'PLEASE HELP ME [name of doctor] LOVE PLEASE HELP ME [name of doctor] You were my best friend [name of doctor]' and 'I just want to be as it was I want to be happy in the job that I loved....Really don't belong anywhere - I am a problem to those who do know me and it would be much easier for everyone if I just went away.' DC Collin Johnson confirmed to the court that not all the babies Letby was accused of harming featured in the handover notes found in her house.

The next day the court heard from Dr Arthurs. He supposed to give evidence before Easter about Baby Q's X-rays but he was unavailable at the time so doing that now. Dr Arthurs said an X-ray of the baby taken after a collapse indicated an abnormality which could have been necrotising enterocolitis. The jury were also given more detail about Lucy Letby's police interviews in relation to the babies she was charged with harming. Of most interest was the revelation that six minutes before Baby C's collapse, Letby sent a bad tempered text to a colleague who she felt wasn't giving her enough support. The police asked Letby if she was in a bad mood and took it out on the baby. Letby said she was in a bad mood but denied harming any of the babies.

Day 86 of the trial continued to focus on Lucy Letby's police interviews. Letby had of course denied harming any babies to the police. Letby's police interviews contradicted a lot of evidence that had been heard in court over the previous months. Letby had denied the (heard in court) claims of Kathryn Percival-Calderbank that she found working outside the intensive care room 'boring'. Letby also denied that Dr Brearey had told her to take a weekend off after the triplet incidents. Letby's police interview also disputed the account by Nurse Ashleigh Hudson of Letby saying Baby I was 'pale' - despite it being dark and Letby being a distance away.

"No," said Letby to the police, "I remember us both going into the nursery together. From memory we were both inside the nursery. I think we put the lights on as we went into the room. Maybe I spotted something that Ashleigh didn't. I'm more experienced than her. And there are varying degrees of paleness – and Baby I was a pale baby anyway. There's always a level of light. She (Baby I) is still facing outwards towards the door. There's still light coming from the main corridor." The police asked Letby if she'd texted about a possible bug or infection in the unit as misdirection. Letby denied this and but staff other than her have speculated about a bug on the ward so she wasn't alone in thinking this as a possible theory.

The next session of the trial heard more details about Letby's police interviews and then moved onto evidence from Eirian Powell (the neonatal unit ward manager at the Countess of Chester Hospital when Letby worked there). Mr Myers asked Eirian Powell if Lucy Letby was a good nurse. Eirian Powell said Letby was a very good nurse. Eirian Powell recalled the meeting where Letby was told she was being moved to a clerical position. The court heard that Letby was quite upset about this. Nicholas Johnson for the prosecution asked Eirian Powell if Lucy Letby had made mistakes. Eirian Powell said all nurses make mistakes sometimes but Letby was good at owning up to them. Mr Johnson asked Eirian Powell what was said at the meeting to decide Letby should come out of the unit. Eirian Powell said it was discussed that Letby seemed to be the common demonitator in the tragic and awful spate of deaths and collapses. This was the last day of the prosecution case. The trial seemed like it had been going on forever but it wasn't finished yet by a long shot. The moment the media and online detectives had been waiting for was about to arrive. The court was going to hear evidence from Lucy Letby herself.

CHAPTER TEN

On Tuesday the 2nd of May there were many more media at Manchester Court than usual. No prizes for guessing why. Lucy Letby was going to speak in court for the first time. Letby, dressed in black, was questioned by Mr Myers about her background. Mr Myers would provide the easy ride. The real test for Letby was going to be when Nicholas Johnson and the prosecution started asking the questions. Letby spoke about her childhood and how she'd always wanted to be a nurse. She said she cared for hundreds of babies in placements before she actually started working full time in the neonatal unit. Letby said she had never harmed a child because this went against everything that a nurse is supposed to be.

    The court heard Letby say she was distraught when she was taken off the unit and put in a clerical job. Letby said she got a letter from the Royal College of Nursing which told her she was going to be 'blamed' for the baby deaths. Letby said she was sickened by this. She got teary eyed in court as she spoke about this.

    Letby told the court that her life had been ruined. Letby said that after she was bailed the police told her not to go back to her house so she had to go and live with her parents. Mr Myers asked Letby about all the medical notes and general notes found in her house. Letby said she was a bit of a hoarder and didn't throw stuff away very often. Myers went through the allegedly self-incriminating notes Letby had written and she said they were not to be taken literally. They were snapshots of her mood and a reflection of the situation she was in. Letby spoke of her training as a nurse and discussed what her duties had been. She said she had loved being a mentor to student nurses. Mr Myers asked Letby about the protocol for nurses making making notes. He asked if it was sinister if something hadn't been signed. Letby said it was not because sometimes nurses are very busy or get distracted by other duties.

Letby was also asked to explain the process for feeding babies in the neonatal unit. Letby, under careful guidance by Mr Myers, also said that observation times (that is the time listed on their medical notes) for nurses were not precise but to the nearest quarter of an hour. Letby said during the time these tragic incidents occurred there were more babies than usual but the staffing levels did not change. She also told the court that you never knew which babies you would care for in advance and there was no formal support process for the staff when a baby died. The staff simply supported each other at difficult times like this. On deaths in the unit, Letby said - "You don't forget things like that, they stay with you."

Letby was asked about her activities outside of work (she went to the gym, salsa classes etc) and said she had about five friends - all of whom were nurses apart from one doctor. Letby was asked about the doctor she confided in through texts during the incidents at the hospital. Letby said they were close friends but nothing more. He later left the hospital. She was asked about her Facebook searches of parents of the babies who died and collapsed. Letby said she had a habit of searching for people who were on her mind. She said there was nothing sinister about it. Letby said she also searched for school friends, people she met at salsa class, and other colleagues and patients. It was just done out of curiosity.

Lucy Letby started crying in court when photographs of her bedroom were shown. The photograph of the bedroom was a reminder of an ordinary life of the kind that Lucy Letby would never experience again. Letby was quizzed more about the notes in her house and imbued them with innocent explanations. Asked why she told the police she didn't have a shredder when in fact she DID have one (the police found that Letby had used the shredder to shred old bank statements), Letby said this was an oversight as the shredder was quite a recent acquisition at the time. Letby was mostly calm and controlled in court during the questions by the defence. Near the end of the day, Mr Myers asked her if she had ever killed any babies. "No," replied Lucy

Letby.

When the trial resumed again on Friday the 5th of May, Letby was asked about Baby A by Mr Myers. As you might expect given that this was her defence barrister, it was again a fairly easy ride. Letby said that after the death of Baby A she had suggested the long line and bag of fluids should be retained so they could be examined but this was not done.

This was clearly the sort of evidence that the defence hoped might sway the jury. It would be up to the jury if they believed Letby was telling the truth. Letby said the death shocked her and was the sort of thing that is hard to get over. Mr Myers asked Letby a lot of medical questions because it allowed Letby to demonstrate her knowledge. Letby knew her stuff and even corrected Myers a few times on something. These were often 'softball' questions designed to make Letby come across as intelligent and professional.

Letby was asked questions about the babies from Baby A to Baby F. Her evidence contradicted some of the things we had heard from other witnesses in the trial. But who was telling the truth? Them or Letby? Who had the better memory? To give an example, in her court evidence Letby said she was in room 3 when Baby C crashed. In her police interview she said she couldn't remember where she was. Letby said she'd had time to think about it now. A nurse (Sophie Ellis) had placed Letby in room one but Letby said this wasn't true. In her evidence under questions by Mr Myers, Letby would often dispute what nurses and sometimes even parents had said concerning their recollections of her movements.

Sophie Ellis had said she found Letby standing over Baby C's cot. Letby told the court she didn't remember this incident and must have responded to a call for help.

Letby also gave the impression that she was rarely alone with a baby in the unit (this observation by Letby, whether true or not, was clearly designed to make it look as if she couldn't possibly have harmed all these babies with other staff constantly around her because surely they would have noticed something). Mr Myers told the court that the mother of Baby D said in her statement that she had a conversation with Letby at 7pm on the

21st of June and saw Letby with a clipboard not doing much when the baby collapsed. Mr Myers said swipe data showed that Letby only entered the unit at 7.26 pm. Letby added to this by saying she was not working in the clinical nursery at this time. The strategy of the defence questioning of Letby that day was to cast doubt on other witnesses and to try and distance Letby from some of the baby collapses. One problem with Letby's evidence though was that too often she would say she couldn't remember something or that she didn't remember much about a specific baby.

The next morning Mr Myers asked Letby if she had done anything to cause Baby F's blood sugar to drop (like give the child insulin - as charged). "No," said Letby. Letby was asked why she did a number of online searches for the family of Baby E and Baby F. "It's just something I do," said Letby. Lucy Letby described Baby G as a premature baby with complex needs. She said she was shocked by the projectile vomiting of the baby - but then downplayed the volume of the vomit. Letby said care for Baby G was swapped around in that sometimes she was the designated nurse and sometimes she wasn't. Letby said she had other babies to care for too besides Baby G.

Letby said she deduced the second desaturation in Baby G herself and administered Neopuff before calling for help. Letby said she had found Baby G alone with the monitor switched off and wasn't very happy about this. Mr Myers was making Lucy Letby look like Florence Nightingale with his defence questioning. The defence even produced a message Letby had got from the hospital management around the time of Baby H which praised Letby for her work. Mr Myers, in relation to Baby H, then prompted Letby to highlight staffing problems on the unit.

One interesting detail in the evidence is that Letby said some colleagues got annoyed that she seemed to often be in room one (the intensive room). The court heard that some nurses wanted to be in this room more because they wanted more experience. The strategy of Mr Myers was twofold. He wanted to highlight incidents of 'mottling' and desaturation which occurred when Letby was not present. He also wanted to point out that Letby spent a lot of time in room one when she was on shift because of her intensive care training. This latter detail was designed to make it seem like less of a statistical red flag that Letby always seemed to be there when a baby died or collapsed. Mr Myers also noted that the nutrient bag for Baby F was 'renewed' - which meant Letby, if she was guilty, would have to have poisoned at least two bags (poisoning two bags at different times would appear to be more difficult than tampering with one). Mr Myers was seeking to add an element of doubt to the case and make those who were leaning towards Letby being guilty have to stop and question this.

Letby was asked again about Nurse Ashleigh Hudson's claim that Letby had said Baby I looked pale - despite the fact it was dark. "Ashleigh was doing something on the worktop," said Letby, "... with her back to the cot. I was in the doorway, talking to Ashleigh. I can see clearly enough that [Baby I] was pale in the cot. [Baby I] was in front of a window. At no point is any nursery in complete darkness. The only time we have that is in room 4, for babies preparing to go home. It's important we need to see them visually. We need to see the monitors and the babies themselves. I could see her face and her hands... she just looked very pale. I said to Ashleigh she looked very pale and we turned the lights up."

The defence questioning of Lucy Letby continued the next day. Letby was asked about sending a sympathy card to the parents of Baby L. Letby said another member of staff had suggested she do this. A photo of this card was found on Letby's phone and she told the police she often took photos of cards she had sent. There was proof of this too because Mr Myers showed the court a photo from Letby's phone of a card she had sent a friend to congratulate them on having a baby. When the evidence moved to Baby J, Mr Myers supplied texts by Letby complaining that the hospital didn't have enough experience of dealing with babies who had stomas.

Mr Myers also said that desaturations took place at times when Letby was not the designated nurse. During the questioning Mr Myers would ask Letby things like "Did you want babies to be hurt?" and the answer of course would be no. Letby said Baby K should have been at a tertiary centre. Baby K was the case where Dr Jarayam said he found Letby standing by the baby's incubator ignoring the desaturations. Lucy Letby said his versions of events was not true and she wasn't there. She was basically saying Dr Jarayam was either a liar or had a terrible memory. Letby also denied dislodging the baby's tube. During her evidence, Letby gave one the impression that 'mottling' on a baby was not unusual. This though was certainly not the view of the numerous doctors and medical experts who had given evidence in the previous months.

Mr Myers asked Letby why, when returning from her holiday in Ibiza, she had texted someone to say "Yep probably be back in with a bang lol". Letby said what she meant by this was that it would probably be a busy shift in the hospital. Texts were read out in relation to Baby O. Letby was saying she had three babies to look after (Letby was also grumbling about having to show a student nurse around - which rather contradicted her earlier evidence about how much she loved being a mentor). Letby told Mr Myers she did not remember noticing a rash on Baby O and was not involved in the CPR. Letby told the court that the needs of Baby P were 'beyond' the medical care the hospital could provide. She said this was why she had made the comment 'he's not getting out of here alive is he?' to a doctor. Letby said that she and the other staff were devastated by this death.

Asked why she had done online searches for the family of Baby O and Baby P, Letby said the family were 'on her mind' because you don't 'forget' things like that.

Letby was asked by Mr Myers about the text she had sent to her doctor friend where she asked if she needed to be 'worried' about Dr Gibbs (who, by now, was concerned about the spate of deaths and collapses on the ward and harbouring some suspicions about foul play). Letby told the court that she'd heard that Dr Gibbs was asking who was present when Baby Q collapsed. Letby said her concern was that Dr Gibbs was going to accuse the nurses of leaving Baby Q unattended. Letby told the court that when she learned she was going to have a meeting with Eirian Powell she was worried it might be because she had made a mistake (though Letby was confident she hadn't).

Letby said she also thought the meeting might be about staffing levels and how the unit was struggling to cope lately. Letby was asked about a Datix form on her phone for Baby O and Baby P but said she couldn't remember if she actually sent these off. Letby said when she was moved to an office role in the hospital she was confused and didn't know what was going on. At the conclusion of the defence questions, Lucy Letby denied harming any babies. "I only ever did my best," she said. The easy part was over. Now came the hard part. Nicholas Johnson, late in the afternoon, was going to begin the prosecution cross-examination of Lucy Letby.

The silver haired Mr Johnson peered down at Lucy Letby over his spectacles. She was still teary eyed after denying any guilt to Mr Myers. The first question of Mr Johnson was devastating. The gloves were off straight away. "Is there any reason," said Mr Johnson, "why you cry when you talk about yourself but not dead or injured children?" Letby said in response that she had cried for the babies. Mr Johnson asked Letby if she wished to change any of her evidence and Letby said no, she didn't wish to change anything. Mr Johnson asked Lucy Letby if she recalled calling Dr Ravi Jayaram a liar who had made up his evidence. Letby said she didn't remember this. "I'm going to suggest a date to you - yesterday," replied Mr Johnson (this was obviously a reference to the fact that the previous day Letby had disputed Dr Jayaram's claim that he saw her standing over a baby's cot seemingly ignoring worrying monitor readings). Letby was a bit stumped by this. She eventually conceded that by saying this she was basically saying that Dr Jayaram had misled the jury with his evidence.

Letby was asked why she kept taking handover sheets home and said it was only a 'few'. Mr Johnson said that 250 sheets was hardly a 'few'. Mr Johnson then asked Letby about saying she didn't take the handover sheets home on purpose. He pointed out that she even took them with her when she moved into her new house. Letby said the sheets were held in confidence. "Held in confidence?" replied Mr Johnson. "They were in a bin bag in your garage! Do you only obey the rules when it suits you?" "No," said Lucy Letby meekly. Nicholas Johnson only had about an hour to question Lucy Letby before the trial wrapped up for the day but Letby had not done terribly well. The next day was going to be a much sterner test for Letby because Johnson would have a full day of cross-examination for the first time.

The next morning Letby wore a pinstripe suit for her first full day of cross-examination by the prosecution. As ever, her parents sat in the background. Mr Johnson began by asking Letby if she wished to change any of her evidence from yesterday. Letby said she did not. Mr Johnson then said that yesterday Letby had said student nurses were not given handover sheets but this wasn't true because many of the sheets found in her house were taken from student nurses. Letby said it was not 'standard practice' for student nurses to have handover sheets and this is what she had meant.

Mr Johnson pressed Letby on the sheets found in her house and said they had prescription and medical notes for the babies she was charged with harming. "They have no meaning to me at all," said Letby. "They're just pieces of paper to me. I didn't know I had handover sheets. They weren't significant." Mr Johnson asked why she shredded bank statements but not handover sheets. Letby said she simply forgot that she had the handover sheets. "Are you really asking the jury to accept that pieces of paper with sensitive information about dead children on them were insignificant?" said Mr Johnson. "They have the names of a lot of children on them," replied Letby, "I agree I shouldn't have taken them home." Mr Johnson suggested that Letby took one sheet out of a hospital bin to take home. This was clearly, if true, highly odd behaviour.

Mr Johnson asked Lucy Letby why she told the police she didn't have a paper shredder - when in fact there was one in her house. Letby replied by saying that she'd just been arrested and had more important things on her mind than a paper shredder that she could barely remember. Mr Johnson asked Letby why she stored some documents at her parents house and had written the word 'keep' on one of them. Letby didn't seem to have an answer to this. Johnson asked Letby about the sympathy card she had sent to the parents of Baby I and said Letby had taken the phone photograph of this card in the hospital where the child died. Mr Johnson asked if this gave Letby a 'thrill'. "Absolutely not," replied Letby.

Mr Johnson asked Letby if she ever went in the neonatal unit late at night even if she wasn't officially on shift. Letby said she had sometimes done this to finish paperwork. Johnson suggested that Letby was then in the neonatal unit even more than we thought. Letby said that electronic swipe cards were needed so her movements were logged. Mr Johnson rather debunked this though by getting Letby to concede that sometimes staff would hold a door open for other staff - so swipe data couldn't possibly have logged ALL of Letby's movements. Mr Johnson asked Letby if she agreed that if babies were attacked then she had to be the attacker - unless there was more than one attacker. Letby replied by saying she'd never attacked anyone. "I understand your case that you've not attacked anyone," said Mr Johnson. "If the jury conclude that a certain combination of children were certainly attacked by someone, then the shift pattern gives us the answer as to who." Letby said she didn't agree.

Mr Johnson asked Letby if she agreed with the principle that she was the common factor in these incidents because she was on shift when when they happened. "I don't think I can answer that," replied Letby. Mr Johnson asked Letby about her relationship with the doctors who formed suspicions about her. He asked her to name them. Letby named Ravi Jayaram, Stephen Brearey, John Gibbs and another doctor who couldn't be named. "What is the conspiracy between the gang of four?" asked Mr Johnson. Letby said the conspiracy was to blame her. Mr Johnson asked what the motive for this conspiracy was. Lucy Letby said the motive was to cover up hospital failings. According to Lucy Letby then, a group of doctors at a hospital were perfectly willing for a kind young nurse to be wrongly convicted of being a serial killer purely so they could prevent the hospital's reputation from being tarnished. Mr Johnson rubbished this theory and suggested it was ludicrous.

Mr Johnson asked Letby if she agreed that Baby E and Baby L were poisoned with insulin. Letby agreed that these babies were given insulin but said it was not by her and unlikely to have been a staff mistake. "Mistake is not an option here," replied

Johnson, "so it was deliberate poisoning by someone, but not you?" Letby replied by saying - "Insulin has been added by somebody but I can't say by who, just that it wasn't me." Mr Johnson asked Letby if she was aware of the dangers in injecting air into patients. "All staff know that air introduced... can lead to death," replied Letby. Johnson asked Letby if she'd ever used her phone or texted while caring for a baby. Letby said she had never used her phone in a clinical area. Mr Johnson asked Letby if she'd ever known a baby to die suddenly hours after birth like Baby A did. Letby said she'd seen several baby deaths at her placement in Liverpool. Mr Johnson then told Letby that she told the police she had only seen a 'few' baby deaths before.

Letby denied that there was discolouration on one of the babies - as described by Dr Jayaram at the trial. Mr Johnson asked Letby if she was again calling Dr Jayaram a liar. At this, Mr Myers got up and complained about Letby constantly being asked if other witnesses were liars. Mr Justice Goss agreed with Mr Myers and said we should leave it to the jury to decide which witnesses they believed the most. Mr Johnson moved onto the babies alleged to have been injected with air and asked Letby if she did this. She said she hadn't. Mr Johnson said that in her police interviews Letby had claimed she didn't know what the dangers of injecting air were. Mr Johnson accused her of playing 'daft' at the interview. "I know the ultimate outcome would be death," said Letby of air embolism, "how that would appear in terms of symptoms for a baby - I don't know."

Letby said she did not know what caused the death of Baby B and said she had no memory of a text where she claimed the father fell on the floor with grief. Mr Johnson then produced a raft of electronic data which showed that Letby texted and made social phone calls while on shift in the unit. Letby said that other nurses did this too and it was normal. She said they did not neglect the babies though. The subtext of Mr Johnson was shrewd. Johnson was basically undercutting the claims of Mr Myers and Letby that the unit was dangerously understaffed. If this was the case, Johnson was arguing, how come the nurses had time to text and make phone calls and Letby also had the time to look after babies that were not her designated patients?

In the case of Baby B, Mr Johnson pointed out inconsistencies between descriptions of the 'mottling' by consultants when compared to Letby. "Do you accept that all the people who saw the skin discolouration, say they hadn't seen that sort of thing before?" asked Johnson. "I have to accept what they say, yes," replied Letby. "Do you accept air was put into the IV lines of both children (A & B)?" asked Mr Johnson. "No," said Letby. "Do you accept that you had the opportunity to access the lines of both children?" asked Johnson. "Yes," responded Letby, "but I didn't access the lines." Mr Johnson also made Letby concede she was in room one with Baby B after its collapse. Letby's answers were becoming very quiet so it wasn't easy to pick up what she was saying at times.

Letby agreed with Johnson that she 'migrated' back to the nursery room where Baby C was but said this was because she didn't think the designated nurse had enough experience. Mr Johnson asked Letby if she accepted the evidence of Nurse Sophie Ellis - who gave evidence saying she found Letby by Baby C's cot. "I haven't accepted it, I've said I don't recall," replied Letby. Letby said she had wanted to look after Baby C to help get over the previous tragedies. She was basically claiming exposure therapy. Exposure therapy is a form of psychological treatment that is commonly used to help individuals overcome anxiety disorders. It involves gradually exposing the person to the feared object or situation, under controlled conditions, in order to reduce their anxiety response.

Mr Johnson pointed out that Baby C collapsed shortly after Letby had a stroppy text exchange where she complained about not being in nursery one. Letby blamed Baby A's death on a lack of fluids and accused her fellow nurse Melanie Tayklor of life threatening incompetence. Lucy Letby came across as stubborn and vain on the stand. A bit delusional even. She was basically accusing all the other doctors and nurses in the hospital of being liars and had, whether unwittingly or not, more or less agreed with Mr Johnson that a serial killer must have been at large in the neonatal unit! It had not been a great performance. The general view is that Lucy Letby damaged her case when she took the stand - although whether or not this made any difference to the verdict is doubtful. It is hard to believe that Letby would have got a not guilty verdict if she hadn't given evidence.

The next morning Mr Johnson pressed Lucy Letby on her denial of having any memory of being in nursery one when Baby C collapsed - despite evidence from another nurse placing her there. "Do you dispute being born?" asked Mr Johnson. "No," said Letby. "But you have no memory of it?" replied Johnson by way of the punchline. Asked about the incident where Letby was asked to stop going in the family room after Baby C died, Letby said "I don't agree with that, I wasn't there a lot of the time" in response to Mr Johnson asking her (in not so many words) if she was some sort of twisted grief tourist. Mr Johnson asked Letby if she was lying when not remembering Baby D in her police interview. Letby denied this and said she remembered Baby D now. Mr Johnson commented that Letby could not remember Baby D's name in police interviews but could remember it for Facebook searches a few years before.

Letby said that Baby D had sub-optimal treatment early in life. In response to this, Mr Johnson said "Lack of antibiotics don't cause air embolous, do they?" Mr Johnson said that Nurse Caroline Oakley's notes showed she was on a break when Baby D collapsed and Kathryn Percival-Ward had confirmed in her evidence that Oakley was on a break. Mr Johnson asked Letby if she accepted all of this evidence. "Yes," said Letby. Mr Johnson said Letby wrote a blood gas reading for Baby D shortly before it collapsed but didn't sign it. Letby said not signing was an oversight. Letby denied looking after Baby D while Oakley was a break. "You were standing over her (Baby D) when the alarms went off, weren't you?" asked Mr Johnson. Letby said she didn't remember. Mr Johnson said the other nurses could be ruled out as going in Baby D's room just before the collapse. He suggested that Letby was 'babysitting' Baby D. Letby said she couldn't remember and had no comment.

Mr Johnson then showed evidence that Letby had been responsible for administering medications to Baby D before the second collapse. Letby said she couldn't remember this. It was a shortened day of evidence and concluded early. That probably came as a relief to Lucy Letby because the day hadn't gone well for her. It is obviously not much of a defence if you keep answering questions by saying that you can't remember anything. Letby had actually requested a break that day - which was why the trial ended early that afternoon. The cross-examination by the prosecution had left Letby frazzled and exhausted. The next morning, Lucy Letby rather implausibly told the court that the plumbing and a sewage problem in the hospital was an 'important' factor in the health problems of the babies. "Did you fill out a Datix form for that?" asked a deadpan Mr Johnson. A rather obvious problem with Letby's sewage theory is that bad plumbing hardly explained why two babies were apparently poisoned with unprescribed insulin.

Mr Johnson then asked Letby why she had signed an alteration to a prescription for Baby E rather than the designated nurse Melanie Taylor. Letby said this was standard practice. Mr Johnson asked Letby if she felt more qualified than the other nurses. Letby answered "No" to this question. Under questioning from Mr Johnson, Letby denied that she'd told Child E's mother the cause of the blood was due to insertion of the naso-gastrinal tube. Mr Johnson's overall strategy that morning was to point out inconsistencies in Letby's evidence - especially in relation to the precise timings of when things happened - in order to chip away at her credibility as a witness. Mr Johnson also went into forensic detail in regard to Letby's nursing notes and how they sometimes failed to record things which were established by other staff in the trial. Letby began to frazzle a bit again under the questioning and began saying "I don't recall" too often as an answer. Mr Johnson asked Lucy Letby why she kept searching for Baby F's parents online - including Christmas Day. "They were on my mind," said Letby.

Mr Johnson moved onto Baby G. Letby told the court that Baby G was premature and had a number of problems. Mr Johnson produced Letby's own nursing notes though which gave the impression that the baby was doing well. Letby had to concede that the readings and notes did indicate this. Letby said it was possible Baby G was overfed by mistake by someone in the unit. Mr Johnson asked is this was a realistic theory. "No," replied Letby. Mr Johnson said that in her police interview, Letby had said Baby G's vomiting was 'inside' the cot. He produced photographic evidence to show it was actually outside the cot. The subtext of this was pretty obvious. Johnson was implying that Letby had downplayed the extent of the baby's ill health.

Mr Johnson went into great detail in arguing the case for why Letby could be tied to the incidents with Baby G. He accused her of falsifying her notes and even attempting to make it look like another nurse had overfed the baby. Letby claimed she was with another colleague during a Baby G collapse but Mr Johnson was easily able to show the colleague she mentioned was feeding a different baby at that time. Mr Johnson said that Baby G later deteriorated very shortly after being fed by Letby. Was this an 'innocent' coincidence? "Yes," said Letby. "It is." In her defence statement, Letby said she had not called for help because she didn't think it was serious. Mr Johnson accused Letby of trying to 'minimise' what had occurred.

Mr Johnson reminded Letby of a text she had sent regarding Baby G which read - '...looked rubbish when I took over this morning and then she vomited at 9 and I got her screened' Mr Johnson said this text was a tissue of lies because the time stated was completely wrong and Baby G was doing fine that day. Mr Johnson accused Letby of attempting to construct an alibi by writing a fluid chart entry for another baby at the same time as Baby G crashed. It was a fairly bizarre performance by Lucy Letby that day in court. At one point she randomly referred to 'experts' during an exchange about Baby G's over-feeding. "What experts?" asked a puzzled Mr Johnson. Letby took a sip of water and didn't respond. It was like she had shut down. The most bizarre thing about this session was that Letby had somehow contrived to - out of the blue - imply that she shared the view of Dr Dewi Evans on key specific details. That was the last Mr Myers wanted her to do. Lucy Letby seemed lost and confused.

The next session of the trial was May the 25th. The jury must have felt like they'd been here forever. They were probably wondering if this trial was ever going to end. The morning session concerned Baby H. Lucy Letby began the day by talking about chest drains and basically suggesting that the doctors at the Chester hospital were incompetent and clueless on this facet of medicine. There were two themes to Letby's evidence under the prosecution cross-examination. Those two themes were that everyone in the hospital not named Lucy Letby was either a liar or useless at their job. The obvious problem with an approach like this is that it makes the jury have to decide which camp they are going to be in. Do they believe all of these experienced doctors and consultants or do they believe a young nurse who is sitting in the dock accused of being a serial killer? That's not really a very difficult decision to make when you boil it down.

Mr Johnson accused Letby of 'cooking the books' when it came to Baby H and manipulating her nursing notes to make it seem as if the child was poorly even before the collapse. Letby denied this was true. Mr Johnson continued to pick apart Letby's nursing notes, pointing out how they often contradicted evidence given by other staff in the hospital and were riddled with errors - especially in relation to the times stated. Letby said that people are 'human' and make mistakes. This was true enough but the volume of Letby's inconsistencies (in relation to accounts by others) and mistakes were not a great help to her case. Mr Johnson was of course, as we have noted, implying that Letby was an unreliable narrator in her nursing notes because she was, the prosecution believed, trying to cover up her tracks. Mr Johnson would often punctuate a series of questions by directly asking Letby if she had harmed the child in question. Letby of course said "no" firmly to these direct accusations but the effect of it was steadily wearing her down.

Mr Johnson asked Letby if she had been bored by her nursing job. She said she hadn't found it boring at all. Mr Johnson said if this was the case why was she 'liking' Facebook posts before Baby H crashed again? Letby said she must have been on a break. Late in the afternoon, Mr Johnson turned to the incident where Nurse Ashleigh Hudson had found Letby standing in the doorway of Baby I and Letby had then said the child looked pale. Hudson had been puzzled by this because she didn't see how Letby could have seen the child in the darkness. In her police interview Letby said they'd put the light on but this contradicted Letby's court evidence.

"Are you trying to massage the evidence by now saying the

lights were on low?", said Mr Johnson "No," said Letby. "What effect does going from a bright corridor into a dark or dimly-lit room have on your eyesight?" asked Mr Johnson. After some prompting, Letby said - "Yes, you wouldn't be able to see as well." Mr Johnson said that Letby knew the child was pale because she was the person that caused it. Letby denied this. Mr Johnson asked why Letby could see the child was pale but Nurse Hudson could not. "I had more experience so I knew what I was looking for - at," said Letby. "What do you mean looking 'for'?" inquired Mr Johnson. Was that a Freudian slip by Letby? "I don't mean it like that," said Letby. "I'm finding it hard to concentrate."

The next session of the trial was on June the 2nd. Mr Johnson again went into intricate detail concerning Letby's medical notes and timings and pointed out a number of areas where he alleged she had 'falsified' evidence or deliberately written something for misdirection. You could only feel sympathy for the poor jury who had to make sense of all this evidence and the complex timelines involved. One of Johnson's common themes was that Letby's notes would sometimes make it seem like a child was stable when they were not. Letby was asked about bathing Baby I after the child died and how the baby's mother had said in court that Letby was inappropriately cheerful when doing this. Lucy Letby told Mr Johnson that this wasn't done because of malice or because she enjoyed that moment. Letby said she was just trying to be nice and kind in difficult circumstances.

Letby said she had no idea why Baby J collapsed but said the unit was not really qualified when it came to stoma care. A stoma is an opening on the surface of the abdomen which has been surgically created to divert the flow of faeces or urine. People who have had stoma surgery are sometimes known as 'ostomates'. Mr Johnson pointed out that the nurse Nicola Dennison was experienced in stoma care and worked in the unit. "This nurse was familiar with stomas, wasn't she?" said Johnson. "In her opinion, yes," replied Letby with detectable sarcasm. In her evidence Letby would often say she wasn't blaming other staff or hospital failings but THEN go on to do exactly that a roundabout understated sort of way.

During the night shift on 21 to 22 October, Letby was designated a baby under transfer to the Royal Stoke University Hospital. Mr Johnson accused Letby of entering a false time for one of the medical charts of this baby to make it look as if she was occupied at a time when she wasn't. "You are altering medical records to put some time between yourself and serious events with Child I?" said Mr Johnson. "No," replied Letby. "I did not deliberately falsify any paperwork." On June the 5th, Lucy Letby was back in court to face Nicholas Johnson again. Mr Johnson produced the neonatal reports for February 17, 2016 and said Letby was in room one at 7-30am - despite being assigned to another room. He suggested she was there to sabotage Baby K. Letby said she couldn't remember why she was in room one and denied any foul play.

Letby denied dislodging the child's tube and said she couldn't remember if the baby's tube was moved or what the desaturation situation was at the time. Letby said she couldn't remember whether or not she was asked to babysit Baby K. Asked about Dr Jayaram's evidence that he had found Letby standing over Baby K's cot, Letby said she had no memory of this incident. Letby (still denying that this incident happened) said that it was standard practice to wait for 30 seconds or so to see if a desaturating baby 'corrected' itself. Letby said she couldn't remember the names of Baby K's parents and they weren't on handover sheets. Mr Johnson asked why she knew their names then for Facebook searches.

During this exchange (and a previous one earlier in the prosecution cross-examination) Mr Johnson actually got Letby to say that, despite the fact she couldn't remember anything, she had a good memory! This made it look as though Letby, whether true or not, was merely pretending not to remember anything. Mr Myers must have despaired as he sat helplessly during the prosecution cross-examination (Letby was not allowed to confer with the defence team at this time - she was on her own). Mr Johnson moved to Baby F and said this would be tied to Baby L (these were the two babies alleged to have been poisoned with insulin). Letby said she did not dispute that insulin was used in these cases but obviously denied it was her that administered this. Letby said she did not remember who put up the nutrition bag for Baby F but did concede she was a co-signer.

Letby said the bag could have come from a part of the hospital outside of the neonatal unit. Letby said she accepted the evidence that insulin was in the bag but did not believe that the baby was deliberately targeted by someone. Mr Johnson said that Letby seemed very eager in her police interview to ask about this contaminated nutrient bag. "Because I was being accused of placing insulin in the bag - I thought someone would have checked the fluids," replied Letby. "I wanted them to check the bag, yes - I thought it would have been standard practice." Mr Johnson accused Letby of knowing full well the insulin bags hadn't been kept. He said her police interview was therefore crafty and calculated to make her seem concerned and innocent. Letby denied this and repeated her theory that the insulin could have come from outside the baby unit.

Mr Johnson said Letby had said in her police interview that she could not recall anything about Baby F having low blood sugar. Mr Johnson said this was a lie because Letby had texted about the baby's low blood sugar when the child was in the neonatal unit. Letby denied trying to suggest other 'natural' causes for Baby F's ill health at the time but then Mr Johnson produced a text from Letby which showed she had done exactly that. Mr Johnson said there were very 'few' candidates who could have tampered with the insulin bag.

Mr Johnson moved onto Baby L. Once again Letby said she did not dispute the evidence that insulin had been administered but that she had had no idea why and it wasn't her. "It follows that insulin was administered while the [dextrose] bag was hanging, doesn't it?" asked Mr Johnson. "I have no idea," replied Letby. "It follows that it was a targeted attack?" inquired Mr Johnson. "I can't answer that," replied Letby.

Mr Johnson told the court the only two staff members on duty for both days, when Child F and Child L were poisoned with insulin, were Letby and Belinda Williamson. Mr Johnson asked Letby if she agreed that the only two people who could have put insulin in the bag were her and Belinda Williamson. "I can only answer for myself," said Letby. Mr Johnson told Letby that when she finished her shift the hypoglycaemia in Baby I gradually resolved itself because new nutrient bags (which didn't have insulin in them) were put up by other nurses. Letby didn't agree that she'd given the baby insulin but she did have to agree that the problem seemed to resolve itself after she'd gone home. Interestingly, Mr Johnson seemed to be saying that three nutrient bags had been injected with insulin though he used the term 'at least two bags' as if he wasn't completely sure of three. The trial ended early that day because a member of the jury was unwell. Lucy Letby was doubtless grateful for the early end.

CHAPTER ELEVEN

When the trial resumed again two days later, the cross-examination moved onto the case of Baby M. Letby told the court she did not know what caused Baby M's collapse but believed that an overstretched unit and staffing levels might have been a factor. Letby said she didn't think that staff incompetence was a factor but it was hard to say what the definitive truth of this was. Letby said she could not remember if she had duties with Baby M and then went into some detail about the condition of another baby (unrelated to this trial) who she was caring for at the time. Mr Johnson dryly commented that Letby had a remarkable memory of this child but not of the babies that had died.

One of the things Mr Johnson did in his cross-examination, and he did it again that day with Baby M, was use timelines to show the babies were usually (allegedly) attacked shortly after the parents had left after a visit. Mr Johnson was arguing that this was no coincidence and that only a member of the neonatal staff would have been able to do this. Mr Johnson said that Baby M's blood gas record, according to evidence heard from a nurse in the trial, was disposed of it a confidential bin. This was later found in Letby's house. Lucy Letby denied that she had fished this blood gas record out of a bin. She said she must have put it in her pocket by mistake. Dr Ukoh's writing was on the resuscitation note for Child M found in Letby's house. Mr Johnson said that Letby must have waited around for some time after her shift waiting for the chance to get this note from the bin. Letby denied this was true although did concede she had to stay late to finish some paperwork.

The cross-examination moved onto the case of Baby N. Letby told the court that the accounts of this baby screaming and collapsing were exaggerated by the trial. She agreed with Mr Johnson that the baby took a turn for the worse when the nurse Christopher Booth went on a break. Mr Johnson turned to the neonatal schedule for June 2-3, He produced a battery of text messages Letby had sent during her shift - including ones for times where she had recorded feeding a baby. Much earlier in the cross-examination, Letby had said she never used her phone while caring for babies - but Mr Johnson was suggesting otherwise and appeared to have the proof to back it up. It was another way to chip away at the credibility of Letby.

At one point there was a seemingly embarrassing text by Letby where she said she would have to google haemophilia because she didn't much about it (it later transpired that this was just a joke by Letby). Letby said that she went into nursery one to look for her nursing friend and it was shortly after that Baby N had a collapse. Mr Johnson asked if this simply bad luck. "Yes," replied Letby. It was just bad luck and coincidence. Mr Johnson pressed Letby on the doctor friend that she often exchanged flirty texts with. Mr Johnson said that Letby had a crush on this doctor but Letby denied that. Letby didn't care too much for being quizzed about this doctor. Mr Myers intervened to say this line of questioning was unfair and not appropriate.

Mr Johnson spent a lot of time on when blood was first noticed on Baby N and also the evidence of the parents in regard to communication with Letby when contrasted with Letby's notes. The aim of this was to point out inconsistencies between what others had said and what Letby was saying. The strategy of Mr Johnson was to make Lucy Letby look shifty and evasive and come across as someone who didn't always tell the truth. It worked too. Lucy Letby's time on the stand during the prosecution cross-examining was probably the most important moment of the trial. Even those who felt the case against Letby was circumstantial and hadn't been proven beyond doubt had to seriously question her innocence after Letby's disastrous time on the stand. In a matter of days, Letby had torpedoed most of the work done by Mr Myers in the previous months.

Letby was asked about the incident where she had seemed agitated by the arrival of a specialist team from Alder Hey. Letby agreed she had been agitated but said this was because she wasn't used to outsiders from other hospitals coming into the unit. She said she asked who these 'people' were because she genuinely didn't know who they were. The strangest point in that day's evidence was when Mr Johnson asked Letby about a jokey text she had got from a friend (concerning the doctor who Letby was fond of) telling her to 'go commando'. Letby had clearly found the text funny at the time but in court Letby said she didn't know what 'go commando' meant when asked.

One would imagine that most people know the phrase 'go commando' means to not wear underwear. Letby clearly knew what it meant in her text exchange. So why was she now pretending to not know what it meant in court? And didn't she realise that things like this just made her look like a liar? Lucy Letby was very strange person. Was she being a prude because her parents were sitting behind her? When Letby said she didn't know what 'go commando' meant, Nicholas Johnson supplied a rare moment of humour in the trial by saying - "Do you think this was an army reference being from Hereford?" (Hereford, for those that aren't aware, is where the SAS are based).

On the 8th of June the trial moved onto Baby O. Letby agreed with Mr Johnson that Baby O and his siblings all seemed to be doing well in the unit at first. Letby had said earlier there was a problem with Baby O's abdomen but Mr Johnson challenged this and said there were no medical reports to back this up. Letby agreed with Mr Johnson that Baby O's liver injury happened on her shift but denied that she was the cause of it. Mr Johnson provided evidence of a battery of texts Letby had sent while on shift and asked her how she found the time to do this texting. Letby replied by saying that she had never used her phone in a clinical area or beside a baby cot.

The jury was shown two feeding charts for Baby O signed by Letby. Letby said the notes above the signature were by student nurse Rebecca Morgan. Letby was asked about the incident reported by Nurse Melanie Taylor where Taylor had suggested moving Baby O to room one to be 'safe' but Letby, in Taylor's account, had been a bit short with her and said no. Letby said she didn't recall being 'dismissive' of Taylor and that this was simply 'Mel's opinion'. Letby said that if Melanie felt that strongly about she could have insisted on moving Baby O and Baby O would have been moved.

Mr Johnson said Letby had written a note about CPAP pressure for Baby O despite the fact that Child O had not been on CPAP breathing support for some time. CPAP stands for Continuous Positive Airway Pressure. It is a form of non-invasive ventilation therapy used to treat sleep apnoea, a condition where the airway becomes partially or completely blocked during sleep, leading to pauses in breathing or shallow breaths. Mr Johnson said this was a false medical report by Letby to cover up giving the baby air. Mr Johnson asked why she had written CPAP in her notes. Letby said she didn't know why she had written that.

Mr Johnson asked Letby why her baby observation notes were timed at the same time as she sent texts. The purpose of this by Mr Johnson was to argue that Letby used her phone while looking after babies. This made Letby look like a liar because she had denied doing that more than once in court. Mr Johnson said just before Baby O collapsed, swipe data showed Letby going back into the neonatal unit from the labour ward. Mr Johnson alleged that Letby had 'nipped' out and then gone back in to make it look like she wasn't there when the baby crashed - though she had caused it and knew it was going to happen.

Mr Johnson then pointed to a discrepancy in the way that Letby and Dr Stephen Brearey had described the rash and discolouration on Baby O. "I don't believe that's what I saw," said Letby. "I saw mottling. If that's what Dr Brearey saw, then if that's what you could take as being true, then yes." Letby then disputed the statements of Baby O's parents concerning the 'bulging veins' they saw on the baby. Letby said she never saw this. Letby also disputed that Dr Brearey asked her to take a few days off at this time.

After the death, Letby had exchanged texts with a colleague

where she suggested sepsis and talked about a 'ballooning abdomen'. Mr Johnson asked her if she was setting up a false narrative. Letby denied this was the case.

Letby was asked about a Datix form she had to fill in after the baby's tragic death. She had written that IV access was lost. Dr Brearey had to amend this form because what Letby had written wasn't true. "You were very worried that they were on to you, weren't you?" said Mr Johnson. "No," replied Letby. Mr Johnson asked Letby if she did CPR on Baby O but she said she didn't. Letby had though seemed to say she was involved in the resuscitation and CPR to the police. The CPR was very confusing but Mr Johnson's approach, at this time at least, seemed to imply Letby had done CPR as a means to cause an injury and thus cover up the real cause of death and now - in court - she was backtracking because she realised this ruse had been detected.

The court now moved to Baby P. Letby accepted that the baby's charts were normal and that the child only took a turn for the worse after Baby O died. Letby denied that she had overfed Baby P - though her signature was on some of the feeding confirmations. Letby was told about the X-ray for Baby P and the evidence of court witness Dr Arthurs. Lucy Lety, in response to this, said she could not comment on how the gas got there but it was nothing to do with her. Letby disagreed with Mr Johnson that Baby P was well at the morning handover time. Mr Johnson said this contradicted what Letby said in her police interview. He accused Letby of enjoying 'crisis' situations because it meant the doctor she was 'sweet' (Mr Johnson used this term earlier in his cross-examination) on might be summoned to the unit. Letby denied and said she and the doctor in question were just friends.

Letby was asked about saying "He's not leaving here alive is he?" about the baby but said she didn't recall this conversation (this again contradicted her earlier evidence). Mr Johnson asked if Baby P was 'bad luck' again. Letby said yes, it was bad luck. Mr Johnson said Letby always sent a flurry of texts after a baby tragedy or collapse because she loved the drama. Letby said that wasn't true. Johnson then moved onto Baby Q. Letby denied injecting this baby with air. Mr Johnson accused Letby of attacking the baby while Nurse Mary Griffith was out. All in all it was another bad day for Lucy Letby on the stand. Her defence team must have been wishing she'd stayed silent.

The next morning, Letby faced cross-examination from Nicholas Johnson again. To the relief of Letby, one would imagine, this was the last day of the prosecution cross-examination. Mr Johnson asked letby about learning that doctors had concerns about her and wanted to take her out of the unit. "You knew they were on to you, didn't you?" said Mr Johnson. "No," replied Letby. Mr Johnson said Letby had completed a Datix form on June 30, 2016 complaining about one of the lumens not having a bung on the end. This was something that might potentially cause an air embolism (which Letby had earlier claimed to know nothing about). "You removed the port and covered it as a clinical incident, didn't you?" said Mr Johnson. "This is an insurance policy - so you could show the hospital was so lax. It was to cover for accidental air embolus." Letby simply answered "no" to all these accusations.

Mr Johnson asked Letby about the 'gang of four' doctors who she claimed had conspired to blame her for hospital failings. Mr Johnson listed the alleged failings in relation to the babies that died or collapsed. Mr Johnson said that for eight of these babies Letby had supplied no evidence for any failings in their care. Mr Johnson said the whole point of this trial was to establish if the babies died or got ill because of sabotage or 'naturally occurring deficiencies' and poor care. He told Lucy Letby she didn't seem able to offer specific reasons for why it was the latter. Mr Johnson asked if the Facebook searches by Letby was a 'killer' looking at their victims. Letby denied this was the case. The prosecution obviously seemed to think that one of the reasons Letby kept handover sheets was for the purposes of doing Facebook searches. The sheets meant she had names and confidential information to hand.

Mr Johnson said that Letby had told a 'sob story' about being depressed, isolated and cut off from friends and colleagues at the unit after she was removed from her duties as a nurse. Johnson said this was a lie and produced photographs of Letby enjoying nights out with colleagues and friends after the suspension. Mr Johnson then accused Letby of lying about just being friends with the doctor she often texted. He produced text and phone evidence to show she had private rendezvous with him and that they even went to London together. The doctor in question was married with kids (so little wonder he wanted to protect his identity in court).

Mr Johnson asked Letby why she said she'd been arrested in her pyjamas. He said she was wearing a Lee Cooper leisure suit and had the police video to prove it. He asked Letby why she lied about this. "I don't know," said Letby. "You tell lies deliberately," said Johnson. "And the reason you tell lies is to get sympathy and attention from people." Mr Johnson ended his cross-examination by saying - "You are a murderer." "I have not murdered or harmed any child," replied Letby. That concluded Mr Johnson's forensic demolition of Lucy Letby. Her performance on the stand had been an absolute disaster for the defence. Benjamin Myers now rose to ask Letby some further questions from the defence. Could Mr Myers salvage anything at this late hour?

Mr Myers pointed out elements in the prosecution cross-examination which he said were untrue. He also asked Lucy Letby why she had seemed to agree with some of these points. "I don't know," said Letby. It was a good tactic by Mr Myers because he portrayed his client as so confused and exhausted she had no idea what Mr Johnson was asking her half the time. Mr Myers asked Letby if she accepted Dr Jayaram's account of her with Baby K. Letby said she did not. Myers produced text messages to dispute the prosecution's claim that Letby had fallen out with Melanie Taylor. He also debunked Mr Johnson's claim that Letby had excitedly texted Sophie Ellis following the death of Child P. Mr Myers produced evidence to show that Ellis had texted Letby - not the other way around.

Mr Myers then disputed the 'folder' the prosecution had showing Letby having a wild time drinking and enjoying herself after her suspension. Mr Myers said many of these were photographs of Letby with family and student friends. He said she was allowed to have a social life and that having a few drinks doesn't mean you are a killer. Letby ended this session by saying she had a happy life before all of this and wasn't a murderer. On the last day before the jury instructions and closing speeches, Mr Myers brought his only witness to court. The witness was a plumber named Lorenzo Mansutti who worked in the Countess of Chester Hospital. That's right. Ranged against all of these doctors and consultants, paediatric specialists, radiologists, blood experts, and professors, all the defence could muster was a plumber. You could probably describe this as something of a mismatch. It seems evident that this plumber was summoned by the defence as a reaction to Mr Johnson ridiculing Lucy Letby's comments about a sewage problem in the hospital.

Mr Mansutti told the court that there were indeed sewage and drainage problems in the hospital. He couldn't supply any specific dates though - which wasn't much help. We learned that the nurse Christopher Booth had once filled out a Datix form about this problem and raw sewage once came out of the neonatal unit sinks. Nicholas Johnson, when called to question Mr Mansutti, didn't have to break sweat. Mr Johnson established that most of the problems never affected the neonatal unit and that there were always hand-washing facilities available with clean water. Mr Johnson also got the plumber to agree that most of the problems were caused by things (like bits of paper towel) being stuffed down sinks and blocking them. Suffice to say then, a drainage problem in the hospital most likely did not cause these tragedies or put insulin in nutrient bags. The Guardian newspaper, in their reporting of the Lucy Letby case, said that Mr Mansutti 'looked as bewildered by his presence in court as those watching on'.

A big problem with the defence in this trial is that they didn't have any expert medical witnesses of their own. It seems that they couldn't find anyone willing to argue that all these doctors and experts were wrong and that Letby's guilt could not be proven - but maybe it wasn't that simple. Some stories say they did have experts willing to testify but chose not to use them because they felt it would be counter-productive. If you put a medical expert on the stand who offers an alternative take to the one by the prosecution, all Nicholas Johnson has to do is ask them if they think the theories of all the other experts are 'possible'. That expert is unlikely to say 'no, they are completely impossible, all those other experts don't know anything about medicine' and so the prosecution would essentially have the defence expert agreeing with the prosecution experts about what MIGHT have happened. Another problem is that one of the main strategies of Mr Myers was to dispute the evidence of the medical experts and even question their impartiality. It's a lot easier to do that if you don't have any medical experts of your own involved in the trial.

It could be the case too that medical experts were 'scared off' the case because they feared their reputation might be damaged if they got involved (this is obviously something that shouldn't happen because a jury in a complex medical trial needs as many expert viewpoints as possible to help them make a decision and Lucy Letby was not a serial killer at this point - she was innocent until proven guilty). The trial undoubtedly would have been more interesting if there were expert witnesses for the defence but for whatever reason it just didn't happen. It is possible that the defence decided putting their own medical expert on the stand would have been more trouble than it was worth. If said medical expert had been demolished by Nicholas Johnson on the cross-examination then the expert would be doing more harm than good. The defence obviously had copious access to medical experts in preparation for this trial. No experts were put on the stand by Mr Myers though. *

On the 15th of June, Mr Justice Goss gave his instructions to the jury. The end of the trial was nearly in sight. "You must not approach the case with any per-conceived views and you must cast out of your decision-making process any response or approach to the case based on emotion or any feelings of sympathy or antipathy you may have," said Mr Justice Goss. "It is instinctive for anyone to react with horror to any allegation of deliberately harming, let alone killing a child – the more so a vulnerable premature baby. You will naturally feel sympathy for all the parents in this case, particularly those who have lost a child and the harrowing circumstances of their deaths.

"You must, however, judge the case on all the evidence in the case in a fair, calm, objective and analytical way – applying your knowledge of human behaviour, how people act and react, using your common sense and collective good judgment in your assessment of the evidence and the conclusions to be drawn from it. Any decision you do make must be based on evidence and not speculation. If you are sure that someone on the unit was deliberately harming a baby or babies, you do not have to be sure of the precise harmful act or acts. In some instances there may have been more than one. To find the defendant guilty, however, you must be sure that she deliberately did some harmful act to the baby the subject of the count on the indictment and the act or acts was accompanied by the intent and, in the case of murder, was causative of death.

"The children were all premature and vulnerable, some had mild respiratory distress syndrome of prematurity and some had specific health issues. There were also a few cases of delays in the administration of appropriate medicine or other clinical failings. Some of the causes of death were unascertained. In the case of each child, without necessarily having to determine the precise cause or causes of their death and for which no natural or known cause was said to be apparent at the time, you must be sure that the act or acts of the defendant, whatever they were, caused the child's death in that it was more than a minimal cause. The defendant says she did nothing inappropriate, let alone harmful to any child. Her case is that the sudden collapses and death were, or may have been, from natural causes or for some unascertained reason or from some failure to provide appropriate care, and they were not attributable to any deliberate harmful act by her. It is for the prosecution to prove the defendant's guilt of any offence by making you sure of her guilt. She has no burden of proving her innocence. If you are not sure she is guilty of any offence, your verdict should be not guilty. If you are sure of her guilt, your verdict should be guilty."

* There were certainly people who have said they would have given evidence if asked. Richard D. Gill is a probability theorist and statistician who helped to exonerate the wrongly convicted Dutch nurse Lucia de Berk. Mr Gill says the trial of Lucy Letby was a miscarriage of justice and said he unsuccessfully tried to contact the defence to offer his services. On his website, Mr Gill offers a number of theories for the baby deaths in Chester such as enterovirus infection. He believes the testing for insulin

and air embolism was faulty. The problem is though that Mr Gill is a mathematician - not a doctor. He was hardly likely to be as credible to a jury as all the medical experts the prosecution lined up (admittedly, Mr Gill in court, unlike on his website, would have been offering only expert statistical analysis and not additional armchair medical conspiracy theories but you get my point). Lucia de Berk was exonerated because it was proven that she wasn't actually there when some of the murders she had been convicted of took place. Lucy Letby on the other hand was on shift in the neonatal unit during all the incidents she was charged with. It seems rather unlikely that a statistical expert as a witness for the defence would have made much difference to the outcome.

CHAPTER TWELVE

On the 19th of June, Nicholas Johnson began his closing speech for the prosecution. Mr Johnson began by asking the jury to consider the similarities in this case and suggested they could not be put down to bad luck or coincidence. He said Letby 'gaslighted' the staff at the hospital and was devious and calculating. Johnson then referenced the fact that the defence had called the plumber Mr Mansutti as their only witness and dismissed this as a waste of time. "His evidence isn't going to help you decide in this case," said Mr Johnson. "He was called, we suggest, to bolster the tattered credibility of Lucy Letby - and you might ask yourself why." Mr Johnson told the court that the insulin poisonings were not caused by bad plumbing.

Mr Johnson talked about how Dr Brearey and Dr Ravi Jayaram had become suspicious of Letby but didn't want to believe it could be true at first - until that is they began to realise the statistical improbability of Letby being the only nurse on shift when all these things happened but having nothing to do with them. Mr Johnson pointed out that the two doctors didn't know about the unprescribed insulin or liver injury to one of the babies at the time. Had they known these things then they would have acted with more urgency to get Letby out of the unit and get the police involved. Mr Johnson told the jury that Lucy Letby's defence was that these incidents and tragedies were caused by hospital failings and natural causes. "The only things that matter is to concentrate on the issues in this case. Concentrate on the 17 children in this case...and see if there are any shortcomings. We suggest that was an uncomfortable exercise for Lucy Letby."

Mr Johnson said that Letby claimed there were long line issues with Baby A. He added that the baby did not die of dehydration and no other nurse besides Letby could have been responsible for air embolus. Mr Johnson said that Letby had offered no explanation for why Baby B and Baby C collapsed in the hospital. In the case of Baby D, Letby had said a delay in antibiotics was a factor. Mr Johnson said this was dubious because Baby D did not die of an infection. Mr Johnson said Letby suggested Baby E died due to the effects of bleeding. Johnson asked the jury to consider what caused that bleeding in the first place. Mr Johnson said that Letby had provided no theories or explanations for the bleeding.

Baby F. Johnson said Letby had tried to blame a colleague for Baby G but then recanted that. Moving onto Baby H, Johnson said Letby had said chest drains were not put in correctly and cited 'potential incompetence'. Mr Johnson sarcastically added that Letby liked the word 'potential'.

Mr Johnson said that Letby had offered no credible explanation for Baby I and that her antibiotics theory was debunked. Johnson said that Letby had provided no explanation at all in the cases of Baby J, Baby K, and Baby L. In the case of Baby M, Letby's only explanation was that the unit was very busy. When it came to babies O, Q, and P, Mr Johnson said that Letby, despite claiming that hospital failings and incompetence was the salient factor in this case, offered no alternative evidence for why these babies might have died or collapsed. Johnson going through all the cases in this way was very effective. Lucy Letby had blamed hospital failings and natural causes for the incidents and deaths. However, when given the chance to elaborate on this in court Letby had almost no evidence for this and very little to say.

"Do you really think the [gang of four] would say things to get Lucy Letby convicted?" Johnson said to the jury. "What did the doctors say that wasn't true?" Mr Johnson said if this was a conspiracy against Lucy Letby the gang of four didn't do a very good job because they missed the insulin poisoning. "All the clues point in one direction, don't they?" said Johnson. "She's sitting in the back of court." Mr Johnson said that Letby attacked Baby A and Baby B because she thought they had a blood disorder that would mask her crimes. Johnson said if Letby had stopped here she might have got away with it.

Mr Johnson said Letby had lied consistently in court and used false data sheets to try and cover her tracks. He then reminded the jury that Letby had disputed the evidence given by Baby E's mother. "This is a head-on credibility contest between [the mother] and Lucy Letby," said Johnson. "You may think [the mother] would have a very good reason to remember this. Either she saw blood or didn't - why would she make it up?" Pointing out further differences between the evidence of Baby E's parents and Lucy Letby, Mr Johnson said - "Have [the parents] made that up, to get at Lucy Letby? Are they in on it? Are they a sub-gang of two?"

Mr Johnson said that in the case of Baby I, Letby 'altered the timing' for her designated baby set to be transferred to Stoke. Mr Johnson pointed how how Letby had disputed the evidence of Dr Harkness in the case of Baby E. Mr Johnson asked the jury if Dr Harkness was part of the conspiracy against Lucy Letby. "How far does this conspiracy go?" Mr Johnson was basically telling the jury again that the notion of a group of doctors framing a young nurse for murder to cover up some medical mistakes was a truly preposterous conspiracy. Johnson said that Baby E took a turn for the worse less than an hour after Letby came on duty. "What are the chances of that?" said Mr Johnson. Mr Johnson said that the point of circumstantial evidence is to connect that evidence and see if it fits into a pattern. He argued that it did indeed fit in this case because was the only person who could be geographically connected to all of these incidents.

Mr Johnson said that the second insulin poisoning had double the dose of the first. This was Letby upping the ante and making sure. Johnson said Letby had 'taunted' the police by asking if they had the bag with unprescribed insulin safe in the knowledge that they did not. He said Letby was only caught out because she didn't understand insulin c-peptide. Mr Johnson said that evidence from the pharmacy team which ruled out prior contamination of the bag had not been contested by anyone. Mr Johnson said only three nurses worked the night shifts for when the two babies were poisoned with insulin. One nurse was proven to be in another room. Another nurse could not be connected to other incidents. That left only Lucy Letby. Mr Johnson went into much detail concerning the insulin poisoning and called Letby 'sick' and 'relentless'.

Mr Johnson said Letby's claim that there was a conspiracy against her was ridiculous because the conspiracists would presumably have had to spike the nutrient bags with insulin to frame Letby. "We suggest that is not a reasonable possibility - that is why all the other cases are so important, they are not coincidences." Moving onto Baby M, Mr Johnson said - "What are the chances of a healthy baby boy collapsing in such an extreme way? The evidence, as you have heard from the doctors, is not very big. What are the chances of this happening at the same time his brother was poisoned...and [point] you to the identity of the attacker?"

Regarding the resuscitation notes for Baby M being found in Letby's house, Mr Johnson was dripping with effective sarcasm. Mr Johnson said the note "... found its way, under its own steam, to Letby's home. Sounds like a dog following home, doesn't it? Her explanation - I collect paper. How long has Lucy Letby had to come up with a reason? Here we are now, 7 years later, and her best reason is 'I collect paper'. Most collectors know what they collect - [it's] absolute nonsense." Mr Johnson then turned to Letby disputing the evidence of Dr Jayaram. "What is Lucy Letby's case, if Dr Jayaram is making things up? We suggest that not only is Letby murdering babies, she is also prepared to trash the reputations of professional people in order to get away with it."

Mr Johnson said Lucy Letby had disputed the evidence of insulin readings in her original defence statement but retracted that if her actual evidence to the court. Mr Johnson said 'it will be interesting to see how the defence get her out of that particular creek'. Moving onto Baby K, Mr Johnson said - "Is Dr Jayaram a wicked liar to make up allegations about one of his colleagues?... or is he telling the truth? What lie did Dr Jayaram tell? We suggest it's all smoke and mirrors, that all these doctors are bad, that they tell lies, that they stitch her up." Mr Johnson's most effective and dramatic moment came when he counted out 30 seconds in court - the time that Letby had apparently watched Baby K desaturating to see if it was 'self-correcting'. "It's uncomfortable isn't it?" said Mr Johnson. "Even talking about it is uncomfortable. That is why it's attempted murder."

The next morning, on his second day of closing the prosecution, Mr Johnson said the liver damage to Baby O was uncontested. Mr Johnson then referenced a post-it-note found in Letby's house which was a message to the triplets. 'Today is your birthday, but you aren't here + I am so sorry for that...I'm sorry that you couldn't have a chance at life.

I can't do this any more. I want someone to help me but they can't. What's the point in asking. Hatemylife.' Mr Johnson said that Baby O and Baby P were doing well before Letby's shifts. He accused Letby of trying to give the impression they had problems and even logging a doctor's examination which didn't actually happen. Mr Johnson said that Letby sabotaged Baby O because she wanted her favourite doctor to have to come to the unit. Mr Justice Goss, in his instructions to the jury, had said the jury need not concern themselves with a motive - merely decide if Letby was guilty or not. Mr Johnson though was clearly happy to speak about his own thoughts on a motive.

Nicholas Johnson gave another impressive performance in court as he pulled together all the strands of the prosecution into a plausible and easy to understand timeline. He made numerous examples of where only Letby could have been responsible for incidents and also went into great depth on why the medical evidence pointed heavily towards foul play. Mr Johnson also went into bat for Dr Evans and said it was ludicrous that the defence attacked him for changing his mind on certain things. Mr Johnson reminded the jury that fresh evidence in this case had consistently come to light since Dr Evans completed his report and continued to do so through the trial. Mr Johnson also made numerous references to times where Letby had made medical notes or observations which were not correct. He argued this was all part of a huge misdirection ruse by Letby. "She was controlling things. She was enjoying what was going on and happily predicting something she knew was going to happen. She, in effect, was playing God."

On his third day of wrapping up the prosecution, Mr Johnson said that Dr Sandie Bohin was, under cross-examination by the defence, told that a genetic problem could explain what happened to Baby A. Mr Johnson reminded the jury that Dr Bohin said she knew of no genetic condition that kills a baby in 24 hours. Of Letby, and by implication the defence, Mr Johnson said - "Letby floats the spectre of possibilities, but there's never anything specific. That's why we tied her down [under cross examination] to the specifics in each individual case." Mr Johnson said there was no evidence that Baby C would have been better off in a tertiary unit. That was simply something floated by Letby and the defence. Mr Johnson told the jury if they decide that hospital failings were the cause of these tragedies then they must acquit Lucy Letby. "We suggest that what's in short supply is specifics," added Johnson ."What specifically caused death in these children? The evidence shows that these children would have been better off anywhere else other than with Lucy Letby."

Mr Johnson told the jury that all the staff in the hospital said Baby C was doing really well during the three days that Lucy Letby was not there. The child died within hours of Letby's arrival in the neonatal unit. Johnson told the jury that Letby had used all manner of fictions to explain these incidents - one of them being to pretend that nursing colleagues were inexperienced or didn't know what they were doing (Mr Johnson said there was never any evidence for this). Mr Johnson said staff at the hospital said Letby was always strangely calm and unemotional - even during emergencies. She also seemed to have a ghoulish fascination with the family room after tragedies. Mr Johnson told the jury that Letby's police interviews and trial evidence seldom meshed. He reminded the jury that Letby often said she didn't remember much about these babies (despite the fact that some of had died while she was at work) and yet this is contradicted by her Facebook searches for them. Mr Johnson said all the 'jigsaw pieces' of this case only told one story. "Lucy Letby tried to murder or murdered these children."

Mr Johnson completed wrapping up his case the following day. His linear approach to the evidence was devastating. The evidence for Baby I was almost unbearable because this child had fought so hard to recover and cling to life. Mr Johnson said these babies would all have gone home to their families were it not for Lucy Letby. He continued to point out the inconsistencies in her evidence and the instances where she appeared to have fabricated her medical notes for the purposes of covering her tracks. This was a truly awful case to have sit through and listen to and rarely had a day of evidence been as heart-wrenching as the final day of the prosecution.

Up until May the 17th a lot of people were still rather on the fence concerning Lucy Letby's guilt. That changed for many of the undecideds after she took the stand to be cross-examined by Nicholas Johnson. Johnson had continued his forensic demolition of Lucy Letby and the defence case in his summing up. Nicholas Johnson had played the long game in this trial. It was as if he saved his most devastating evidence and material for the end. Few could have envied Benjamin Myers now. Mr Myers was going to have do the closing speech for the defence and somehow undo all the damage that Nicholas Johnson had done. By this stage of the trial the defence team needed a couple of snookers.

Benjamin Myers began his closing speech for the defence on June the 26th. Mr Myers started by thanking the jury for the way they had endured this marathon and 'distressing' trial. He then said the thing which struck him the most about the prosecution case is the way literally everything was cited as a reason for Letby's guilt. If she turned up for work that was deemed guilt. If she left the unit to do something else that was deemed guilt. If she didn't cry that was deemed guilt. If she DID cry that was deemed guilt. If she signed medical records that was deemed guilt. If she didn't sign medical records that was deemed guilt. A baby in her care doesn't show signs of deteriorations - that was deemed guilty. A baby does show signs of deteriorations - that was deemed as guilt too. "Just about everything became an allegation against Lucy Letby," said Mr Myers.

Mr Myers said the prosecution was using the presumption of guilt but the principle of the legal system is supposed to be innocent until proven guilty. Mr Myers said the information the jury had heard in court in the previous months was often a 'spaghetti soup' of data and evidence which had no real relevance. Mr Myers said that during the prosecution cross-examination, Letby was asked questions which she had no chance of answering. Questions, for instance, about hospital staffing. This, Myers was plainly arguing, was a way to trick Letby into appearing evasive and confused.

Mr Myers said that the trial had been heartbreaking and nothing could diminish the sense of loss felt by the parents. Mr Myers said that the defence team have shared the sadness of the trial's evidence and had nothing but sympathy for the parents of the babies discussed in the case. Mr Myers said the 'emotional' reaction to a case as awful as this is to look for someone to convict. Mr Myers said that was a dangerous reaction and one should look at the evidence very carefully before making any conclusions. Myers said that prosecution had used all manner of unpleasant words in describing Letby - like gaslighting, manipulative, sabotage, enjoying killing, and so on, but all on the thinnest of evidence.

Mr Myers said there were two possibilities in this case. One possibility is that these deaths and collapses were a result of infant medical fragility and failings in the unit and hospital. The other possibility is that a nurse, for no apparent reason and completely 'out of the blue', suddenly decided to start killing babies - despite the fact she had safely looked after hundreds of babies previously in her career and was respected by other staff. Mr Myers said there was a marked increase in the number of babies admitted to the neonatal unit when Letby was there and it 'boggles the mind' to hear the prosecution and medical witnesses in the trial give the impression that these babies were all fine and had nothing wrong with them. Mr Myers said it is vital that the issue of 'sub-optimal' care is not 'brushed' aside in this case.

Mr Myers said there is no evidence of any acts of harm being done - DESPITE the scrutiny that Letby was under from suspicious doctors. Mr Myers said none of the evidence against Letby amounted to her being caught in the act. He pointed out inconsistencies in the medical reports of some of the doctors and said that just because a lot of evidence is presented it doesn't mean that evidence is right. Mr Myers said the defence has a right to be critical of a neonatal unit and a hospital and this should not provoke any 'outrage'. Myers than ran through some examples of what he felt constituted sub-optimal care in the unit. These were basically the same things he had said earlier in the trial. The delay in fluids to Baby A and the chest drains, poor management of stomas for Baby J, Baby K should have been in a tertiary centre, getting the doses of adrenaline wrong for Baby P, and so on. Mr Myers said that some of these babies were also looked after by staff who were not sufficiently qualified to handle their specific needs. "There is plenty of sub-optimal care knocking about in this unit," said Mr Myers.

Mr Myers said that Dr Dewi Evans had said - "One tends not to spread news about the mistakes we make." Mr Myers said the jury should remember that quote. Mr Myers said doctors tend to be resistant to criticism. "Don't think the senior doctors came here without motives of their own. However you look at it, there was a terrible failing of care" at the unit." Mr Myers said that doctors apparently suspected Letby of foul play for months without actually doing anything about it. He said that was 'staggering'. "You will understand the stakes [in this trial] are very high. We don't say 'doctors bad'. We say for those senior consultants who presided at that unit... Lucy Letby getting the blame matters."

Mr Myers seemed to be leaning into the 'hospital conspiracy' angle here - which was a questionable strategy. After this he returned again to the hospital staffing levels, citing evidence from doctors that the unit was very 'busy' at times. Mr Myers said that when the neonatal unit was upgraded to handle more types of babies it only got two new consultants. After lunch, Mr Myers reminded the jury that the burden of proof in a trial is with the prosecution not the defence. He said the prosecution, to secure a guilty verdict, have to make the proof of guilt absolutely clear. Mr Myers said that the evidence for guilt in this case was not clear at all. He said they must be sure of an 'intent to kill'.

Mr Myers said that if air embolus was such an effective way to kill someone why switch to insulin poisoning? This felt like a weak point because wouldn't it make sense for a medical serial killer to alter their methods in order to muddy the trail? Mr Myers then claimed that, contrary to what the prosecution had claimed in their closing speech, the second insulin incident in this case (Baby L) only had a quarter of the insulin found in Baby F. Mr Johnson had claimed that double the amount of insulin was found in the second case. Mr Myers asked the jury why there was only a quarter of the insulin used if the intent was to kill? There was certainly some confusion about the insulin claims by Mr Myers but neither the judge nor Mr Johnson made an intervention at this time. It could be the case that Johnson and Myers were using different measurements - hence the confusion.

*Mr Myers said there were things the prosecution brought up in the trial which were not in the indictment. He also accused the prosecutor Mr Johnson of putting words into Lucy Letby's mouth when he cross-examined her. Mr Myers told the jury there was a problem with missing electronic swipe card data for the neonatal unit from July-October 2015. As such, Mr Myers argued that the evidence for Letby's exact movements and location during this period is questionable and flawed. Mr Myers said there was also missing post-mortem evidence for Baby E. The subtext of Mr Myers was that the prosecution had filled in the blanks where there was missing evidence merely to bolster their own theory.

Mr Myers said there was a presumption in this case that Lucy Letby must be guilty because she was in the unit when all of these incidents happened. Mr Myers said this was a dangerous generalisation. Just because Letby worked in the unit and did a lot of shifts it doesn't automatically follow that she was responsible for everything that went wrong. He also cited an incident where Baby N was unwell at night but Lucy Letby wasn't on shift at the time - she was at home. Mr Myers was saying that if Letby had been on shift at the time then the prosecution would now be blaming her for Baby N being unwell overnight. Mr Myers then suggested there were 'two or three' missing incidents in this case. Cases where babies got ill or projectile vomited but it had nothing to do with Letby because she wasn't on shift. Mr Myers said the prosecution had no interest in these incidents because Lucy Letby wasn't on duty.

Mr Myers said that the prosecution had cited 'similarities' in the cases of the babies as compelling evidence for Letby's guilt. Mr Myers said there was no pattern of similarities which suggested guilt. Quite the opposite. He said there wasn't even a consistent description of the discolouration and rashes that doctors say they saw. In the afternoon, Mr Myers spoke about Lucy Letby as a person. He said the glum Lucy Letby you saw in court was misleading. The real Letby, captured in old photographs, was happy and smiling. She had never been in any trouble in her life and cared for hundreds of babies in her training and beyond. Everyone who worked with Letby said she was kind and dedicated.

Mr Myers said that Letby did extra shifts because she was single and flexible and saving up for a house. He said this - and not sinister reasons - was why she seemed to be in the neonatal unit a lot. Mr Myers said the notes found in Letby's house reflected her dismay at being removed from her job and her fear that the babies might have been affected by a poor standard of care in the unit. Mr Myers said there was no way to establish where Letby was at any specific time in the unit so evidence concerning her movements is a hit and miss affair. Mr Myers said the incident in the prosecution cross-examination where Lucy Letby claimed she didn't know what 'go commando' meant happened because Letby was embarrassed with her parents sitting not far away. Mr Myers said that questions like this and references to Letby's 'doctor boyfriend' were inappropriate.

Mr Myers said of the Facebook searches that Letby did not search for all the families of the babies and the searches she did were indicative of sentiment for the babies - not a ghoulish form of voyeurism. He said that the police found Letby had made over 2,000 Facebook searches but only 31 related to families in this case. Myers said that Letby was never found to have googled things like air embolus or anything sinister. She never googled 'haemophilia' (in relation to Baby N) either - this was just a joke. On the issue of handover sheets found in Letby's house, Mr Myers pointed out that many sheets related to babies who had no relation to this case. He said only 10% of the sheets related to babies in this case.

Mr Myers then moved onto the medical experts used by the prosecution. Mr Myers said the jury should take the evidence of 'experts' into account but that doesn't you have to accept it. Mr Myers said that Dr Sally Kinsey was an expert in haematology but that didn't mean she knew much about air embolus. Myers openly wondered whether Dr Sandie Bohin and Dr Andreas Marnerides provided impartial evidence but saved his biggest attack for Dr Evans. Mr Myers went back to Dr Evans being criticised by a judge in another case and told the jury that Evans was not a neonatologist. Mr Myers said that Dr Evans had no current clinical practice and was an 'expert in being an expert'.

Mr Myers then reminded the jury of how Dr Evans had 'touted' for work on this case - a fact which Myers argued made Mr Evans impartial. Mr Myers said that Dr Evans said in evidence that he came up with the theory of air embolus independently. Mr Myers disputed this and said Dr Jayaram suggested air embolus to the police before Dr Evans got involved in this case. Mr Myers said that Dr Evans was impartial and dealing with evidence beyond his medical competence. He said that the other medical experts (including Dr Bohin) had been guided in their conclusions by the work done by Dr Evans. Mr Myers was aruing that if the work of Dr Evans was flawed then that meant the whole prosecution case was flawed because Dr Evans was the original foundation stone underpinning the entire case against Lucy Letby.

Mr Myers was clearly wheeling out a 'greatest hits' package in his first day of cross-examination in that the court had heard most of this stuff before. His attack on Dr Evans was predictable and something he'd done throughout the trial. It was an obvious strategy because if you can cast doubt on the expert witnesses then this gives the jury pause for thought. The problem with this approach though was that Mr Myers was basically lumping all these medical witnesses in with the conspiracy against Letby -

which felt far-fetched. The jury might have been forgiven too if they wondered why, given that he disputed the impartiality and evidence of these experts, Mr Myers hadn't produced any medical experts of his own to offer alternative explanations. Overall though, the performance of Mr Myers was highly professional and he made some interesting points about things which may have happened when Letby was not actually there.

Mr Myers began the second day of his closing speech with the case of Baby A. Myers said it was not acceptable to have one nurse looking after two babies and returned to his by now familiar theme of problems with the long line. He added that there was no evidence that Letby injected this baby with air. Mr Myers said that the prosecution evidence on air embolus was based on a 1989 research paper and as such was mostly 'guesswork'. Mr Myers was sort of saying that no one actually knows anything about this subject. Mr Myers said 'unexpected collapses' can happen to neonatal babies and reminded the jury that there was no consistent description of the discolouration suffered by the babies. Mr Myers disputed that the air embolus evidence case matched other photographic examples of air embolus and said they can happen by 'accident' and don't necessarily indicate foul play.

Mr Myers told the jury that Dr Evans alleged Baby B might have been smothered at one point and but this theory was quietly 'abandoned'. He reminded the jury that a nurse said the neonatal unit was like a 'bus station' when it got busy. Mr Myers wondered how Lucy Letby could have taken insulin and done all these other things in a busy unit. Mr Myers said that, contrary to the picture painted by the prosecution, Lucy Letby's nursing notes were often 'unremarkable' and dovetailed with those of doctors. He said that Dr Evans sometimes cited no cause of death in his report and then arrived at air embolus in court. Mr Myers said Sophia Ellis should not have been looking after Baby C because she was too inexperienced. Myers also said that Nurse Melanie Taylor's evidence in court did not mesh with her police interviews. Mr Myers was now attacking not just the medical experts and doctors, but the nurses too.

On this second day of his summing up, Mr Myers didn't really offer anything new. It was again a rehash of his common themes - the hospital was understaffed, these babies were not as healthy as everyone says, some of the babies should have been in another hospital, Dr Evans is wrong about everything, and so on. Mr Myers was cleary trying to paint this hospital as dangerous and dysfunctional but he failed to provide any concrete evidence that negligence caused these tragedies. The case of Mr Myers would obviously have been stronger if he had produced a neonatologist in court who agreed with this view. Another problem is that people know your average NHS hospital isn't perfect. The defence failed though to provide proof that it was a full blown sub-optimal care scandal in Chester. Mr Myers did have more success though in regard to returning to air emboli (again). He (again) argued that this was a vague science (in terms of our knowledge) when it came to research and literature and argued that it was therefore questionable to convict a person on air embolus theories proposed by people who (according to Myers) were not experts in this field.

On day three of his closing speech, Mr Myers began by talking about the insulin results. He said the prosecution said Letby made 'concessions' about the insulin readings (which was true - she did) but Mr Myers said Lucy Letby and the defence 'make it clear' they are not admitting that Letby administered the insulin. Mr Myers then said Lucy Letby was in no position to agree to the insulin readings because she was hardly in a position to test them. Mr Myers then said the insulin results were not 'agreed' evidence. Mr Myers said Letby was accused of spiking insulin bags already put up in the case of Baby F and re-spiking a bag about three times for Baby L. Mr Myers said that these accusations were artificial and unrealistic. Myers said it was striking that neither baby, besides low blood sugar and some vomiting, seemed to display any serious side effects from the alleged insulin attack.

Mr Myers disputed that the two babies displayed the symptoms of serious insulin poisoning. "The evidence has demonstrated that there have been bag changes when Ms Letby wasn't present," said Mr Myers. He said that Baby F's bag was changed after Letby finished her shift. Mr Myers said Letby would have needed to be Nostradamus to know that the 'random stock bag' would be used. Mr Myers also asked why none of the 'random bags' allegedly tampered with had harmed other babies in the hospital. "There is no evidence that Miss Letby interfered with any bag of TPN," said Mr Myers. "None. Blink, ladies and gentlemen, and you will miss that point. We say there would be nothing quick about what the prosecution allege. It involves getting a syringe and the bag, drawing up the insulin and injecting it without arising suspicion and getting caught. The prosecution have suggested alternatively that the insulin was introduced when the bag was hanging. It still involves getting insulin from the fridge, having a syringe, getting it in the bag without detection when there is no reason for anyone to put insulin into a hanging TPN bag.

"It's quite easy to make the allegations but it would be quite difficult to carry out. We say it's incredible to maintain she is responsible for this. How can Miss Letby be held responsible for that second bag on any fair or logical basis? A high level of insulin in a bag that no-one could have foreseen would have been used which comes into play hours after she has left? So even if somebody guessed that a maintenance bag may be needed in an unexpected way, they are not to know what bag would be taken. They would have to do the lot to make sure. You will keep in mind that stock bags are not stored in any particular order. It's like a series of Russian dolls of improbability. There is no evidence that any other baby was affected at this time and you can be sure we would be told if there was. This is not party games – let's get Letby. We are not here to invent explanations and ignore the evidence. Whatever happened to the TPN bag, or bags, there is no sensible way of claiming that Miss Letby could have been responsible for putting insulin in the second bag. That fundamentally undermines the accusation she put it in the first bag."

It's probably safe to say that evidence concerning the insulin bags had long since become confusing. It could be that Mr Myers was bambozzling the jury with a blizzard of brain melting detail by way of strategy but he did genuinely manage to claw back some hope for the defence. He cast a few doubts - and that's exactly what a defence barrister is supposed to do. Mr Myers spoke of the incident where the monitor was found to be switched off in the neonatal unit. He said that if two doctors hadn't said they did that then the prosecution would almost certainly have blamed Lucy Letby for that and given it a sinister sheen.

This was the underlying strategy of Mr Myers in his closing speech. He was arguing that literally everything in this hospital was blamed on Lucy Letby and suggested that this was not a plausible proposition. Mr Myers also refuted the prosecution's claim that Letby had falsified a report on Baby I and said that Baby I's mother, in part of a statement not heard in court, had corroborated Lucy Letby on this detail. Day three had been a strong performance by Mr Myers. He was certainly earning his money. One thing which didn't come across well though was Mr Myers casting doubt on the evidence of the mother of Baby E about her baby screaming. Mr Myers evidently believed this was an important and necessary thing for the defence but it did unavoidably leave a sour taste to have this mother's memories of her precious baby dismissed as inaccurate.

Mr Myers began day four of his closing speech with Baby K. He said that the evidence of the mother of Baby K had been critical of the care in the Countess of Chester Hospital and that doctors had also said in evidence that it was 'challenging' to provide stoma care. Mr Myers told the jury that this was proof of what the defence have been saying all along - that the care in the neonatal unit was sub-optimal. Mr Myers said that desaturations for Baby J when Lucy Letby was not on shift passed by without any scrutiny whereas desaturations for Baby J when Letby WAS on shift were later judged as foul play. Mr Myers said this was unfair.

Mr Myers said that Baby K should have been in a tertiary unit and that Dr Jayaram's evidence, which implied he'd caught Letby in the 'act' of doing some harm, was not 'worthy of belief'. Mr Myers said that if a doctor suspected a nurse of deliberately harming a baby surely that doctor would have been watching that nurse 'like a hawk' for the rest of the day and then had her removed and called the police. Myers cast doubt on the incident even happening at all and said a nurse had given evidence that

Dr Jayaram asked her who was in the room (the room where he allegedly found Letby acting weird). On the case of Baby L, Mr Myers said that the baby displayed no clear serious symptoms of insulin poisoning. Mr Myers also again cast doubt on the mechanics of how a nurse would poison a baby with unprescribed insulin in a busy neonatal unit. Mr Myers believed that it was implausible that Letby could have done this without other members of staff becoming aware that something dodgy was going on.

Mr Myers disputed the air embolus theory for Baby M and alleged that this theory was something later 'worked in' by Dr Evans and Dr Bohin. Mr Myers also disputed the air embolus theory with Baby N and questioned if Lucy Letby was even there when she was alleged to have sabotaged the baby. Mr Myers said that Alder Hey consultant anaesthetist Dr Francis Potter said that it had been 'easy' to intubate Baby and expressed surprise that the Countess of Chester Hospital staff found this task so difficult. Mr Myers said that Dr Bohin had disagreed with Dr Francis Potter on this because she had to 'come to the rescue of the prosecution'.

The next morning, on the last day of his closing speech, Mr Myers discussed the case of Baby O. Mr Myers said we could not rule out CPR for the liver injury and also cast doubt on whether the electronic swipe data for Letby would even have given her time to sabotage the baby in the timeframe alleged by the prosecution. Mr Myers argued that Baby P had undiagnosed pneumothorax and was also the recipient of substandard care in Chester. Mr Myers cited the evidence given by the mother of seeing a doctor googling chest drains. Mr Myers suggested the doctors in Chester were 'out of their depth'. Mr Myers said that Baby Q's medical charts were 'consistent with early stage Necrotising enterocolitis (NEC)' and said it was preposterous that Letby was alleged to have attacked this child. "'What an earth is Miss Letby meant to have done? There's no evidence of an attack."

Mr Myers ended his speech by saying that the medical experts in this case and were not neutral and - in the case of Dr Evans - highly partisan. "We say there were terrible failings in care on that unit that have nothing to do with Lucy Letby. Between June 2015 and June 2016 the neonatal unit at the Countess of Chester took more babies than it would usually care for and took babies with greater care needs. In that same year there was an increase in the number of deaths and the types of collapses we're looking at in this trial. Those two facts are connected, we would say."

Mr Myers asked the jury to "apply a presumption of innocence and not a presumption of guilt, if you do that you will reach the right verdicts, verdicts of not guilt and those are the verdicts we ask you to return." Mr Myers had given a highly detailed and committed closing speech for the defence but was it enough? Had he planted enough doubts in the minds of the jury? Perhaps the biggest weakness of his closing speech was to again lean into the hospital conspiracy angle. It was not far-fetched at all to believe that medical mistakes had been made in this hospital but it was somewhat more of a stretch to believe that the doctors had all got together and thrown Lucy Letby under a bus to save their reputations. The work of Mr Myers and Mr Johnson was finally done. It was now up to the jury to decide the fate of Lucy Letby.

* It transpired that Mr Myers was wrong about the insulin measurements and had to admit this. This might explain why the last day of the defence closing speech didn't seem as strong as the start. It could be that Mr Myers was planning to use the insulin measurements as a big part of his last speeches to court but then had to abandon this. This is purely speculation though.

CHAPTER THIRTEEN

The jury, who must have felt like this trial had been going on for decades by now (this was the longest murder trial in British legal history), still had a vitally important task before they retired to discuss their verdict. That task was to listen to the five day summing up of the case by Mr Justice Goss. This was important because the clear, linear, summing up of Justice Goss was very helpful as a sort of refresher course in all that had happened over the previous months. Mr Goss went through the case of each baby and reminded the jury of what was said by witnesses. He set out what the prosecution had argued and he set out what the defence had argued. He said that the jury must be fair, calm, objective and analytical.

"The defendant has never been in trouble with the police and has no criminal convictions, reprimands and cautions recorded against her," he said. "Not having any previous convictions does not provide someone with a defence but it is something you should take into account in her favour in two ways. First, it may make it less likely that she would deliberately harm any babies she cared for at the hospital. Second, it is also something that you should consider in her favour when deciding her credibility, in other words, whether she was being truthful in her evidence to you about these events. It is entirely for you decide what weight, if any, you attach to the defendant's previous character." At the end of his detailed summation of the case, Mr Justice Goss told the jurors to be respectful of one another and keep their deliberations confidential. He advised them to reach unanimous verdicts on each count on the indictment.

In all, the jury would take 21 days to reach all of their verdicts. During this time one of the jurors was discharged on August the 3rd for what the judge described as 'good personal reasons'. That left eleven jurors to decide the fate of Lucy Letby. On the 8th of August the jury were told they could reach majority verdicts. Lucy Letby was found guilty of seven counts of murder of seven babies. Letby was also found guilty of seven counts of attempted murder of six infants. She was found not guilty on two counts of attempted murder. The jury was unable to reach verdicts on six further attempted murder charges. The guilty verdicts were staggered and revealed to Letby and the court before it became public due to reporting restrictions. On August 8, Letby was unanimously found by the jury to have poisoned Child F and Child L with insulin. Letby was unemotional at first but then began crying.

On August 11, the jury unanimously found Letby guilty of murdering Child O, and by a 10 to one majority, of murdering Child C, Child I and Child P. The jury also found Letby guilty by a

10 to one majority of attempting to murder Child M and Child N. Once again Letby cried in court and her mother was audibly heard to express disbelief at the verdicts. On August the 16th, Letby was not in court when more verdicts were read out. Letby was found guilty, by a majority of 10-1, of murdering Child A, Child D and Child E, and of attempting to murder Child B. She was also found guilty on two counts of attempting to murder Child G.

Letby was found not guilty on a third count of attempting to murder Child G. On August 17, Letby was found not guilty on one count of attempting to murder Child H. She was absent from court again on this date. On the 18th it was revealed that the jury could reach no verdicts on the remaining six charges. At this the jury was finally discharged. This was all highly emotional for the jury but most of all the parents of the babies involved. This had been an awful and distressing trial to have to sit through. Mr Justice Goss told the court Lucy Letby would not be back. She had declined to attend sentencing and refused to appear by videolink. The judge said he had no power to force Letby to attend - which most people felt was rather strange. One naturally assumes that convicted criminals have no say in these matters but that obviously wasn't the case. Of the six charges where the jury could not reach a verdict, the prosecution was given 28 days to decide if it wanted a retrial on these specific allegations.

Senior investigating officer, Detective Superintendent Paul Hughes, said of the verdicts - "This has been a highly complex and extremely sensitive investigation over the past six years. We had to go right back to the start, keeping an open mind and being careful not to draw any conclusions. The last thing we expected to find was a suspect responsible for these deaths and non-fatal collapses. It was a long, drawn-out process but no stone was left unturned. We had to do it right – not rush it. This has been an investigation like no other – in scope, complexity and magnitude.

"We had to deal with this as 17 separate investigations – we are normally used to dealing with one murder or attempted murder investigation at a time let alone something on this scale. What started out as a team of eight quickly increased and, at the height of the investigation, featured almost 70 officers and civilian staff working together – in a bid to unearth the answers that the families so desperately deserved. Turning up at the home of a family who have lost a baby, grieved for their loss and are trying to move on from that is difficult enough. But having to tell them that someone who was meant to be caring for their little one could ultimately be responsible for their death – is not an easy task. I want to say thank you to the whole investigation team in recognition of all of their dedication and hard work – without you we wouldn't be in this position today."

Cheshire Constabulary family liaison co-ordinator Janet Moore read out the statement on behalf of all the families in the case. "Words cannot effectively explain how we are feeling at this moment in time. We are quite simply stunned. To lose a baby is a heart-breaking experience that no parent should ever have to go through. But to lose a baby or to have a baby harmed in these particular circumstances is unimaginable. Over the past seven/eight years we have had to go through a long, torturous and emotional journey.

From losing our precious new-borns and grieving their loss, seeing our children who survived – some of whom are still suffering today, to being told years later that their death or collapse might be suspicious. Nothing can prepare you for that news. Today, justice has been served and a nurse who should have been caring for our babies has been found guilty of harming them.

"But this justice will not take away the extreme hurt, anger and distress that we have all had to experience. Some families did not receive the verdict that they expected and therefore it is a bittersweet result. We are heartbroken, devastated, angry and feel numb. We may never truly know why this happened. Words cannot express our gratitude to the jury who have had to sit through 145 days of grueling evidence, which has led to today's verdict – we recognise that this has not been an easy task for them and we will forever be grateful for their patience and resilience throughout this incredibly difficult process. The police investigation began in 2017 and we have been supported from the very beginning by a team of experienced and dedicated Family Liaison Officers. We want to thank these officers for everything they have done for us.

"Medical experts, consultants, doctors and nursing staff have all given evidence at court, which at times has been extremely harrowing and distressing for us to listen to.

However, we recognise the determination and commitment that each witness has shown in ensuring that the truth was told. We acknowledge that the evidence given by each of them has been key in securing today's verdict. Finally we would like to acknowledge and thank the investigation team and, more recently, the prosecution team who have led the trial to a successful conclusion. The search for the truth has remained at the forefront of everyone's minds and we will forever be grateful for this. We would now ask for time in peace to process what has happened as we come to terms with today's verdict."

A statement from the liaison officers on Operation Hummingbird was also read out. "On behalf of our team of dedicated Family Liaison Officers, I would like to thank all of the families for the immense fortitude and extreme resilience that they have shown over the years. They have acted with dignity and reservedness during a very long trial, whilst hearing the most horrendous evidence. We are all extremely humbled by them. I hope that the support that we have provided to all of the families has been of some comfort to them during an incredibly difficult journey. We have worked closely alongside His Majesty's Court Service to ensure that the families have been able to watch court proceedings in Manchester as well as remotely over the past 10 months. This has assisted them greatly in being able to view the trial with more ease. We would like to thank court staff for all of their help with this. Whilst today's verdict can by no means relieve the suffering that families have gone through and are still going through, we hope that it will bring them some comfort. Our thoughts remain with you all."

There was no need for anyone to call for an inquiry because it was blindingly obvious one would happen. Health Secretary Steve Barclay said: "I would like to send my deepest sympathy to all the parents and families impacted by this horrendous case. This inquiry will seek to ensure the parents and families impacted get the answers they need. I am determined their voices are heard, and they are involved in shaping the scope of the inquiry should they wish to do so. Following on from the work already underway by NHS England, it will help us identify where and how patient safety standards failed to be met and ensure mothers and their partners rightly have faith in our healthcare system."

Lady Justice Thirlwall was later appointed to lead the public inquiry into Lucy Letby's crimes.

It was announced that there would now be an investigation too into Letby's time at Liverpool Women's Hospital during training placements. The police said they would also look to investigate all the babies admitted at the Countess of Chester during Letby's time there. A few days after the verdict, Dr Dewi Evans told a newspaper - ""I shall write to Cheshire police and ask them, from what I have heard following the end of the trial, that I believe that we should now investigate a number of managerial people in relation to issues of corporate manslaughter. I think this is a matter that demands an investigation into corporate manslaughter. Failing to act was grossly irresponsible – let's make it as clear as that. We are talking about a serious emergency. It's grossly irresponsible."

Tony Chambers, the ex-chief executive of the Countess of Chester Hospital NHS Foundation Trust and one of those who 'failed to act', was quick to release a statement. "All my thoughts are with the children at the heart of this case and their families and loved ones at this incredibly difficult time. I am truly sorry for what all the families have gone through. The crimes that have been committed are appalling and I am deeply saddened by what has come to light. The trial, and the lengthy police investigation, have shown the complex nature of the issues raised. I will co-operate fully and openly with any post-trial inquiry." Chambers worked as head of a trust in West Sussex after leaving Chester. Kim Thomas, chief executive of the Birth Trauma Association, said of Chambers - "It's worrying NHS trusts seem happy to appoint somebody who has already been shown to fail in another trust and there are questions about their competence. You have to wonder what kind of due diligence is going on there."

Ian Harvey, the medical director of the Countess of Chester

Hospital when Lucy Letby was working there, swiftly retired after Letby was arrested and moved to the south of France with his £1.8 million pension pot. In 2018, Dr Stephen Brearey had referred to Harvey to the GMC over Harvey not taking any action over warnings about Letby but the GMC decided the complaint didn't meet the threshold for any punishment. After Lucy Letby's conviction, Harvey told the media - "It has been alleged that the paediatricians informed me of their concerns in February 2016 but a meeting was not arranged until May 2016. I do not recall any such communication. It is surprising, given the level of concern that some of the paediatricians professed to have had at the time, that there was no follow-up to chase a response, either with my secretary or with me."

The lawyer Richard Scorer, who represents some of the families involved in this case, said of Harvey - "Our clients received a series of anodyne letters from Harvey containing no proper explanation or clarification. The letters invited them to contact Harvey for more explanation and they tried to contact him repeatedly, but despite many attempts to get through to him they never received a return call. Our clients have described his response as a 'total fob off'. It seems that Harvey had little interest in passing any meaningful information to the parents, responding properly to any of their concerns, or complying with any duty of candour to them." In response, Mr Harvey said he was sorry they felt he didn't provide enough communication. He said his ability to respond was constricted by the police investigation.

Karen Rees, the head of nursing at the Countess of Chester Hospital's urgent care division at the time of Letby's crimes, went on Sky News to try and explain why Lucy Letby was not taken off duty sooner - despite warnings from doctors. "Ravi (Dr Jayaram) wouldn't give me any information to explain why Lucy Letby should be removed from the unit. He said nothing about air embolus, or over-feeding. He did not even mention babies dying and Lucy Letby being present. He just asked for Lucy Letby to be removed from the NNU (neo-natal unit). Dr Stephen Brearey was measured throughout... I said that if there were issues, then I needed to know what they were.

Despite that, he refused to give me any more information. He said that he had evidence, but he refused to show it to me. At no point did he say that he suspected she had been purposely harming babies. If he had said that there had been 16 deaths, and that she was present for all of them, then my actions may well have differed. If Stephen Brearey had given me whatever evidence he said he had, that may have meant that a further death could potentially have been prevented." There certainly seemed to be a game of pass the parcel going on when it came to anyone accepting any blame for what had happened in the Countess hospital.

Karen Rees said she was taking legal action over Dr Brearey claiming at the trial that she (Rees) said she would accept 'responsibility' for any that happened from Letby staying on duty. Karen Rees said this conversation never happened. Alison Kelly, an NHS manager alleged to have ignored warnings about Letby in evidence at the trial, later became director of nursing at the Northern Care Alliance NHS Trust located in the Manchester area. in August 2023 she was suspended due to the allegations that she didn't take any action against Lucy Letby despite warnings from doctors.

A few days later, Dr Jayaram told ITV News - "I think throughout this whole process there have been opportunities for those people who are at the top of the Countess of Chester to be able to put their hands up and admit that they got it wrong and apologise. They could have done this very early on, the very moment that Operation Hummingbird was launched. They could have done it at the point that Lucy Letby was first arrested. They could have done this at the point she was first charged. They could have done it as the trial progressed and more and more evidence came through. They certainly had a massive opportunity to do it when the verdicts were announced. And part of being a professional is being able to admit you got it wrong, it's about being able to admit, and have the balls to actually put your hands up and say 'we made a terrible mistake, we can't undo it, but we apologise'. But instead, and this is what's incensed me more than anything, they are still trying to find reasons why what they did was the right thing. For example, one of them said we weren't loud enough in expressing our concerns. How much louder could we be?"

On 21 August 2023, Lucy Letby was sentenced to life imprisonment with a whole life order, the most severe sentence possible under English law. Only three other female criminals had ever received a whole life order - Myra Hindley, Rose West, and Joanna Dennehy. Among the male criminals who got whole life orders are Peter Sutcliffe, Dennis Nilsen, Ian Brady, and Harold Shipman. Lucy Letby was now officially ranked in the same league as some of the worst killers in history. Letby was not in court for sentencing - which was understandably controversial. In response to this controversy, Prime Minister Rishi Sunak announced that the government would bring forth legislation that would compel convicted criminals to attend their sentencing hearings. Mr Justice Goss directed his sentencing remarks as if Letby was in court. He said that Letby would be given a transcript of his comments and the victim statements.

It was a long sentencing statement and a sobering and moving one too. "You acted in a way that was completely contrary to the normal human instincts of nurturing and caring for babies and in gross breach of the trust that all citizens place in those who work in the medical and caring professions. Loving parents have been robbed of their cherished children and others have to live with the physical and mental consequences of your actions. Siblings have been deprived of brothers and sisters. You have caused deep psychological trauma, brought enduring grief and feelings of guilt, caused strains in relationships and disruption to the lives of all the families of all your victims.

There was a deep malevolence bordering on sadism in your actions. During the course of this trial you have coldly denied any responsibility for your wrongdoing and sought to attribute some fault to others. You have shown no remorse. There are no mitigating factors. In their totality, the offences of murder and attempted murder were of exceptionally high seriousness and just punishment, according to law, requires a whole life order."

The victim statements were unbearably poignant and moving. The mother of Baby F and Baby E said - "I would like to thank Lucy for taking the stand and showing the court what she is really like once the 'nice Lucy' mask slips. It was honestly the best thing she could have done to ensure our boys got the justice they deserve. We have been living a nightmare but, for me, it ends today. I refuse to wake up with my first thought be about my boys being harmed. Lucy no longer has control over our lives. She holds no power or relevance in anybody's life. She is nothing." The mother added that she now never allows her surviving son to be alone with medical staff. The mother of Baby I said - "When they handed (Child I) to us we never wanted to let her go, we held her so tight. She was our gorgeous little princess and I can't even begin to explain the pain. When we lost her a part of us died with her." The father of the triplets Lucy Letby targeted gave a heartbreaking statement in which he said he'd felt guilt at experiencing joy when one of the triplets survived. The surviving babies will all have their identities protected until they are eighteen. What they will be told about these events and when will obviously be something that the parents will have to decide one day.

  Lucy Letby was back in HM Prison Low Newton in County Durham while this was happening. Her parents lived in Manchester during the trial to support Letby. It was said in the media that they were going to move north so they could be close to Letby's prison. It can't have been easy for them because they were not rich. Letby's parents couldn't accept that she might be guilty - which is, as we noted earlier in the book, perhaps understandable. Letby was in a maximum security area of the prison and spent most of the day in her cell. She was permitted two visits a month from loved ones. Joanna Dennehy was also at Low Newton. In March 2013, Dennehy embarked on a killing spree in and around Peterborough, Cambridgeshire. Over a period of 10 days, she murdered three men and attempted to kill two others. She targeted her victims at random and showed no apparent motive for her actions. Dennehy's victims were all adult men. She stabbed and killed Lukasz Slaboszewski, 31; John Chapman, 56; and Kevin Lee, 48. All three victims were found dumped in ditches near Peterborough. Dennehy also stabbed and injured Robin Bereza and John Rogers, but they managed to escape and survive. It was incredible really to think that this smiling young nurse from Hereford had ended up with Dennehy, Hindley, and Rose West in a little exclusive club of evil. True crime can truly be stranger than fiction.

CHAPTER FOURTEEN

As we have noted earlier at various points, medical killers have been a subgenre of true crime for many years. There are a fair number of famous examples of this type of criminal. Elizabeth Wettlaufer was born on Ontario, Canada in 1967. She studied nursing as a young woman and was eventually employed in a care home. Her time at Caressant Care though was plagued by problems related to her drug and alcohol addictions. She was eventually fired for various infractions - which included getting medications mixed up and being found passed out drunk in a storeroom. Wettlaufer was then employed at the Meadow Park Care Center but her time there was cut short when she had to have treatment for her drug problems. After this Wettlaufer had a battery of medical positions in different places but - once again - never lasted very long. She was caught stealing from one care home and her habit of turning up for work drunk or high meant she was not a very reliable employee to say the least. The last thing a medical business (not to mention the patients) needs is the nurses turning up to work drunk or high on drugs. This was only the tip of the iceberg though. Turning up for work drunk or stealing was one thing but Wettlaufer was also trying to kill patients with injections of insulin.

Wettlaufer's first murder is believed to have occurred in 2007 when she killed a World War 2 veteran who was being looked after at Caressant Care. Elizabeth Wettlaufer killed eight patients in various places and attempted to kill a further six. In 2016, Wettlaufer checked into a drug rehabilitation centre and confessed to her crimes. She said the motivation for the murders was a strange 'surge' and compulsion which she couldn't control. Wettlaufer said that when this surge gripped her she could hear cackling laughter which seemed to be coming from the bowels of hell. Elizabeth Wettlaufer was clearly highly disturbed and just about the last person in the world you'd want working in a medical care home. Staff who worked with Wettlaufer later said she was a friendly woman who would often bring the patients gifts. They had no idea that she was secretly killing them. Wettlaufer, like other Angel of Mercy medical killers, was said to be obsessed with death and intoxicated with the power she had over the fate of her patients. She had this deluded sense that she was sparing people from pain by killing them.

Wettlaufer was charged formally with eight counts of murder and (later) six more charges consisting of four counts of attempted murder and two counts of aggravated assault. Elizabeth Wettlaufer was then sentenced to life imprisonment and later sent to a secure facility in Montreal to receive medical treatment. In a report on the case, Commissioner Eileen E. Gillese admitted that Elizabeth Wettlaufer might not have been caught if she hadn't confessed (which was a rather disturbing admission). 'The evidence,' said Gillese, 'showed that no one suspected that Wettlaufer was intentionally harming those under her care — not the residents or their families, not those who worked alongside Wettlaufer, and not those who managed and supervised her.' Wettlaufer was found to be suffering from antisocial personality disorder and is believed to have killed the patients purely for her own gratification. Ultimately, this was a highly disturbed and troubled woman who couldn't seem to distinguish right from wrong anymore. If she hadn't been caught there is no telling how many people she might have killed in the end. This case recieved much publicity in Canada because it was revealed that Wettlaufer's previous infractions at medical facilities were not reported to the College of Nurses of Ontario. If they had been she might have been banned from working as a nurse much sooner and thus prevented some of these tragedies.

Charles Edmund Cullen was born in West Orange, New Jersey, in 1960. Cullen was a male nurse who was discovered to have deliberately given dozens of patients lethal overdoses in a number of hospitals. He is believed to have done this for the first time in 1988 but he was only convicted in 2008. Cullen apparently tried to commit suicide when he was nine years-old by drinking dangerous chemicals. When he grew-up he joined the United States Navy but attempted suicide again and had to spend some time in a psychiatric ward. After he left the navy, Cullen decided to take a nursing course and became qualified in 1986. He got married and found employment at a hospital. Cullen left his first hospital because of an incident where he was found to be tampering with IV drips. He may have killed dozens of patients already though. His next post was at Warren Hospital in Phillipsburg. He killed three patients there by giving them too much heart medication. Once again, there were almost certainly more victims. The family of one of the elderly victims were very suspicious of the hospital and Cullen in particular. Members of staff had to take a lie detector test as part of an investigation. No action was taken in the end but Cullen had to move on anyway and leave the hospital.

Charles Edmund Cullen came under suspicion in most of the hospitals he worked in but somehow managed to survive numerous investigations. Tragically, it is believed that the chronic shortage of nurses was the main reason why he kept being employed again. He continued to work in hospitals in the 1990s and also continued to kill patients. He later told prosecutors that he killed five patients in 1996 alone. While at St. Luke's Hospital in Bethlehem, Cullen killed five more patients and was the focus of an investigation that lasted nearly ten months. He was dismissed from the hospital but no criminal action was taken against him. Cullen then got employment at the Somerset Medical Center in Somerville, New Jersey. He killed a dozen or more patients at this facility with digoxin, insulin, and epinephrine. The staff at the Somerset Medical Center became suspicious of Cullen because he often seemed to be the rooms of patients that were not assigned to him. This feeling of suspicion was heightened when they noticed that he would sometimes ask for a medication that hadn't been prescribed to anyone under his care. More patients continued to die in suspicious circumstances and the police were called in. The police put Cullen under surveillance and made other nurses wear wire taps. They collected enough evidence to charge Cullen and he made a full confession.

Cullen told prosecutors that he had sought to mitigate the

pain and suffering of patients but this evidence was thrown out because of the fact that many of these patients had no critical or terminal condition and would have recovered if he hadn't killed them. In 2006, Cullen was sentenced to eighteen consecutive life sentences in New Jersey. Prompted by the Cullen case, Pennsylvania, New Jersey, and 35 other states adopted new laws which encourage employers to give honest appraisals of workers' job performance and which give employers legal protections when they provide a truthful employee appraisal. It is not known exactly how many patients Cullen killed in the end but a conservative estimate is most likely over forty at the very least.

Kimberly Clark Saenz was born in Fall River, Massachusetts in 1973. Saenz was another of those awful medical killers. She used her position as a nurse to murder patients. Saenz killed five patients and is believed to have attempted to murder five more. Although she was married with two children, Saenz was a troubled woman who was hooked on prescription drugs and had a conviction for public intoxication. Saenz had a battery of nursing jobs in her life but was fired more than once. She was dismissed from one hospital for stealing Demerol and then trying to fake the drug test she was subsequently obliged to take. Saenz ended up at DaVita's Lufkin clinic in Texas - which dealt with patients on dialysis. A strangely high number of patients at the clinic began to suffer from cardiac problems after Saenz began working there. Paramedics were bewildered and very concerned by this sudden spike in cardiac incidents and asked the hospital to launch an investigation. DaVita consequently sent some surveyors to the clinic to see if they could find out what the problem was. The investigation established that Kimberly Clark Saenz had been on shift for 85% of the cardiac emergencies. This was clearly highly suspicious and probably not a coincidence.

Two patients then gave statements in which they claimed they had seen Saenz injecting other patients with sodium hypochlorite. Sodium hypochlorite is better known as bleach. The clinic was closed after syringes used by Saenz showed clear traces of bleach. It was then established that in google searches on the personal computer of Saenz she had researched if bleach could kill someone if it was injected. Other nurses also gave accounts of how Saenz would talk about which patients she didn't like and show no remorse when they went into cardiac arrest or died. Although this all sounds like an open and shut case it wasn't quite that simple in the end. There was relatively little scientific research in detecting bleach in the blood so they had to get in scientific experts to build a case. These experts had to prove and explain how an agent like bleach would produce a reaction in the body that could result in cardiac arrest. They thankfully managed to do this in the end. Prosecutors wanted the death penalty for Saenz but at her 2012 trial she received life in prison. Kimberly Clark Saenz appealed her conviction in 2015 but to no avail. The evidence against her at the trial was simply too overwhelming and conclusive.

Vickie Dawn Jackson was born in 1966. In 2006 she pleaded no contest to charges that she had murdered ten patients at Nocona General Hospital in Texas. Jackson worked as a vocational nurse at the hospital and would use an overdose of Mivacron (a muscle relaxant) to kill the patients. Jackson had always wanted to be a nurse and worked hard to pass her exams. However her daughter later said that Vickie Dawn Jackson was always a strange and unpredictable woman prone to rages. She didn't seem surprised at all to learn that her mother had been killing patients. The hospital Jackson worked in was very small and so the workers there were on intimate terms with their patients. Over the course of 2000 and 2001, twenty patients died on the ward during the night shifts covered by Jackson. In that same time frame, not a single patient died during the night shifts not covered by Jackson. A lot of these patients were in the hospital for very minor conditions or injuries so the deaths were obviously suspicious to say the least.

In 2002 it was discovered that twenty bottles of Mivacurium had gone missing at the hospital. Syringes with traces of this drug were found in Jackson's trash. Exhumations of the patients who had died then revealed Mivacurium overdoses as the cause of death. The hospital had been subject to a negligence lawsuit from relatives of those that had died there in the past but Jackson kept working throughout this time. What was especially chilling about Jackson's activities is that she targeted a number of people who she thought had slighted her. She tried to kill one patient who had called her fat and also killed her estranged husband's grandfather. The motivation for some these murders was petty to say the least. Jackson was arrested in 2002. After a mistrial (caused by a prosecutor's comments) she pleaded no contest in 2006. Jackson received life in prison for ten murders.

Not all of Vickie Dawn Jackson's victims were named due to privacy laws. Jackson clearly killed many more than ten patients but identifying how many is very complicated. Vickie Dawn Jackson never admitted any guilt and never offered any explanation as to why she killed these patients. It is believed that she pled no contest because her daughter was going to testify against her and say she was a dreadful mother. Vickie Dawn Jackson knew that she was going to be convicted whatever happened at the trial so she simply decided to cut to the chase and avoid the trial altogether.

Richard Angelo was born in Long Island in 1962. He was a model boy scout and a good student by all accounts. As a young man entered a two-year nursing program at Farmingdale State College and then worked at a number of medical facilities. Angelo became known as a nurse who was good during a crisis. Angelo even volunteered as an EMT with the fire department in his spare time. However, as his colleagues were soon to discover, it was usually Angelo who created the crisis in the first place. In 1987 he was accused of poisoning a patient at then Good Samaritan Medical Center in West Islip, Long Island by injecting Pavulon through his I.V. The elderly patient immediately became ill as a consequence. Angelo had the been the night supervisor in a special unit full of vulnerable and elderly patients. This was a recipe for disaster to say the least because it gave him free access to a unit full of patients who had come to trust him - which turned out to be a big mistake. What had rumbled Angelo was the fact that one of the patients he had injected with a dangerous and paralysing cocktail of drugs had managed to press the assistance button before he succumbed to the effects of the drugs and this had made a nurse rush to the scene. The nurse decided to take a urine sample from the patient for tests. The tests were positive for the drugs Pavulon and Anectine - both of which were then found in Angelo's locker and house.

Angelo was arrested and the full catalogue of his wicked medical activities soon came to light. A number of dead patients were exhumed after Angelo confessed that this wasn't the first time he had done something like this. Angelo is believed to have poisoned over 30 patients - which resulted in at least ten deaths. Angelo said that his motivation was that he liked to play the 'hero' and bring a patient to the point of death and then save them. "I wanted to create a situation where I would cause the patient to have some respiratory distress or some problem, and through my intervention or suggested intervention or whatever, come out looking like I knew what I was doing. I had no confidence in myself. I felt very inadequate." A number of medical killers have this psychology. They like to play God with the lives of their patients and become addicted to the power they wield over life and death. Angelo was initially well respected by his colleagues at the hospital because of his calmness and apparent dedication. However, the unusually high number of patient emergencies during his shift eventually began to attract suspicion.

In December 1989, Angelo was found guilty on two counts of murder, one count of manslaughter, and one count of criminally negligent homicide. Sadly, it is believed he may have killed more patients than his official tally indicates. On January 25, 1990, he was sentenced to 50-years-to-life in prison. Angelo was only 27 years-old at the time of his sentencing. Angelo's defence team had claimed in court that he suffered from a form of multiple personality disorder and didn't really know what he was doing. This defence obviously proved futile in the end. The court was convinced that Angelo knew exactly what he was doing when he poisoned those patients.

Michael Swango was born in 1954 in Tacoma, Washington. Swango was a good student, played the clarinet in a band, and joined the Marines when he left school. You might think this would be a good start in life and set him on the straight and narrow forever but, sadly, you'd be completely wrong about. Swango was, it seems, what you might justifiably call completely crazy. It is said that Swango's personality seemed to change when a girlfriend left him. As a consequence of this he became reclusive and abandoned college for the army. His father had been an officer in the army though so this was by no means an eccentric or strange career path to take. Swango studied chemistry and biology at Quincy University after leaving the Marines although early clues about his character were retrospectively apparent here because he lied about his time in the army and claimed to have won various awards for bravery. In reality Swango had seen no combat at all during his time in the Marines.

Swango then attended the Southern Illinois University School of Medicine - though his time here was difficult because his grades were poor and he began to display a rather morbid fascination with gruesome imagery and death. In his third year Swango began to spend more and more time with ill patients and several of these seemed to die in a manner that is suspicious today (now that we know of the true nature of Swango) but didn't attract any attention at the time. Swango was hired as a surgical intern at the Ohio State University Medical Center in 1983 and then entered a neurosurgery residency. Swango soon attracted suspicion due to patients dying in his care but, in what would sadly be a recurring pattern, he was able to get away with his activities and keep working in medicine. One of the odd things about Swango is that he didn't simply target his patients but also poisoned co-workers. Swango was simply addicted to poisoning people and seemed fascinated by the affects it had. In this he had some similarities with the British killer Graham Young.

Swango became an emergency medical technician with the Adams County Ambulance Corps in Quincy but his colleagues soon deduced that whenever Swango gave him any food or drink to consume they fell ill thereafter. In 1985, Swango was convicted for poisoning co-workers and sentenced to five years in prison. Swango served four years of his sentence and then got as a job laboratory technician for ATICoal in Newport News. Well, you can probably guess what happened next. That's right. His work colleagues seemed to come down a mysterious illness whenever they worked with Swango. He was up to his old arsenic themed tricks again. Swango decided to make a sharp exit. What he desired more than anything was to get back into medicine but his criminal past obviously made this impossible. So he decided to change his name to Daniel J. Adams and even forged a document to pretend that his criminal offense had been a six month minor charge for nothing serious. Amazingly, Swango managed to secure a battery of medical jobs again in various places - where naturally he was up to his old tricks again and patients began dying dying in suspicious circumstances.

Swango eventually attracted the attention of investigative reporters and the American Medical Association. Swango had also had a relationship with a nurse named Kristin Kinney who later committed suicide. Kristin was found to have arsenic in her system when when she died. Her mother spoke out against Swango - joining the growing chorus against him. Swango must have realised by now that the net was tightening around him. He fled to Atlanta and got a job as a chemist but he was fired after the FBI (who were now also investigating Swango) warned his employer that Swango was a dangerous man suspected of many crimes relating to poison.

The old saying that truth is stranger than fiction certainly applies to Michael Swango because what he did next sound like the plot of a far-fetched television thriller movie. Swango fled to Zimbabwe and got a job in a hospital! As you can probably imagine, patients at the hospital soon started to get sick. Swango even poisoned his landlady - which was a big mistake because this attracted the attention of the local police. They quickly deduced that Swango was a dodgy character and got in touch with the FBI. Swango made a doomed attempt to flee to Saudi Arabia but he was arrested at Chicago-O'Hare International Airport. Michael Swango was sentenced to three years for fraud but he knew a much more serious case against him for his medical crimes was being prepared and so accepted a plea deal. He was eventually sentenced to three consecutive life terms. It is believed that Swango may have killed as many as 60 people but - as ever in case like this - the true figure could be much higher than that.

Harold Shipman was born in Nottingham in 1946. Shipman was a GP in Manchester who murdered (at least) 218 of his patients with injections of diamorphine (heroin) from 1975 to 1998. He was known as Doctor Death in the British media when his shocking secret came to light. Shipman trained at the Leeds School of Medicine and became a qualified doctor in 1970. He was married with children and loved rugby. Harold Shipman seemed like the most normal person in the world. The chances of him one day becoming one of the most notorious serial killers in history must have seemed laughable at this stage of his life. After working at a hospital, Shipman became a GP at a medical centre in Yorkshire. In 1975, Shipman was found to be addicted to a pain reliever called Pethidine (Demerol). He was forced to go to rehab for this addiction. Shipman then worked at the Donneybrook Medical Centre in Hyde, Manchester. Shipman appeared on the ITV documentary television show World in Action in 1982 talking about new treatments for the mentally ill - thus joining that select group of serial killers who appeared on television before their crimes came to light.

By the early 1990s, Shipman had three hundred patients at his practice and was a respected pillar of the local community. However, unknown to his patients and the community, Shipman was secretly killing his elderly patients by the dozen. Shipman first aroused suspicion in 1988 when a funeral home noted that he seemed to order a strangely high number of cremations. The police were called in but found no firm evidence of anything criminal or suspicious. Shipman was caught in the end because he murdered an elderly woman who used to be the local Mayor. The woman's daughter was a lawyer and became very suspicious of Shipman. This suspicion was confirmed when she discovered that her late mother's will had been recently changed so that Shipman received the inheritance (which amounted to £386,000). The victim's daughter demanded that a medical examination of her late mother should take place to investigate evidence of foul play. The body was dug up and - sure enough - found to contain diamorphine. Dr Harold Shipman was naturally arrested.

People who knew Shipman were absolutely bewildered by the revelation he had been secretly killing his patients. They simply couldn't believe it. He was known by everyone to be a kind man who spent his spare time growing vegetables in his garden. No one had ever detected anything sinister or troubled about

Harold Shipman at all. The body count is so high that we might never know just how many people Shipman killed. It is possible that Shipman's true kill count might be pushing 300. And yet, Shipman never confessed to anything. He never admitted killing a patient (despite the overwhelming evidence against him) and never provided any explanation for why he had done these awful things. His wife stood by him too. Mrs Shipman maintained that her husband was innocent and stood by him during the trial. Harold Shipman was convicted in 2000 on fifteen counts of murder but hung himself (using bed sheets) in prison in 2004. He was 57 years-old. Shipman was reading Henry IV by Shakespeare in his cell when he committed suicide.

Shipman could not be buried for fear that his grave would be attacked. In the end he was secretly cremated with only his wife and children in attendance at the service. It remains a mystery why Harold Shipman did what he did but one theory pertains to the death of his mother from cancer when he was a boy. She required sedatives and regular medication. It is speculated that Shipman, who was clearly not the most mentally stable man, had an enduring obsession with putting people to 'rest' as had happened to his mother. Another theory as regards the motivation of Shipman is (of course) financial. After Shipman was arrested, the police found that he had a large stash of jewelry he'd taken from victims and hidden in his garage. As a result of the Harold Shipman case, death certificate practices and the paperwork needed for a cremation in England were both reviewed and changed. The story of Harold Shipman remains very strange and unfathomable - not to mention very disturbing. True crime bios sometimes refer to him now as The Doctor Jekyll of Hyde. Harold Shipman truly was a bizarre and inexplicable killer.

Ludivine Chambet was born in France in 1983. Chambet worked in a number of nursing homes around Jacob-Bellecombette in Savoie and was the employed at Chambéry hospital. Chambet had a form of gigantism which gave her a very oversized body and some deformations. As a result of this she suffered from ridicule at school - which must have left mental scars. She was later an unlicensed nursing assistant and seemed like a perfectly kind and caring woman to those that knew her. It is speculated that Chamet's mental health began to erode after the death of her mother in 2013. Chambet was exceptionally close to her mother and felt lost and adrift in the world after her mother passed away. Chambet had no friends or love life and her world revolved around her mother. After her mother passed away, she suffered from a deep depression and - eventually - began to do some unexplainable and tragic things.

Chambet began killing patients in the nursing home l'Ehpad du Césalet at Chambéry she worked in by giving them large quantities of drugs like neuroleptics and antidepressants. These patients, many of whom were elderly, fell into comas from which they never recovered. The patients killed by Chambet were not terminal and would have got better were it not for Chambet murdering them. What rumbled Chambet was the death of an 83 year-old woman who had Parkinsons. The nursing home had experienced a number of patient deaths which seemed somewhat mysterious and they soon deduced that the common factor was Ludivine Chambet. Chambet had been on duty for all of these slightly strange patient deaths.

In 2013, Chambet was arrested. She confessed to killing a number of patients but said she had done so to alleviate their suffering. This defence is one that many medical serial killers seem to use and in Chambet's case, as with most others, it simply didn't wash.

What had really killed these patients it seems was Chambet's descent into mental illness. In 2017 Ludivine Chambet was found guilty of ten homicides and sentenced to 25 years in prison. Chambet's treatment by the authorities was humane because of her obvious fragility and mental health problems. It was argued in court that she wasn't really a serial killer because, in her deluded mind, she thought she was helping these patients. However, Chambet did say that she was compelled to kill by a split version of herself she called the 'personality'. A number of serial killers have said something like this after they were captured. Though convicted of ten murders, investigators at the trial believe that Ludivine Chambet probably killed thirteen people. She clearly would have killed a lot more if she hadn't been caught. Ludivine Chambet became known as The Poisoner of

Chambéry in the French media.

Gwendolyn Graham (born 1963) and Cathy Wood (born 1962) became known as The Lethal Lovers after killing five patients in Michigan's Alpine Manor. This diabolical duo were nursing aides and lovers. The victims were - Mae Mason, 79, Edith Cole, 89, Marguerite Chambers, 60, Myrtle Luce, 95, and Belle Burkhard, 74. Graham and Wood first met in 1986 and moved in together. They killed their first victim at the start of 1987 and got away with it because the death was deemed to have been as a result of natural causes.

Graham and Wood wanted to choose victims whose names spelled out MURDER as part of a sick private game but they abandoned this plan in the end because it proved too difficult. The patients were suffocated by the duo. They believed that by killing together they would cement an unbreakable bond. The murderous duo eventually went their separate ways though and this split led to their downfall. That unbreakable bond obviously wasn't as unbreakable as they thought. Gwendolyn Graham began a relationship with another nurse and then moved to Texas.

The crimes of Wood and Graham came to light because of Wood's ex-husband. Cathy Wood had confessed the murders to him and he went to the police. When the police interviewed Wood she confessed to the murders and said they suffocated the patients with washcloths. Wood testified against Graham at the trial and as a consequence Graham was convicted of first-degree murder of all five victims and handed five life sentences. Wood received a sentence based on her guilty plea of one charge of conspiracy to commit murder and one charge of second-degree murder. Cathy Wood was granted parole by the Michigan Department of Corrections in 2018 and in 2020 she was released. The relatives of the victims were very upset by this and believe that Wood downplayed her own role in the murders to get a lesser charge than Gwendolyn Graham. Some retrospectives of this case have argued that Wood was the most dangerous of the duo and the brains and driving force behind the whole murderous operation. Gwendolyn Graham, in a prison interview, said that Cathy wood was 'evil' and expressed astonishment that her partner in crime was now a free woman.

Retired police officer Roger Kaliniak, who was involved in the case when the two women were investigated and arrested, said he was rather surprised to learn that Cathy Wood had been released. "She's a serial killer and she could do it again, and most of them do," he said. "I believe that Cathy Wood was the mastermind, she was the one that was pulling strings on Gwendolyn Graham. Gwendolyn Graham handled the dirty work and Cathy Wood was the brains behind it." Court documents from the trial suggested that the two women tried to kill at least ten patients in all. The only crumb of comfort from this awful case is that the two women went their separate ways fairly quickly. The body count would have been considerably higher if they hadn't. Graham and Woods were later the inspiration for a 2016 episode of American Horror Story where two nurses named Miranda and Bridget decide to kill their patients.

When it comes to medical professionals, Miyuki Ishikawa is up there with the worst killers in terms of numbers. Ishikawa (born in 1897) killed more than 103 newborn children in Japan in the late and post-war years. She is known as Oni-Sanba (which translates as Demon Midwife). Ishikawa was a hospital director in the Kotobuki maternity hospital and highly experienced and respected. During the war and in the years that followed a large number of infants ended up in the hospital where Ishikawa was in charge. Japan's cities pretty much destroyed in the last years of World War 2 and the death and destruction created many orphans and many destitute transient people who couldn't care for a child.

Many of the parents of these infants had no money (some of them didn't even have homes) and Miyuki Ishikawa found that the hospital was overloaded with babies.

However, rather than seek to establish or find places where the overflow of babies could be looked after, Miyuki Ishikawa decided there was nothing she could do for them so she started to allow the babies to die. She simply neglected them on purpose so they would perish. The amount of infants who died as a result of this cold hearted decision is sometimes estimated to be around 160 but the general number of victims is usually credited at around a hundred. The other staff members at the hospital were outraged when they learned of Ishikawa's conduct and many resigned. There were accomplices though and some doctors participated in forging death certificates. Miyuki Ishikawa even claimed payments from the parents for taking in these infants and allowing them to die. She told the parents she would be saving them money in the long run.

In a sense then Miyuki Ishikawa was not completely dissimilar to one of those awful Victorian baby farmer killers. Strange as it might seem the fate of infants at the time was of no great concern to the Japanese authorities. They didn't really seem to care. Miyuki Ishikawa was finally arrested in 1948 when two police officers found two dead infants and medical tests indicated they had not died of natural causes. This was merely the tip of the iceberg though. There were tends of dozens of dead infants found in the hospital mortuary. The weirdest part of this tale is surely the sentence handed to Miyuki Ishikawa. She was given eight years in prison but then had this sentence halved to four years after an appeal!

Miyuki Ishikawa's defence in court was that the parents of these infants were responsible for the deaths by passing them onto the hospital. Incredibly, this defence actually seemed to work and Miyuki Ishikawa attracted some public sympathy. It is remarkable in the case of Miyuki Ishikawa that this cold and heartless woman didn't get a sterner sentence and wasn't more despised in Japan for her awful crimes. She is one of the worst medical killers in history. While her job was not exactly easy it seems clear that she made no real concerted effort to save these babies or find alternative arrangements for them. In the end she was strangely indifferent to their fate and ended up facilitating their deaths by the dozen. Whatever way you look at it, this was evil and wicked. Ishikawa's coldness and indifference was unfathomable and unforgivable.

Donald Harvey was born in Butler County, Ohio, in 1952. Harvey is another of those 'Angel of Death' medical killers. He claimed to have killed nearly 90 people in the end although the true number is almost impossible to ever know. It honestly wouldn't surprise you though if Harvey had killed close to a hundred people. Harvey dropped out of high school and didn't have the greatest education. As an adult he worked as an orderly at hospitals and this enabled him to kill dozens of patients. Many of his victims were cardiac patients. His first medical job was as an orderly at the Marymount Hospital in London, Kentucky. He said this is where he started killing.

Harvey was said to love going to the morgue in the hospital and always dispensed a lot of black humour about death to colleagues. His methods of murder were not limited to any one means. He turned off ventilators, used arsenic, suffocation, sabotaged catheters, and even injected people with hepatitis. Rather like Jane Toppan, his murders were not confined to hospitals either. He poisoned his roommate, his roommates father, and two neighbours. These actions completely contradicted his later claim that he had only done 'mercy' killings of sick patients. That was blatantly not true. Donald Harvey was perfectly capable of killing anyone anywhere. Harvey was finally rumbled when an autopsy on a patient found large traces of cyanide. The police decided to investigate the staff at the hospital and they found out that Donald Harvey had once been dismissed from a hospital after he was caught stealing body parts. This, at the very least, made Harvey sound odd and suspicious.

When the police questioned Harvey he confessed to giving the patient cyanide and claimed to have killed dozens of people. Subsequent investigations into suspicious deaths at the hospitals he had been employed in showed that he was probably wasn't lying. As for how he got away with his crimes for so long, Donald Harvey later said - "Most of the doctors would be so overworked, so busy, that a patient could die and the family doctor would not come in and pronounce the person dead. They'd have a resident do that. They just pronounce him dead and send him straight to his funeral home. The doctors go and spend all these years in school. And they'd always come in with this kind of - superior attitude. You know, 'I know everything.' But yet, they didn't know nothing." Harvey said he enjoyed the power and control that the murders gave him.

Donald Harvey agreed to confess to as many murders as he could remember (with names and dates of course) as part a bargain to avoid the death penalty. In 1987, Harvey pled guilty to 24 counts of first-degree murder. In accordance with the plea agreement, he was sentenced to three concurrent terms of life in prison. Harvey's lawyer later wrote that Harvey told him he used to light a candle, put it on top of a skull, and then draw up a list of people in the hospital he was going to kill. Donald Harvey was simply obsessed with killing people. In 2017, Donald Harvey was found beaten to death in his prison cell. He was 64 years-old.

The Lainz Angels of Death were Maria Gruber, Irene Leidolf, Stephanija Meyer, and Waltraud Wagner. This quartet were Austrian nurses who murdered dozens of patients at a Vienna hospital by giving them overdoses of morphine or putting water into their lungs. Waltraud Wagner was the first of the women to kill but they all conspired and worked together in the end when it came to killing patients. Three of the women were very young (Maria Gruber in particular was only a teenager) but Stephanija Meyer was in her forties and her age made her the most charismatic of the group. She arguably wielded the most influence. The nurses would pinch the nose of victims and pour water in them. Many of these patients were very feeble and unable to struggle. Few of these patients were terminally ill and they would have lived to leave hospital were it not for these evil women.

Waltraud Wagner, who recruited the other nurses into this heartless activity, had classic symptoms of God complex - a familiar trait of serial killers who work in the medical profession. Wagner loved the sense of power she had over these patients and clearly enjoyed taking lives. The Lainz Angels of Death were captured when they were overheard bragging about their murders in a pub. They were thankfully taken into custody very quickly. It later transpired that investigators had raised alarm bells about a suspicious death at the hospital in 1988 but couldn't go very far in their investigation because of the lack of cooperation from the hospital (who clearly wanted to brush the suspicious death under the carpet lest there be any legal complications). The women confessed to over forty murders but the true figure is impossible to say. Some accounts of this case they might have potentially killed over a hundred people.

Wagner was convicted of 15 murders, 17 attempts, and two counts of assault. She was sentenced to life in prison. Irene

Leidolf also received a life sentence for five murders. Wagner and Leidolf tried to claim the murders had been mercy killings of terminally ill patients but this simply didn't wash when subjected to sustained scrutiny in court. Meyer and Gruber received twenty years in prison for manslaughter and attempted murder. Meyer and Gruber were released fairly soon and given new identities. That was surprising but even more controversial was the release of Wagner and Leidolf in 2008 for 'good behaviour' in prison. The early release of these women caused outrage in Austria and made both the media and public alike wonder if the country's justice system was too soft and forgiving. It hardly must have seemed fair to the relatives of the victims that these four awful women had barely spent any time in prison at all for their dreadful and chilling crimes. It is amazing really to think that they were all released from prison so soon - as if their crimes had been petty or not that serious. It is hard to think of many more serious crimes than murdering helpless patients in a hospital.

Here is the thing one must remember about medical killers though. They are exceptionally rare. The chances of you encountering any serial killer are very remote and the chances of you encountering a medical serial killer are even more unlikely. The killers we've mentioned above are anomalies or aberrations. They are the exception - not the rule. The staff in hospitals represent the best of humanity and are kind, decent, and highly professional. In the long history of true crime a few bad apples have (sadly) used the medical world as a facility for murder and got notoriety and (dark) fame as a consequence but they represent only the tiniest imperceptible fraction of all the millions of doctors and nurses who do so much to look after us.

CHAPTER FIFTEEN

In September, 2023, a candlelight vigil was held at Chester Cathedral for the victims of Lucy Letby. Seven candles, each for one of the victims, was lit. Dr John Gibbs and Dr Ravi Jayaram were among those who attended. The Right Reverend Mark Tanner, the Bishop of Chester, said after the service - "It is really important we gather at a time when people are despairing, when they don't know where to turn, when there is anger, confusion and grief because the church exists to hold those kind of things, to introduce some kind of hope." The case of Lucy Letby was still recent and painful. It was also a surreal sort of case in that it was hard to fathom how this young woman from Hereford had gone down a path that connected her to notorious monsters like Rose West and Beverly Allitt.

Who is Lucy Letby and why did she do those awful things? The answer to both of those questions is that we don't really know. The reason why many seemed to find it difficult to believe that Letby could be guilty is because she looked so ordinary and seemed to have such an ordinary normal life. There was nothing in Letby's past which can be retrospectively viewed as weird or some sort of warning sign. Nothing at all. In the wake of Letby's conviction, political activist Dr Shola Mos-Shogbamimu said that it was Letby's 'white privilege' which enabled her to get away with her crimes. This view was echoed by the president of the Royal College of Nursing, Sheila Sobrany.

Their theory was that due to the fact that Letby was blonde and blue eyed no one believed she could be a serial killer (this isn't actually true because we know of at least three doctors who reported their suspicions about her). Dr Shola Mos-Shogbamimu and Sheila Sobrany suggested that if Lucy Letby was a black nurse she'd have been taken off duty and banged up a lot sooner. Well, who knows? Maybe. Maybe not. Whether or not any of this is true, it seemed rather distasteful timing to suddenly try and make a point about race in the immediate aftermath of a trial about dead babies. At least wait for a respectable period of time to pass. The nurse Rebecca Leighton was white but she got wrongly charged with crimes she didn't commit. Leighton's privilege didn't do her much good.

Famous convicted serial killers become a sort of weird nightmare folk memory in the end. They also attract morbid bad taste humour. Lucy Letby attracted this latter phenomenon rather quickly during a football match when Chester City fans taunted Hereford fans with Letby themed chants. That wasn't just bad taste - it was idiocy and insensitivity on a moronic scale. Still, it was proof that Letby has now entered the dark pop culture world of notorious serial killers. One imagines that in the near future you'll be able to purchase things on 'murderabilia' sites alleged to have once belonged to Letby. Someone will probably start selling jars of dirt online and say it was dug up in Letby's old garden in Chester.

In the wake of Letby's conviction, some of the newspapers said that a few old nursing colleagues of Lucy Letby think she is innocent and still can't believe she could have done those awful things. Lucy Letby's childhood friend Dawn Howe also refused to accept that Letby was guilty after the trial. "Unless Lucy turned around and said "I'm guilty" I will never believe that she's guilty. We know she couldn't have done anything that she's accused of, so without a doubt we stand by her. I grew up with Lucy and not a single thing that I've ever seen or witnessed of Lucy would let me for a moment believe she is capable of the thing's she's accused of. It is the most out-of-character accusation that you could ever put against Lucy. Think of your most kind, gentle, soft friend and think that they're being accused of harming babies."

Dawn is not alone in thinking that Letby is innocent. There is a veritable battery of armchair amateur doctors, forum addicts, and online detectives who insist Letby is innocent. Numerous (and often crackpot) reasons for Letby's guilt have been offered by these groups. The insulin readings were wrong, the hospital had a superbug infection, there was conspiracy by Freemasons in the medical establishment to frame Letby, and so on. Sarrita Adams, a California-based scientific consultant, announced in August that the conviction of Letby was the greatest miscarriage of justice in British history and that she would be raising money for an appeal. The claim that this nine month trial was a sham miscarriage of justice would certainly be news to the jury, Mr Justice Goss, and the families of the children involved.

While there are clearly a large number of unsavoury, misguided, and bonkers people online making, for reasons best known to themselves, all manner of unsupported claims about Letby's innocence and the trial, it would be unfair to dismiss all doubters as 'nutters'. Some people, who are perfectly rational and reasonable, believe the trial did not prove guilt beyond any doubt and that the case against Letby was a trifle circumstantial in places. These observers are in the minority but they are perfectly entitled to hold that view and can make some good points. A lot of observers were on the fence for much of the trial. You also had two brilliant and persuasive barristers in court for the prosecution and defence respectively so it was natural to sway back and forth and at times genuinely have no idea whether Letby was guilty or not.

The trial was incredibly complex and concerned with events which happened several years ago. It was never going to be straight forward and easy. There were no CCTV pictures of Letby committing crimes. However, the linear and intelligent prosecuting of Nicholas Johnson, especially near the end, banished any sense of doubt for most people. There was no fight in Letby when she took the stand. She seemed resigned to her fate. Lucy Letby did not come across as an innocent woman in court. She contradicted herself, couldn't remember much, and only showed any emotion when her doctor friend gave evidence. The decision of Lucy Letby to give evidence at the trial was clearly a mistake. Letby taking the stand and being cross-examined by the prosecution was highly damaging for the defence.

It is certainly true to say that, sadly, there have been scandals when it comes to NHS care of children. The Shrewsbury and Telford maternity scandal refers was a series of allegations of poor maternity care at the Shrewsbury and Telford Hospital NHS Trust. It is considered one of the largest maternity scandals in the history of the National Health Service. The scandal came to light in 2017 when a group of parents known as "The Shrewsbury and Telford Hospital NHS Trust (SaTH) Maternity Review" raised concerns about the care they received during childbirth. The review was launched to investigate the allegations and uncover the extent of the poor care provided. The initial review found several instances of negligence, including cases of avoidable deaths and permanent disabilities to both mothers and babies. The investigation uncovered a pattern of poor communication, inadequate monitoring of fetal well-being, failure to escalate concerns, and inadequate investigations into adverse outcomes.

As the investigation progressed, the number of cases continued to rise, and it was discovered that the scandal stretched back over several decades, affecting over 1,800 families. The cases included stillbirths, neonatal deaths, brain injuries, and other serious birth injuries. Many families affected by the scandal have criticised the trust for its lack of transparency and failure to learn from past mistakes. They have highlighted issues of poor record-keeping, mishandling of complaints, and a defensive culture within the trust. In June 2020, the Healthcare Safety Investigation Branch (HSIB) launched an independent investigation into the maternity services at the Shrewsbury and Telford Hospital NHS Trust. In November 2020, the independent review of the scandal concluded that the trust had shown a failure at every level to deliver appropriate care to mothers and babies over a period of 40 years. The review made a range of recommendations to improve maternity care and prevent similar incidents from occurring in the future.

We know that health scandals can happen. They can be awful and tragic. However, the defence in the trial and Letby's 'supporters' (if we can use that term) failed to establish proof that the spike in deaths and non-fatal collapses at the Countess of Chester Hospital was because of a major care scandal and incompetent staff. Where was the evidence for this? Mr Myers had nine months in court to make this case but there he was at the end of the trial bringing in a plumber to talk about the sinks in the hospital. It is clear that not everything was perfect in the Countess of Chester Hospital and the staff were not infallible but there is no evidence that the tragedies and collapses happened through staff incompetence and that a little group of doctors got together and decided to blame everything on Lucy Letby in order to mask these failings.

It is ludicrous to believe that a doctor would happily get an innocent young nurse sent to prison for life merely to protect the reputation of themselves and a hospital. To believe such a thing we would be to believe that these doctors had hearts of stone and no compassion at all. The failure of management to heed the warnings about Letby are, sadly, far less implausible. These hospital bigwigs were rather like Mayor Larry Vaughn in Jaws, refusing to close the beach because they didn't want to believe there was a shark. The most difficult question of all in the Lucy Letby case is motive. The crimes that Letby was convicted for are so evil and tragic one is truly lost for words. They are the worst crimes that anyone can imagine. Letby is often called Britain's worst child killer in articles and while that strictly isn't true (Amelia Dyer became known as the Reading Baby Farmer and the Angel Maker for her horrendous crimes in Victorian England looking after illegitimate babies - it is estimated that Dyer killed 400 babies) it is accurate enough when it comes crime in the modern era.

We've already mentioned Munchausen syndrome by proxy and theories that Letby was a closet sadist and psychopath. Some experts believe Letby had a hero complex. The term "hero complex" refers to a psychological condition in which a person feels an overwhelming need to be a hero or to save others. This often stems from a deep-seated need for validation, a desire for control, or a fear of failure. As we've noted, medical killers like playing God and enjoy the drama of emergency situations. The prosecution at the trial often leaned into the theory that Letby was engineering these baby collapses in order to get the doctor (she was clearly so fond of) to come to the unit. In court, Letby said her friendship with this doctor 'fizzled out' in the end. One would imagine that Letby being arrested probably had a lot to do with that! It's hard not to feel sympathy for the doctor in question. He must have felt dreadful when it dawned on him that Letby might actually have done these terrible things.

The truth is that we don't really know why Letby did the things she was convicted of doing. To any normal person it is completely beyond comprehension. The term the 'beige killer' was apt for Letby because she was not someone who ever stood out. If you look at pictures of Joanna Dennehy she looks totally insane. Dennehy looks like the last person you would ever want to meet in real life. She's straight out of central casting for a serial killer. Even frumpy Rose West in her granny spectacles seems sinister and full of dark inner secrets. When one looks at photographs of Letby though there is nothing of the night about her at all. That is unavoidably part of the morbid fascination with Letby. It's as if she was a sleeper agent impersonating a human being for 25 years. There were no clues at all before the events that made Letby notorious. When it comes to Lucy Letby you can only say that she hid her darkness well.

The case of Lucy Letby is truly one of the most awful and tragic true crime cases in modern British history. The enduring sympathy of anyone who followed this case is with the parents of the children involved. It would be comforting to think they can find some small degree of solace from the sense that justice was done and things will change as a consequence in the NHS. At the Countess of Chester Hospital now, beds for visitors have been put near incubators so that parents can stay in the unit and watch over their babies at all times. Our thoughts and best wishes are also of course with the precious children who survived. The children that did not survive will never be forgotten. We can only hope there is a better place somewhere and that one day they will all be reunited with their parents and relatives again.

REFERENCES

https://www.bbc.co.uk/news/topics/cvp59396q42t
https://www.cps.gov.uk/legal-guidance/witness-protection-and-anonymity
https://7hs.co.uk/members/mr-nick-johnson-kc/
https://www.cheshire.police.uk/police-forces/cheshire-constabulary/areas/cheshire/about-us/about-us/operation-hummingbird/
https://www.theguardian.com/uk-news/2023/aug/19/doctors-were-forced-to-apologise-for-raising-alarm-over-lucy-letby-and-baby-deaths
https://www.dailymail.co.uk/news/article-5921303/Police-dig-garden-home-neonatal-nurse-28-arrested-baby-deaths-Chester.html
https://www.herefordtimes.com/news/23049595.full-list-deaths-collapses-lucy-letby-accused-causing/

Milton Keynes UK
Ingram Content Group UK Ltd.
UKHW042006281024
450365UK00003B/227